Management and Organization: Various Approaches

Yasin Cakirel (ed.)

Management and Organization: Various Approaches

PETER LANG

Bibliographic Information published by the Deutsche Nationalbibliothek
The Deutsche Nationalbibliothek lists this publication in the Deutsche Nationalbibliografie; detailed bibliographic data is available online at http://dnb.d-nb.de.

Library of Congress Cataloging-in-Publication Data
A CIP catalog record for this book has been applied for at the Library of Congress.

ISBN 978-3-631-78282-8 (Print)
E-ISBN 978-3-631-78869-1 (E-PDF)
E-ISBN 978-3-631-78870-7 (EPUB)
E-ISBN 978-3-631-78871-4 (MOBI)
DOI 10.3726/b15579

Peter Lang – Berlin · Bern · Bruxelles · New York · Oxford · Warszawa · Wien

This publication has been peer reviewed.

www.peterlang.com

Foreword

Within the limited pages of this book, we have tried to address some of the concepts and issues that have been discussed in the field of management and organization in recent years—of course not all. A total of 28 authors contributed to our work. I thank all of them.

In the context of this book, readers are encouraged to focus on new career approaches and emotional work; they will come up with a lot of human resource concepts from job alienation to whistleblowing. In the area of organizational behavior, they will examine topics such as responsible leadership, cyberloafing, job crafting, organizational trust, and career sales. Organizational DNA about the organization will offer a perspective.

The book is waiting for you with these topics and more.

Views and ideas expressed in parts of this book represent the personal thoughts of the authors and may be used as a reference. And I would like to thank the staff of Peter Lang Publishing House for their rigorous work and assistance.

Sincerely
Yasin Cakirel

Yasin Çakırel works at Kırklareli University. He holds a PhD in Business Administration and Organization. He carries out studies on strategy, leadership, knowledge management and competition.

Contents

List of Contributors

Fahri Erenel
Assoc. Prof. Dr.; Istinye University,
Faculty of Economics and
Administrative Science,
Department of Business Management
fahrierenel59@gmail.com

Tahsin Akcakanat
Asst. Prof. Dr.; Süleyman Demirel
University,
Faculty of Economics and
Administrative Science,
Department of Business Management
and Organization
tahsinakcakanat@sdu.edu.tr

Hasan Huseyin Uzunbacak
Asst. Prof. Dr.; Süleyman Demirel
University,
Faculty of Economics and
Administrative Science,
Department of Business Management
and Organization
hasanuzunbacak@sdu.edu.tr

Mehmet Dinc
PhD; Süleyman Demirel University,
Faculty of Economics and
Administrative Science,
Department of Human Resources
Management
mehmetdinc@sdu.edu.tr

Basak Dogan
Asst. Prof. Dr.; Kırklareli University,
School of Applied Sciences,
Department of International Trade
and Logistics
basakdogan@klu.edu.tr

Murat Yorulmaz
Asst. Prof. Dr.; Yalova University,
Yalova Vocational School,
Department of Maritime
Transportation and Business.
myorulmaz@yalova.edu.tr

Adviye Asli Denizli
Research Assistant Dr.; Marmara
University,
Vocational School of Social Sciences,
Department of Management and
Organization
asli.denizli@marmara.edu.tr

Gonen İlkar Dundar
Professor Dr.; İstanbul University,
Faculty of Business Administration,
Department of Human Resources
Management
gdundar@istanbul.edu.tr

Ozge Can
Asst. Prof. Dr.; Yasar University,
Faculty of Business,
Department of Business
Administration
ozge.can@yasar.edu.tr

Burcak Vatansever Durmaz
PhD.; Bahçeşehir University
burcak.vatansever@gss.bau.edu.tr

Anil Boz Semerci
Asst. Prof. Dr.; Hacettepe University,
Faculty of Economics and
Administrative Sciences,
Department of Business
Administration,
anilboz@hacettepe.edu.tr

Guller Banu Karaman Menemencioglu
Dr.; İzmir Kavram Vocational College of Higher Education
Department of Property Protection and Security
Occupational Health and Safety Program
banu.menemencioglu@kavram.edu.tr

Ahmet Sait Ozkul
Assistant Professor: Suleyman Demirel University,
Faculty of Communication,
saitozkul@sdu.edu.tr

Omer Lutfi Antalyali
Associate Professor: Suleyman Demirel University,
Faculty of Communication,
omerantalyali@sdu.edu.tr;
Kyrgyz-Turkish Manas University,
omerlutfi.antalyali@manas.edu.kg

Ayse Gokcen Kapusuz
Asst. Prof. Dr.: Selçuk University
Beyşehir Ali Akkanat Faculty of Tourism
Department of Tourism Management
Konya/Turkey
aysegokcenkapusuz@gmail.com

Alptekin Develi
Lecturer: Tokat Gaziosmanpasa University,
Resadiye Vocational School,
Tokat, Turkey,
alptekin.develi@gop.edu.tr

Bilal Ezilmez
Lecturer: Bandırma On Yedi Eylül Üniversitesi
bezilmez@bandirma.edu.tr

Canan Çetin
Prof. Dr.:
Marmara University (retired)
canancetineylul@gmail.com

Ezgi Dede
PhD, MEB
ezgi.math@gmail.com

Gaye Özçelik
Assoc. Prof. Dr.; Istanbul Bilgi University
gaye.ozcelik@bilgi.edu.tr

Mustafa Babadag
Lecturer Dr.: Mugla Sitki Kocman University, mustafababadag@mu.edu.tr
Orcid ID: 0000-0002-0198-7105

Gokhan Kerse
Asst. Prof.: Karamanoglu Mehmetbey University, gokhankerse@hotmail.com,
Orcid ID: 0000-0002-1565-9110

Gozde Kosa
Asst. Prof. Dr.; Kafkas University,
Faculty of Economics and Administrative Science,
Department of Management and Organization
gozdekosa@gmail.com

Hakan Aslan
Marketing Coordinator, Graduate School of Social Sciences
Bahçeşehir University
hakan.aslan@gss.bau.edu.tr

Meryem Aybas
Asst. Prof. Dr.; Kafkas University
Faculty of Economics and
Administrative Science,
Department of Business Management
and Organization
meryemaybas@kafkas.edu.tr/
meryemaybas@gmail.com

Resul Baltaci
Bahçeşehir Üniversitesi,
rbaltaci@yahoo.com

Mehmet Yorulmaz
Assist. Prof.:
Selçuk University
Faculty of Health Sciences-Turkey
mtyorulmaz@hotmail.com

Burhanettin Uysal
PhD.
General Health Department-Turkey
burhaneddin.uysal@gmail.com

Adviye Asli Denizli

New Career Approaches and Career Capital

1 Introduction

The term *career* is derived from the Latin word *carraria*, which means road. However, different meanings have been attributed to this term in time. With this evolution, the modern meaning of the word "career" refers to an occupation or employment type that involves an opportunity to advance (Arthur and Lawrence, 1984). Career may also be defined as accumulations of information and knowledge embodied in skills, expertise, and relationship networks acquired through an evolving sequence of work experiences over time (Bird, 1994).

Although the concept of career had emerged and been discussed by different disciplines such as psychology and sociology earlier, it was addressed by studies focusing on the right interaction between individuals and organizations and career management in the late 1970s. Starting from the 1980s, the subject of career has become a separate field of study under business administration and part of the human resources management system (Adamson, Doherty, and Viney, 1998).

The perspective toward the concept of career, which is of interest to many different disciplines, has changed with developments that affect professional life, and the traditional career approach has been replaced by new career approaches. This section primarily focuses on the change in the nature of career as a concept and the emergence of new career approaches. It then explains new career approaches, introduces the concept of career capital, and finally discusses the role of this concept with regard to new career approaches.

2 The Evolving Nature of Career and the Emergence of New Career Approaches

Advancements in information and communication technologies, changes in the structure of organizations due to economic and technological developments, and the changing structure of psychological contract can be suggested as the most significant reasons behind the change observed in the nature of the concept of career. The traditional career approach, which involves an employee spending his or her entire professional life in one or two organizations and displaying a linear advancement in hierarchical ranks within the organization, has been abandoned due to the aforementioned reasons. This traditional approach has been replaced by new career approaches that involve multiple organizations and is even shaped independent of organizations, support not only vertical movement, but also horizontal and diagonal movements, and allow employees develop in more than one area.

Today, organizations resort to practices such as reengineering, business process reengineering, downsizing, delayering, and outsourcing in an attempt to deal with turbulent conditions. Such practices are directly reflected and cause instability in relationships between individuals and organizations (Brousseau, Driver, Eneroth, and Larson, 1996). Narrowing horizons in planning and uncertainties regarding the labor force needs of organizations in the future have brought along changes related to the concept of career (Adamson, Doherty, and Viney, 1998).

Economic developments have led to emergence of some novelties in the concept of career as well. The new information-based understanding of economy has caused structural differences in both jobs and labor force and changed the outlook of the concept of career in the business world (DeFillippi, Arthur, and Parker, 2003). In light of intensive developments in information and communication technologies, the ability to produce and use information constitutes the main dynamics of the new economy, which has led to a more equipped labor force as well as allowed employees to acquire competencies other than those specific to the organization. Hence, individuals are able to shape their careers independent of organizations.

Flexible forms of employment (gigs, part-time work, freelancing, etc.) are becoming more widespread due to market fluctuations, uncertainty, intensive use of technology, and other similar reasons. Concepts such as employability, network connections, and career mobility have become more significant with the prevalence of flexible forms of employment, and concepts emphasized by the traditional career approach such as stability and continuity have lost their meaning. This transformation has weakened the validity of the traditional career approach and resulted in new career approaches replacing the traditional approach (Marler, Woodard Barringer, and Milkovich, 2002).

Changes in the structure of psychological contract, which represents unwritten expectations between the employer and the employee, are being associated with new career approaches. While the expectations of the employee from the employer include long-term employment and job security according to the psychological contract of the traditional career approach, today these expectations have transformed into learning and performance opportunities that improve employability and flexibility. The organization's expectation of loyalty from the employee has weakened as well; instead, the expectation of high performance during the employee's time in the organization has become stronger (Sullivan, 1999).

Concepts such as downsizing and delayering have become more widespread with technological changes, which prevent the organization from employing the same individual throughout their career and providing job security. In the traditional career approach, the employee's career involves an ascending level of capacity through hierarchical ranks within the same organization. However, the concepts of job security and loyalty have been abandoned due to the intense atmosphere of uncertainty surrounding businesses today; instead, employees are expected to have a wide variety of skills and present this variety in an appropriate way. While linear career paths are still valid for some employees, this is not the case for many employees in such an environment. Careers of employees may develop in multiple ways and involve different organizations in today's business world (Gomez-Mejia, Balkin, and Cardy, 2012). In line with these developments, the concept of career has been handled differently and new career approaches have emerged.

3 New Career Approaches

The perspective of the traditional career approach is insufficient to shed light to careers of today's employees, which has led to a need for new career approaches. New career approaches suggested in the relevant literature include boundaryless career, protean career, portfolio career, and post-corporate career (Baruch and Peiperl, 2000). Researchers and practitioners seem to show a great deal of interest in the concepts of boundaryless career and protean career. It can be said that boundaryless career and protean career are concepts that significantly affect the theory and research on new career approaches considering that they are quite frequently the focus of various studies (Briscoe and Hall, 2006).

The concept of boundaryless career has emerged as an extension of the concept of boundaryless organization, which is in contrast with traditional organization structures (Inkson, 2006). Boundaries of organizations have become blurred due to reasons such as increased strategic alliances and joint ventures between businesses, higher rate of outsourcing, and higher popularity of flexible forms of employment. Thus, rules related to membership, department identity, and job responsibilities—definitions within organizations have become indistinct. The concept of boundaryless career refers to a career that unfolds unconstrained by clear boundaries around job activities, by fixed sequences of such activities, or by attachment to one organization (Miner and Robinson, 1994). The idea of boundaryless career goes beyond job opportunities presented by a single organization and offers employees the chance to acquire new experiences in different organizations or jobs. For employees who have flexible accumulations of information and improve their professional and sectoral network, boundaryless career means a career identity beyond organization and hierarchy (DeFillippi and Arthur, 1994). In other words, traditional career paths' losing their significance due to changes in the structure of organizations is not perceived as a threat by employees who keep their knowledge and equipment up-to-date as well as expand their professional network. On the contrary, it creates a wide range of opportunities for individuals who assume responsibility of their career.

Conceptualized by Hall (1996), the protean career is defined as a career that is driven by the individual and not by the organization unlike the traditional career approach, a career that is reconstructed as a result of the changing individual and environment. The word "protean" is derived from "Proteus", the Greek sea-god mentioned in Homer's Odyssey who could change and transform in many shapes at will. The concept of protean career emphasizes the individual's ability to transform according to their conditions and needs; in other words, the ability to adapt (Inkson, 2006). In today's world where economic uncertainties and economic crises lead to an increased threat of unemployment, the protean career orientation plays a very significant role. In such an environment, employees must shape their careers themselves. Another noteworthy factor related to the protean concept is that it is driven by the individual's values. Being values driven makes career decisions closely aligned with one's own personal values, rather than being driven by objective rewards such as material gains, promotion, or power (Waters, Briscoe, Hall, and Wang, 2014). To summarize, the protean career emphasizes the individual's defining their career success based on their own values and shaping their own career with this mentality.

Boundaryless career and protean career, which receive the highest interest among new career approaches, seem to offer a flexible and harmonic perspective and focus on sustaining employability through career self-management, life-long learning, psychological career success, and career mobility between organizations (Clarke, 2009).

4 The Concept of Career Capital

Career capital refers to the sum of knowledge, skills, experiences, and connections that individuals acquire throughout their career and lead them to success (Inkson and Arthur, 2001). Individuals accumulate career capital by consciously investing in career competencies suggested by DeFillippi and Arthur (1994), which represent three forms of knowing (Tams and Arthur, 2010). These competencies that allow individuals to be employed and guide their career include knowing-why, knowing-how, and knowing-whom. Knowing-why refers to the individual's career identity, values, and areas of interest; knowing-how refers to the individual's knowledge, skills, talents, expertise, and experiences regarding their career; and knowing-whom refers to the individual's professional network in and out of the organization (DeFillippi and Arthur, 1994). Today, career is seen as a process where individuals equip themselves with knowledge and progress by this means. The capital that carries individuals forward in this process is made up of their motivation and awareness regarding their career (knowing-why), their knowledge in their area of expertise (knowing-how), and their professional network connections (knowing-whom).

Each of the three forms of knowing that constitute the career capital may affect one another and this interaction may be constant. Further, the three forms of knowing complement each other because new career experiences are acquired by re-interpreting the previous experiences. For example, job skills (knowing-how) followed by the individual to focus on and achieve a task (knowing-why) provide the individual with new connections and collaborations (knowing-whom), and the extent to which the individual defines themselves with their job increases or decreases based on the messages or feedbacks received from such collaborations (DeFillippi, Arthur & Parker, 2003). In this way, it is possible for the individual to prepare themselves for different roles other than their current one and seize opportunities that they encounter.

Mayrhofer et al. (2004) have offered a different perspective related to the concept of career capital and suggest that the capital that supports the individual's success and that the individual may invest in consists of economic capital, social capital, and cultural capital based on definitions of Bourdieu, a sociologist, regarding types of capital. Economic capital refers to the individual's financial capacity, which may be acquired or inherited. Income is regarded as the most significant element of economic capital, and economic capital may be transformed into other forms of capital. Social capital is made up of relationships, social connections, and group memberships. Cultural and informational capital, on the other hand, refers to those the individual acquires through education and nurture. It is suggested that every career actor has a unique portfolio of career capital made up of a mixture of these capital types. Career capital is decisive in career choices and success of the individual.

5 The Role of Career Capital with Respect to New Career Approaches

The traditional career approach has lost a significant portion of its validity due to factors such as transition to the information economy, more dynamic structure of the business world, employability, and increased career mobility (Kuijpers and

Scheerens, 2006). The responsibility related to career management and development has shifted from organizations to individuals with the emergence of new career approaches (Pang, Chua, and Chu, 2008).

Among the concepts suggested as new career approaches, the boundaryless career emphasizes career flexibility in an atmosphere of uncertainty surrounding organizations, while the protean career focuses on the individual's shaping their own career. Career capital, on the other hand, points out to sustaining employability and progress throughout one's career (Harris and Ramos, 2013).

The concept of career has become unpredictable and multidimensional under the uncertain and ever-changing conditions of today's business world and economy. Employees can only seize important career opportunities to the extent that they are able to adapt to the change (Zhu, Wolff, Hall, Heras, Gutierrez, and Kram, 2013). At this point, the capital (knowing-why, knowing-how, and knowing-whom) in which employees invest throughout their career is very important. Competencies that make up the career capital allow employees to predict and seize career opportunities.

Career capital is regarded as a significant determinant in career success of individuals. Employees who are aware of their strengths and weaknesses, set realistic career goals, improve their knowledge and skills to reach these goals, and have network connections required for their career have an easier time to achieve success within the framework of new career approaches. In addition, the marketability of the individual's capital, which is made up of such investments into one's career, is an important factor in the individual's success (Eby, Butts, and Lockwood, 2003). The Internet has led to undeniable changes in how career works. Today, individuals who wish to improve their career are able to build their professional network where they can manage their profile and reputation through channels that involve potential employers and resources of information. In this way, individuals are able to emphasize their strengths, expand their social network consisting of professionals, and seize opportunities that appeal to them (Hooley, 2017). In other words, the Internet serves as a facilitator for increasing career capital and ensuring marketability among organizations in today's business world, which offers boundaryless and protean career opportunities. Employees must be careful and use their career capital effectively.

From the organization's point of view, the changing nature of career as a concept requires a different approach from the organization-oriented career development managed by the human resources department that consists of career paths standardized with the participation of line managers. Today, organizations seem to drift away from the "best practice" approach in terms of career management. It is suggested for organizations that they focus on improving their human capital consistent with the dynamics of labor market and adopt supportive and development-oriented practices rather than organization-oriented, "one size fits all" perspective such as career coaching (De Vos and Cambré, 2017). Individuals create value by carrying competencies that make up their career capital to their work environment. Thus, organizations, too, benefit from the development of their employees' career capital. Hence, similar to employees, those who assume the responsibility of human resources management within the organization must focus on the concept of career capital (Sutherland, Naidu, Seabela, Crosson, and Nyembe, 2015). Awareness regarding career capital makes it easier to create an employer brand that attracts successful career capitalists and makes organizations superior to their competitors, thanks to employees with top-tier skills (Lamb and Sutherland, 2010).

6 Conclusion

Current career approaches require employees to construct their career-related knowledge, skills, and network in a flexible, harmonic way that supports mobility between organizations. By constructing their own career capital, employees are able to shape their career according to their goals independent of the organization and find employment opportunities and gain experiences at different organizations. Additionally, employees who sustain a high level of employability, thanks to their career capital, become prepared against threats to their job security due to economic crises, market fluctuations, and organizations' practices such as downsizing, delayering, and outsourcing.

New career approaches require individuals to assume responsibility in shaping their career and encourage them to be adequately equipped and keep their knowledge and skills up-to-date at all times. In this sense, absolute commitment to the organization has been replaced by an opportunity for individuals to choose the organization that will support their career goals and increase their career capital. Thus, organizations should adopt practices that take this matter into account in terms of career management, which will lead to positive outcomes for both individuals and organizations.

References

Adamson, S. J., Doherty, N., & Viney, C. (1998). The meanings of career revisited: Implications for theory and practice. *British Journal of Management*, *9*(4), 251–259.

Arthur, M. B., & Lawrence, B. S. (1984). Perspectives on environment and career: An introduction. *Journal of Organizational Behavior*, *5*(1), 1–8.

Baruch, Y., & Peiperl, M. (2000). Career management practices: An empirical survey and implications. *Human Resource Management*, *39*(4), 347–366.

Bird, A. (1994). Careers as repositories of knowledge: A new perspective on boundaryless careers. *Journal of Organizational Behavior*, *15*(4), 325–344.

Briscoe, J. P., & Hall, D. T. (2006). Special section on boundaryless and protean careers. *Journal of Vocational Behavior*, *1*(69), 1–3.

Brousseau, K. R., Driver, M. J., Eneroth, K., & Larson, R. (1996). Career pandemonium: Realigning organizations and individuals. *Academy of Management Perspectives*, *10*(4), 52–66.

Clarke, M. (2009). Plodders, pragmatists, visionaries and opportunists: career patterns and employability. *Career Development International*, *14*(1), 8–28.

De Vos, A., & Cambré, B. (2017). Career management in high-performing organizations: A set-theoretic approach. *Human Resource Management*, *56*(3), 501–518.

DeFillippi, R. J., & Arthur, M. B. (1994). The boundaryless career: A competency-based perspective. *Journal of Organizational Behavior*, *15*(4), 307–324.

DeFillippi, R., Arthur, M., & Parker, P. (2003). Internet odysseys: Linking web roles to career and community investments. *International Journal of Human Resource Management*, *14*(5), 751–767.

Eby, L. T., Butts, M., & Lockwood, A. (2003). Predictors of success in the era of the boundaryless career. *Journal of Organizational Behavior*, *24*(6), 689–708.

Gómez-Mejía, L., Balkin, D., & Cardy, R. (2012). *Managing Human Resources* (7th ed.). NJ: Pearson Education.

Hall, D. T. (1996). Protean careers of the 21st century. *Academy of Management Perspectives*, *10*(4), 8–16.

Harris, R., & Ramos, C. (2013). Building career capital through further study in Australia and Singapore. *International Journal of Lifelong Education*, *32*(5), 620–638.

Hooley, T. (2017). Developing your career: harnessing the power of the internet for "digital career management". *Development and Learning in Organizations: An International Journal*, *31*(1), 9–11.

Inkson, K., & Arthur, M. B. (2001). How to be a successful career capitalist. *Organizational Dynamics*, *30*(1), 48–61.

Inkson, K. (2006). Protean and boundaryless careers as metaphors. *Journal of Vocational Behavior*, *69*(1), 48–63.

Kuijpers, M. A. C. T., & Scheerens, J. (2006). Career competencies for the modern career. *Journal of Career Development*, *32*(4), 303–319.

Lamb, M., & Sutherland, M. (2010). The components of career capital for knowledge workers in the global economy. *The International Journal of Human Resource Management, 21*(3), 295–312.

Marler, J. H., Woodard Barringer, M., & Milkovich, G. T. (2002). Boundaryless and traditional contingent employees: Worlds apart. *Journal of Organizational Behavior, 23*(4), 425–453.

Mayrhofer, W., Meyer, M., Iellatchitch, A., & Schiffinger, M. (2004). Careers and human resource management—a European perspective. *Human Resource Management Review, 14*(4), 473–498.

Miner, A. S., & Robinson, D. F. (1994). Organizational and population level learning as engines for career transitions. *Journal of Organizational Behavior, 15*(4), 345–364.

Pang, M., Chua, B. L., & Chu, C. W. (2008). Learning to stay ahead in an uncertain environment. *The International Journal of Human Resource Management, 19*(7), 1383–1394.

Sullivan, S. E. (1999). The changing nature of careers: A review and research agenda. *Journal of Management, 25*(3), 457–484.

Sutherland, M., Naidu, G., Seabela, S., Crosson, S., & Nyembe, E. (2015). The components of career capital and how they are acquired by knowledge workers across different industries. *South African Journal of Business Management, 46*(4), 1–10.

Tams, S., & Arthur, M. B. (2010). New directions for boundaryless careers: Agency and interdependence in a changing world. *Journal of Organizational Behavior, 31*(5), 629–646.

Waters, L., Briscoe, J. P., Hall, D. T., & Wang, L. (2014). Protean career attitudes during unemployment and reemployment: A longitudinal perspective. *Journal of Vocational Behavior, 84*(3), 405–419.

Zhu, G., B.Wolff, S., T.(Tim) Hall, D., Las Heras, M., Gutierrez, B., & Kram, K. (2013). Too much or too little? A study of the impact of career complexity on executive adaptability. *Career Development International, 18*(5), 457–483.

Adviye Aslı Denizli and Gönen İlkar Dündar

Human Resources Development Climate: Characteristics and Related Employee Behaviors*

1 Introduction

Human Resources Development (HRD) practices in organizations focus on developing performance by enhancing the links between knowledge and performance. HRD practices allow for behavioral changes in individuals, and such changes affect primarily individual performance and consequently organizational performance. In today's environment of rapid development and change, establishments need to develop their human resources to reach their goals, achieve competitive advantage, and ensure sustainability. The success of efforts related to HRD depends on creating an appropriate climate within the organization. HRD climate is an interesting subject since it allows efforts related to development to be successful, and it is related with many employee behaviors valued by today's organizations. This chapter explains the theoretical background and characteristics of HRD climate as well as discusses related employee behaviors.

2 Theoretical Background of Human Resources Development Climate

In order to accurately identify and guide behaviors of individuals, it is necessary to investigate circumstances related to the environment where these behaviors take place. This perspective has provided the foundation for the development of the concept of climate in the relevant literature and has been often discussed within the context of explaining and shaping employee behaviors (Soudek, 1983). Schneider and Reichers (1983) suggest that organizational climate involves common perceptions shared by members of the organization regarding organizational practices, policies, and processes. According to Moran and Volkwein (1992), organizational climate is a concept that involves relatively permanent characteristics that distinguish the organization from others as well

* This chapter is derived from the PhD thesis completed by Adviye Aslı Denizli under the guidance of Gönen İlkar Dündar.

as common perceptions about autonomy, trust, collaboration, support, innovation, and justice.

Although a long history of research on organizational climate fails to establish which organizational characteristics make up this concept, HRD climate, which represents employee perceptions related to the development environment within the organization, is accepted as an integral component of the general organizational climate (Chaudhary, Rangnekar, and Barua, 2013). HRD climate focuses more on employee development and, therefore, is a subset of organizational climate. The work environment within the organization is affected by HRD practices, which bring along the HRD climate, referring to an understanding of organizational climate from an HRD perspective (Mittal, Gupta, and Mottiani, 2016a).

Employees of the organization acquire shared experiences, and such experiences lead to a shared perception. Accordingly, it is possible to say that certain organizational climate conditions yield certain results, and shared perceptions of employees can be improved by guiding them in a similar way using certain tools (Anderson and West, 1998). Therefore, it is important to create an ideal environment of development within the organization and integrate this into the establishment's philosophy in order to create a healthy organizational climate and obtain the desired results from HRD practices aimed at improving the organization's human resources (Mufeed and Gurkoo, 2006). HRD climate has been valued by organizations since it was first suggested and became a necessary tool for organizations to develop and motivate their employees (Babushe and Narendranath, 2013).

HRD climate is defined as perceptions of employees about the environment of development within the organization. HRD climate is deemed as an integral part of organizational climate, and it is stated that a positive HRD climate facilitates achieving the goals of HRD practices (Rao and Abraham, 2010).

Muduli (2015) defines HRD climate as assumptions, values, and beliefs carried by the organizational participants about a work environment conducive for development of human resources.

Mariyappan (2010) states that the climate may affect motivation, performance, and job satisfaction by creating certain expectations regarding results of different actions. For an ideal HRD climate, top management needs to see human resources as the most important resource of the organization; managers need to develop competencies of their subordinates and help them recognize their strengths and weaknesses; the organization needs to provide an environment of open communication, team spirit, and trust; risk-taking needs to be encouraged; and the organization needs to implement development-oriented policies and practices (training, job rotation, career planning, potential appraisal, and rewarding).

Hyde et al. (2016) state that HRD climate emphasizes elements such as considering employees as human capital, recognizing and having confidence in the skills and capabilities of employees, communicating openly, encouraging risk taking and experimenting, making efforts to help employees recognize their capabilities and weaknesses, creating an environment of trust and collaboration, implementing sound HR policies, and accommodating HRD practices.

3 Characteristics of Human Resources Development Climate

Characteristics that positively affect HRD perceptions of employees and allow for a positive HRD climate within the organization fall under three headings: General (supportive) climate, HRD culture (OCTAPACE culture), and HRD mechanisms.

3.1 General (Supportive) Climate

One of the characteristics of a positive HRD climate, general (supportive) climate, deals with the commitment of the management toward developing the organization's human resources and providing genuine support for employees to this end (Mohanty, Parija, and Sahu, 2012).

General (supportive) climate within the organization is important for effective implementation of HRD activities. It focuses on the importance placed by top management and line managers on the development of human resources. However, such an environment that will ensure HRD practices achieve their goals does not only involve the commitment of the management, but also the main philosophy of the organization regarding the development of human resources, human resource policies, and attitudes within the organization related to the subject (Rao and Abraham, 2010). Core elements of general (supportive) climate include the perspective and attitude of the top management, human resource policies of the organization, commitment of line managers, and positive attitude of employees toward development (Lakkoju, 2014).

Beliefs and ideas of managers regarding HRD are reflected in their interactions with subordinates. This process influences whether employees will develop a positive attitude toward and internalize HRD. Consistency plays a key role in this sense; when messages from all sources are consistent and reliable, it becomes possible for employees to internalize this concept (Mittal, Gupta, and Mottiani, 2016a). For example, top management's and line managers' belief in and support for the performance management system and determined and consistent behaviors while running the system will ensure that employees internalize the system. In this way, the performance management system implemented in the organization will contribute to the development of employees and serve as a facilitator in achieving organizational goals.

3.2 Human Resources Development Culture

Developing and sustaining employee competencies within the organization require creating an appropriate culture. While HRD culture is a term with a broad meaning, researchers try to provide a framework for this concept by focusing on the most prominent values of HRD culture. HRD culture represents a framework that values and encourages openness, confrontation, trust, autonomy, pro-activity, authenticity, collaboration, and experimentation within the organization. HRD culture is known as the OCTAPACE (derived from the first letters of the aforementioned values) culture in the relevant literature.

The OCTAPACE culture is necessary for facilitating HRD activities within the organization. Openness refers to an environment in which employees can express their feelings and ideas freely, without any reservation. Confrontation means that employees face issues within the organization squarely and try to find solutions without hiding them or avoiding them for fear of hurting each other. Trust means an environment in which employees value and believe in each other. Authenticity refers to the willingness of employees to do what they say. Pro-activity means encouraging employees to take the initiative and risks. Autonomy is allowing members of the organization freedom to assume responsibility and work independently. Collaboration refers to an environment in which employees accept their mutual relationships, help each other, and work as a team (Rao and Abraham, 2010). Experimentation refers to the ability to view events from new perspectives and being creative when solving problems (Mittal, 2014). These values contribute to the creation of an environment of constant development for employees of the organization. A culture built on these values strengthens open communication, innovation and creativity, trust, participation in decision-making, and positive attitudes toward development. These values must be accepted within the organization and ultimately adopted in the organization's culture. However, the level of significance attributed to these values varies between organizations. For example, pro-activity and experimentation may be more dominant in HRD cultures of organizations operating in industries where uncertainty is prevalent, while authenticity and trust may be expected to be more dominant in more stable industries.

Rao, who conceptualized the HRD culture, notes that openness and confrontation, autonomy and collaboration, trust and authenticity, and pro-activity and experimentation go together. He states that these four pairs are the four building blocks of the HRD culture. He suggests that if these values are prioritized in an organization, it will develop its human resource potential and benefit from the competencies of its human resources at a maximum level (Rao, 2014).

In today's world where customer demands and expectations and technological developments are rapidly transforming, it is evident that organizations need to be flexible and innovative to achieve and sustain competitive advantage. Being flexible and innovative depends on creating a development-oriented culture and improving human resources constantly. HRD culture is regarded as the building block of a positive HRD climate, which allows for increased efficiency and achievement of goals related to growth and profitability (Jain, 2013).

3.3 Human Resources Development Mechanisms

In order to create a positive HRD climate within the organization, it is necessary to implement mechanisms aimed at development of organization's human resources effectively and consistently. It is crucial for HRD policies and practices to address the development of employees seriously in order to create a positive perception among employees regarding the organization's development environment. This allows for creating a positive HRD climate within the organization and increasing the organization's efficiency by ensuring development of employees (Jain, 2014).

It is necessary to adopt an integrated perspective toward HRD mechanisms in order to implement HRD activities successfully within the organization. HRD mechanisms include constructs such as performance appraisal, potential appraisal, rewards, career development, feedback and counseling, training, work rotation, and employee welfare for increased quality of work life (Rao and Abraham, 2010). It can be suggested that these mechanisms comprise subsystems of the HRD system. Implementing these mechanisms effectively, consistently, and impartially in conjunction with each other ensures the functionality of the organization's HRD system.

It is noted that all HRD mechanisms must be implemented together by considering links between them to achieve the desired results. For example, the results obtained from performance appraisal must be used in career development system, determination of training needs, and rewards (Jain, 2014).

HRD mechanisms create an organizational environment that makes it easier for employees to develop themselves, and the HRD climate is enhanced with these mechanisms (Dash, Mohapatra, and Bhuyan, 2013). It is advocated that HRD mechanisms lead to an efficient organization through HRD climate and HRD outputs. HRD mechanisms and processes provide a foundation for the development of the HRD climate, and a positive HRD climate facilitates the implementation of HRD systems (Mittal, Gupta, and Motiani, 2016b).

Organizations need to create a positive HRD climate in order to obtain the desired results from their HRD efforts, reap the fruits of their investment in HRD, and make efficient use of their human resources. To this end, top management and line managers must give due importance to HRD, believe in their employees' skills, and give genuine support to their development; the organization must spread values of the HRD culture and implement HRD mechanisms effectively (Jain, 2014).

4 Relationship Between Human Resources Development Climate and Employee Behaviors

Studies on the relationship between the HRD climate and employee behaviors deal with the relationship of this concept with job satisfaction, work engagement, organizational commitment, and organizational citizenship behavior. This section contains findings obtained in some of these studies.

Solkhe and Chaudhary (2011) conducted a study with 71 executives from various departments and different hierarchical levels of a public sector undertaking located in India and found a positive and strong correlation between their perceptions regarding HRD climate and job satisfaction levels and that the perception of HRD climate had a positive effect on job satisfaction. Dash, Mohapatra, and Bhuyan (2013) performed a study with 60 administrative personnel at Mahanadi Coalfields Ltd. in India and found a strong correlation between employees' perceptions regarding HRD climate and job satisfaction levels and that the perception of HRD climate had a positive effect on job satisfaction. Babushe and Narendranath (2013) performed a study with 539 employees from public institutions in Ethiopia and found a strong correlation between employees' perceptions regarding HRD climate and job satisfaction levels and that the perception of HRD climate had a significant effect on job satisfaction.

Chaudhary, Rangnekar, and Barua (2011a) conducted a study using data obtained from 85 business executives working in private and public sector manufacturing and service firms in India and found a positive correlation between perception regarding HRD climate and employee engagement. Further, the researchers found that the perception regarding HRD climate had a positive effect on employee engagement. In another study conducted by the same researchers in India in 2011, the HRD climate and occupational self-efficacy perceptions were considered as predictors of work engagement. It was found that there was a positive and moderate correlation between the perception of HRD climate and work engagement and that the perception of HRD climate had a positive effect on work engagement (Chaudhary, Rangnekar, and Barua, 2011b).

Akinyemi and Iornem (2012) performed a study with 303 employees from the banking industry in Nigeria and found a positive correlation between the perception regarding HRD climate and organizational commitment level, the affective commitment being the dimension where this correlation was the strongest. Mittal, Gupta, and Montiani (2016b) performed a study using data derived from 203 bank employees in India and found a positive correlation between the perception regarding HRD climate and organizational commitment.

Ewis (2015) conducted a study investigating the effect of the HRD climate on organizational commitment, work engagement, and organizational citizenship behavior with 246 employees from three Saudi telecommunication companies. The results of the study revealed that there was a positive and strong correlation between the HRD climate perception and the aforementioned variables and that the HRD climate perception had a significant effect on these variables. Manzoor and Shah (2015) performed a study with 613 employees from public banks in India and found a positive and moderate correlation between the perception regarding HRD climate and organizational citizenship behavior. However, the researchers did not find the effect of perception regarding HRD climate on organizational citizenship behavior to be significant.

5 Conclusion

The literature on human resources management seems to have shifted its focus to the distinction between intended human resources practices, implemented human resources practices, and perceived human resources practices. According to this distinction, it is advocated that perceptions regarding human resources practices determine reactions to such practices. Reactions of employees change depending on how they perceive these practices (e.g., constructive or destructive), and these reactions are reflected in their attitudes and behaviors toward the job and the organization (Brewster, Gollan, and Wright, 2013). It is not enough for organizations to design and carry out such practices to make the most of their human resources and get the desired results from their HRD practices aimed at achieving current and long-term goals. Perception of employees regarding such practices—aimed at ensuring development by creating behavioral change—must be considered as well. In this context, it is important to study the HRD climate, which reflects perceptions of employees regarding the development environment and HRD practices within the organization, and reveal its relationship with employee behaviors.

Findings obtained in studies on the subject show that the perception regarding HRD climate has a positive correlation with concepts such as job satisfaction, work engagement, organizational commitment, and organizational citizenship behavior. Thus, attention paid to the HRD climate within the organization will facilitate achieving these behaviors that are of utmost importance for organizations. Human resources practices are necessary to encourage and support employee behaviors required for businesses to achieve their goals. It is necessary to create an appropriate climate and culture within the organization to get the desired results from these practices (Schuler and Jackson, 2014). The relationship between the HRD climate and employee behaviors constitutes the focal point of recent studies on HRD climate. Studies on HRD climate are often performed in India; therefore, conducting studies in different countries will be beneficial in terms of illuminating the subject. Further, it is believed that addressing the relationship of HRD climate with organizational justice, organizational support, organizational trust, and organizational identification will contribute to the literature.

References

Akınyemi, B. & Iornem, D. (2012). Human Resource Development Climate and Employee Commitment in Recapitalized Nigerian Banks, *International Journal of Business and Management, 7* (5), 91–99.

Anderson, N.R., & West, M.A. (1998). Measuring Climate for Work Group Innovation: Development and Validation of the Team Climate Inventory. *Journal of Organizational Behavior, 19* (3), 235–258.

Babushe, M.T. & Narendranath, K. (2013). HRD Climate and Job Satisfaction in the Public Sector of Ethiopia: An Empirical Study in Amhara and Benishangul-Gumuz Regions, *IOSR Journal of Business and Management (IOSR-JBM), 13* (6), 121–131.

Brewster, C., Gollan, P. J., & Wright, P. M. (2013). Guest editors' note: Human Resource Management and the Line. *Human Resource Management, 52* (6), 829–838.

Chaudhary, R., Rangnekar, S., & Barua, M. (2011a). Relation between Human Resource Development Climate and Employee Engagement: Results from India. *Europe's Journal of Psychology, 7* (4), 664–685.

Chaudhary, R., Rangnekar, S., & Barua, M.K. (2011b). HRD Climate and Occupational Self-efficacy as Predictors of Employee Engagement. *Review of Management, 1* (3), 16–28.

Chaudhary, R., Rangnekar, S., & Barua, M. (2013). Human Resource Development Climate in India: Examining the Psychometric Properties of HRD Climate Survey Instrument. *Vision, 17* (1), 41–52.

Dash, S., Mohapatra, J., & Bhuyan, L.L. (2013). A Correlation of HRD Climate with Job Satisfaction of Employees: An Empirical Investigation on MCL, Burla, Sambalpur, Odisha. *International Journal of Research in Business Management (IJRBM), 1* (2), 11–26.

Ewis, M.Z. (2015). The Role of Human Resources Development Climate in Building Positive Job Attitudes and Extra-Role Behaviors. *International Journal of Business and Management, 10* (5), 153–167.

Hyde, A.M., Singhai, M., Ubeja, S.K., & Patel, R. (2016). HRD Climate: A Literature Review. *Research Journal of Management Sciences, 5* (9), 63–65.

Jain, V.K. (2013). HRD Climate Factors in Indian Industries-A Case Study. *International Journal of Development Research, 3* (12), 43–56.

Jain, V.K. (2014). An Overview of Human Resource Development Programmes in Indian Industries. *IOSR Journal of Business and Management, 16* (3), 21–31.

Lakkoju, S. (2014). HRD Climate in Indian Banks: a Comparison between SBI & KVB, *The Indian Journal of Industrial Relations, 50* (2), 280–292.

Manzoor, S. & Shah, P.A. (2015). Exploring Relationship between Human Resource Development Climate and Organizational Citizenship Behavior: A Study of Banks. *International Journal of Human Resource & Industrial Research, 2* (7), 1–12.

Mariyappan, M.S.R. (2010). HRD Climate in Co-Operative Dairy Union – A Case Study. *Global Management Review, 4* (2), 33–36.

Mittal, S. (2014). Does Employee Characteristics Impact HRD Climate? A Study in Banking Sector. *The Indian Journal of Industrial Relations, 50* (2), 270–279.

Mittal, S., Gupta, V., & Mottiani, M. (2016a). HRD Climate & Customer Satisfaction in Indian Private Banks. *The Indian Journal of Industrial Relations, 51* (3), 447–459.

Mittal, S., Gupta V., & Motiani, M. (2016b). Relation between Human Resource Development Climate and Organisational Commitment: Empirical Study in Indian Banking Sector, *International Journal of Indian Culture and Business Management, 12* (2), 204–223.

Mohanty, B., Parija, S., & Sahu, G. (2012). An Empirical Study on HRD Climate and Its Impact on Job Performance in Private Insurance Companies in Odisha. *International Journal of Multidisciplinary Research, 2* (5), 15–28.

Moran T.E. & Volkwein, J.F. (1992). The Cultural Approach to the Formation of Organizational Climate. *Human Relations, 45* (1), 19–47.

Muduli, A. (2015). High Performance Work System, HRD climate and Organisational Performance: An Empirical Study. *European Journal of Training and Development, 39* (3), 239–257.

Mufeed, A.S. & Gurkoo, A.F. (2006). Enhancing Educational Institutions Effectiveness through HRD Climate: An Empirical Assessment. *Management &Change, 10* (2), 25–64.

Rao, T.V. & Abraham, S.J., (2010). HRD Climate in Organizations. In T.V. Rao (Ed.), *Readings in Human Resource Development* (pp. 36–45). New Delhi: Oxford & IBH Publishing.

Rao, T.V. (2014). *HRD Audit: Evaluating the Human Resource Function for Business Improvement* (2nd ed.). New Delhi: SAGE Publications.

Schneider, B. & Reichers, A.E. (1983). On the Etiology of Climates. *Personnel Psychology, 36* (1), 19–39.

Schuler, R., & E. Jackson, S. (2014). Human Resource Management and Organizational Effectiveness: Yesterday and Today. *Journal of Organizational Effectiveness: People and Performance, 1* (1), 35–55.

Solkhe, A. & Chaudhary, N. (2011). HRD Climate and Job Satisfaction: An Empirical Investigation. *International Journal of Computing and Business Research, 2* (2), 1–20.

Soudek, M. (1983). Organizational Climate and Professional Behavior of Academic Librarians. *Journal of Academic Librarianship, 8* (6), 334–338.

Anıl Boz Semerci

Cyberloafing in Organizations: Job Quality and Job Involvement as Predictors of Employees' Cyberloafing Behaviors

1 Introduction

In recent years, as technology is increasingly utilized in workplaces, there has been a growing interest on the abuse of organizations' Internet resources. Although the Internet is an important tool for businesses to perform efficiently and effectively, it is also a tool that employees can spend their personal resources through rather than meeting work demands (Lim and Chen, 2012). The term cyberloafing is defined as "*any voluntary act of employees' using their companies' Internet access during office hours to surf non-job related Web sites for personal purposes and to check (including receiving and sending) personal e-mail as misuse of the Internet*" (Lim, 2002, p. 677). That is cyberloafing is the non-work-related Internet usage of employees during working hours.

Many debates are still going on whether cyberloafing has a negative impact on employees' productivity or not. Some scholars have indicated that cyberloafing leads to time loss and impacts productivity negatively. Cyberloafing activities have been found as having a diminishing role on work performance (Ramayah, 2010), job engagement (Lim and Chen, 2012), and organizational commitment (Niaei et al., 2014). On the other hand, in some studies, it is stated that cyberloafing is beneficial to for decreasing employees' work stress (Stanton, 2002), helping them to deal with work problems (Lim and Chen, 2012), and increasing innovative work behaviours (Yogun, 2015) and organizational learning capacity (Keklik et al., 2015). Although the findings related to cyberloafing consequences are not conclusive, a meta-analytic investigation by Mercado et al. (2017) revealed that cyberloafing is strongly correlated with overall counterproductive work behaviours. From this perspective, examination of cyberloafing behaviours becomes crucial for organizations in order to understand its predictors and develop strategies according to these predictors.

This chapter seeks to offer an integrated approach to explore the predictive roles of job quality and job involvement on employees' cyberloafing behaviours. More specifically, the employees' perceptions of job quality and job involvement are examined by considering their impacts on cyberloafing. Such an investigation is necessary to examine possible reasons behind why some employees are so engaged in cyberloafing behaviours than others. It is also valuable to understand how supportive sources of employees as job characteristics affect their job involvement and non-work-related behaviours. Such knowledge can provide a wider perspective and help managers to control employees' Internet usage.

2 Literature Review

Previous research examining the antecedents of cyberloafing activities can be categorized as personal, organizational, and job-related variables. However, there is scarce research on the relationship between job-related factors and cyberloafing. Job quality, as one of the job-related variables, has become an important indicator for employees' productive or counterproductive behaviours. Job quality is defined as "*sets of work features which foster the wellbeing of the worker*" (Strazdins et al., 2010, p. 2052). Job quality is considered as a combination of many factors that are important for employees. Some of these factors are job control, job security, flexible working hours, family-friendly policies, and workload. Employees' perceptions of these job features can result in positive or negative organizational outcomes. Therefore, it is proposed that employees who perceive their job quality as high are less likely to engage in counterproductive behaviours. That is, poor quality jobs compound employees' cyberloafing behaviours.

Hypothesis 1: Job quality negatively affects employees' cyberloafing behaviours.

Job quality is especially important for today's employees since they are spending longer hours at work. Employees as sources of organizations perceive job characteristics and in turn develop positive or negative job attitudes (Barling et al., 2003). The job characteristics associated with meaningfulness of job, greater responsibility and safety and balance in work and family life lead to positive job attitudes. Many studies have revealed that good job characteristics lead to high job satisfaction (Judge et al., 2000) and job engagement (Schaufeli and Bakker, 2004). In this chapter, it is proposed that job quality will have a positive impact on employees' job involvement.

Hypothesis 2: Job quality positively affects employees' job involvement.

Job involvement is defined as a "*cognitive belief state of psychological identification with one's job*" (Kanungo, 1982, p. 80). It is considered to be an important factor influencing organizational outcomes. Many researches revealed the positive role of job involvement on job satisfaction, performance and effort, while some others indicated negative relationships with absenteeism and turnover intention. It is stated that employees who have higher levels of job involvement spend most of their time on performing job demands and do not have as much time to engage in workplace deviance (Ketchen et al., 2008). Studies have shown that when employees are disengaged at work they will be more likely to participate in non-work-related activities (Galperin and Burke, 2006). Based on these findings and literature review, it is proposed that job involvement will negatively affect employees' cyberloafing behaviours.

Hypothesis 3: Job involvement negatively affects employees' cyberloafing behaviours.

3 Methodology

3.1 Sample

Data were obtained from 382 academicians working in three public universities in Ankara, Turkey. The population consists of all academicians in these three universities, which is approximately 10,000 people. Krejcie and Morgan (1970) population and sample size table was used to determine the sample size. At 95 % confidence level, the calculation gives minimum sample size as 370. Of the 552 questionnaires distributed, 385 were returned with a response rate of 69.7 %. Data obtained from three participants were not included in the analysis because of the 40 % and above missing values on the items.

In the data collection procedure, academicians were contacted via email and online survey link was send. The purpose of the study was explained and the possibility of sharing the results was offered. Data collection lasted one year, starting in August 2017 till August 2018. The mean age of the participants was 47.6 years and of these 65.9 % were female and 34 % were male.

3.2 Measures

Job quality was measured with the scale developed by Strazdins et al. (2007) and this brief version was used by Charlesworth et al. (2011). The scale consists of six items, which are related to work conditions: *job control, job security, flexibility* (flexible start and finish times), *family friendly leave* (family-related paid leave) and *workload.* Sample items include "I have a lot of freedom to decide how I do my own work", "I never have enough time to get everything done in my job." Participants were asked to rate their perceptions using a 5-point Likert scale format, ranging from 1 (strongly disagree) to 5 (strongly agree). The coefficient alpha score of the scale was $\alpha = .81$

Job involvement was measured with the scale developed by Lodahl and Kejner (1965). The scale consists of two items, which are "I'll stay overtime to finish a job, even if I'm not paid for it" and "I used to care more about my work, but now other things are more important to me" (reverse-coded). Each of these items was measured on a scale ranging from 1 (strongly disagree) to 5 (strongly agree). The coefficient alpha score of the scale was $\alpha = .70$

Cyberloafing was assessed with the scale developed by Lim (2002), which included eight items referring to browsing activities and three to e-mailing activities. Sample items include "Browsing sports-related web sites" "Downloading non-work-related information" and "Sending non-work-related e-mail." The responses were rated on a 5-point Likert scale ranging from 1 (never) to 5 (constantly).The coefficient alpha reliabilities of the scale was $\alpha = .89$.

4 Results

Structural equation modelling was used in the analytical procedure of this study. This is appropriate for data in which a series of regressions are being performed. Prior to applying the structural equation model, which defines the predictions among latent variables, confirmatory factor analyses (CFA) were performed in order to examine how well the observed items serve as a measurement instrument for the latent variables. The sufficiency of sample size for factor analysis was measured by the Kaiser-Meyer-Olkin (KMO) test, for job quality (0.68), job involvement (0.81) and cyberloafing scales (0.88). The CFA results revealed that a 3-factor model fits the data adequately ($\chi^2/df = 1.98$; GFI= 0.95; CFI=0.95; NFI= 0.96; SRMR= 0.05; RMSEA= 0.05). That is, all variables (job quality, job involvement and cyberloafing) were assumed to be independent. The standardized factor loadings of the items' were above 0.40 and loaded significantly on their underlying factors, which is satisfactory for construct validity. With regard to the composite reliability (CR), it showed that most of the indicators exceeded 0.7 (for job quality 0.78, for job involvement 0.72, and for cyberloafing 0.76), which indicates good internal consistency. The average variance extracted (AVE) from all the latent variables was higher than 0.5, which shows convergent validity. Tab. 1 presents the mean, standard deviation and correlations of the variables. The diagonal elements in Tab. 1 are the squareroots of AVEs and they are greater than the inter-construct correlations, which supports the discriminant validity. The correlations also show that the bivariate relations among several of the variables were in the expected direction and statistically significant.

After the examination of factor structures, the structural model was assessed for testing hypothesized relations between latent variables. The empirical findings on Fig. 1 support the first hypothesis (H_1), which posits that job involvement influences cyberloafing behaviours negatively ($\beta = -.42$, $p < .01$). The path between job quality and job involvement is statistically significant and

Tab. 1: Means, Standard Deviations and Correlations of the Variables

	Mean	S.D.	1	2	3	C.R.
1. Job quality	3.56	0.84	(0.55)			0.78
2. Job involvement	3.59	1.15	0.43**	(0.91)		0.72
3. Cyberloafing	4.05	1.02	-0.36**	-0.29**	(0.92)	0.76

Note:, ** p< .001

S.D: Standard deviation, C.R: Composite reliability

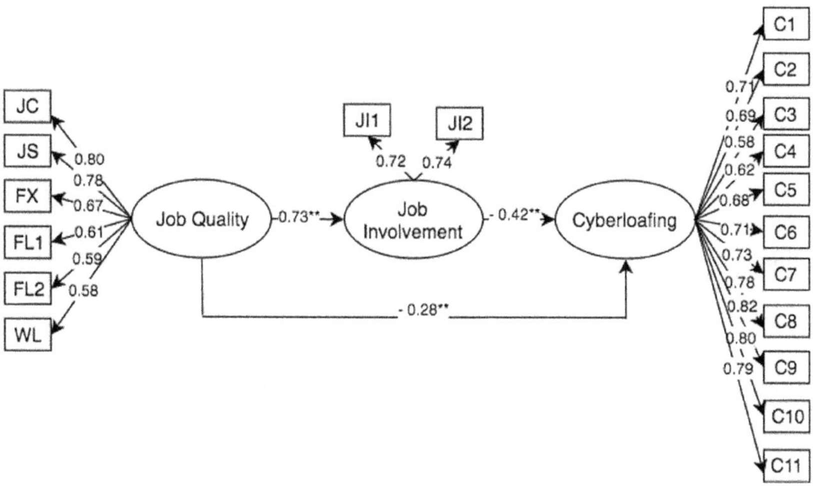

Fig. 1: Results of Structural Equation Modeling. Note: JC: Job control, JS: Job security, FX: Flexibility, FL: Family friendly leave, WL: Workload, JI: Job involvement, C: Cyberloafing. * p< .05, ** p< .001

positive ($\beta = .73$, $p < .01$), which supports H_3. The direct link from job quality to cyberloafing was also statistically significant and negative ($\beta = -.28$, $p < .01$). Thus, this result provides support to H_2. All the indicators, related to overall fit of the model, showed an acceptable fit ($\chi^2/df = 2.01$; GFI= 0.95; CFI=0.90; NFI= 0.93; SRMR= 0.05; RMSEA= 0.06).

5 Discussion and Conclusion

The results of this study address several issues and can be interpreted in terms of the two relationships: the relationship between job quality and cyberloafing, and the one between job involvement and cyberloafing. The results obtained show that job quality has a significant negative influence on the cyberloafing behaviours of employees, which supports Hypothesis 1. This emphasizes the importance of developing job characteristics to reduce employees' misusing of the Internet. Managers should make some interventions to offer more favorable job characteristics for their employees. Managers should consider different job designs, flexible working times and pay attention to the balance between job demand and control and employees' work and family lives. Although cyberloafing is likely to have a positive impact on employees' work stress (Henle and Blanchard, 2008; Lim and Chen, 2012), it also reduces the amount of resources (energy and time) that employees will use for work demands. Therefore, formal and informal interactions in organizations and planned social activities can help employees to perceive their job as more meaningful and less stressful.

The results show that Hypothesis 3 was supported, demonstrating that job involvement has a negative impact on employees' cyberloafing behaviours. That is, employees who have high job involvement are less likely to cyberloaf. These results also indicate consistency with previous studies that demonstrate job attitudes influence cyberloafing (Garrett and Danziger, 2008; Liberman et al., 2011). However, few studies addressed the role of job attitudes in cyberloafing activities. Future studies can examine other job-related attitudes such as job satisfaction and job engagement. Moreover, the results indicate that job quality positively impacts employees' job involvement, which was proposed in Hypothesis 2. This finding is also complementary to Liberman et al. (2011), who found that job involvement and intrinsic involvement lead to low cyberloafing activities. The results indicate that job involvement may play a different role as a mediator and transform the employees' perceptions of job quality to a lower level misusing of the Internet.

Although the present study provided comprehensive findings, they should be interpreted in light of its limitations. It is noteworthy to consider that a larger sample with higher response rates might increase the generalizability of the findings and help to reduce potential method bias. Although confirmatory factor analysis and Harman's one-factor test results indicated that common method bias is not a serious problem, future studies' data from different sources may help to reduce measures concerns. Furthermore, the cross-sectional design of this study does not allow proposing and testing the causality. Future studies may incorporate experimental or longitudinal research methodologies, which would enable researchers to control other influential variables and to explore the changes in variables during specific time periods. The other limitation concerns the participants' variety. Focusing on the education sector and a small set of universities may limit the interpretation of studied variables in the model. Data obtained from participants coming from variety of industries would help to provide more comprehensive results.

As a result, despite all limitations, this research can help to increase awareness on job characteristics and employees' involvement in cyberloafing literature. A deeper study on the job designs and person–job fit could explain to what extent the job characteristics and employees' perceptions affect the acts of workplace deviance. Also, what is the influence of managers on these processes? Another suggestion that could be offered for future research is the analysis of moderator variables in the relationships of this model. Future studies should explore to what extent the results obtained are contingent on several moderator variables.

References

Barling, J., Kelloway, E. K., & Iverson, R. D. (2003). High-quality work, job satisfaction, and occupational injuries. *Journal of applied psychology*, 88(2), 276.

Charlesworth, S., Strazdins, L., O'Brien, L., & Sims, S. (2011). Parents' jobs in Australia: Work hours polarisation and the consequences for job quality and gender equality. *Australian Journal of Labour Economics*, 14(1), 35.

Galperin, B. L., & Burke, R. J. (2006). Uncovering the relationship between workaholism and workplace destructive and constructive deviance: An exploratory study. *International Journal of Human Resource Management*, 17, 331–347.

Garrett, R. K., & Danziger, J. N. (2008). On cyberslacking: Workplace status and personal Internet use at work. *CyberPsychology & Behavior*, 11(3), 287–292.

Henle, C. A., & Blanchard, A. L. (2008). The interaction of work stressors and organizational sanctions on cyberloafing. *Journal of Managerial Issues*, 20(3), 383–400.

Judge, T. A., Bono, J. E., & Locke, E. A. (2000). Personality and job satisfaction: The mediating role of job characteristics. *Journal of applied psychology*, 85(2), 237.

Kanungo, R. N. (1982). Measurement of job and work involvement. *Journal of Applied Psychology*, 67(3), 341.

Keklik, B., Kiliç, R., Yildiz, H., & Yildiz, B. (2015). Sanal Kaytarma Davranislarinin Örgütsel Ögrenme Kapasitesi Üzerindeki Etkisinin Incelenmesi/An Investigation of the Effect of Cyberloafing Behaviors on Organizational Learning Capacity. *Business and Economics Research Journal*, 6(3), 129.

Ketchen, D. J., Craighead, C. W., & Buckley, M. R. (2008). Time bandits: How they are created, why they are tolerated, and what can be done about them. *Business Horizons*, 51, 141–150.

Krejcie, R. V., & Morgan, D. W. (1970). Determining sample size for research activities. *Educational and psychological measurement*, 30(3), 607–610.

Liberman, B., Seidman, G., Mckenna, K. Y., & Buffardi, L. E. (2011). Employee job attitudes and organizational characteristics as predictors of cyberloafing. *Computers in Human behavior*, 27(6), 2192–2199.

Lim, V. K. (2002). The IT way of loafing on the job: Cyberloafing, neutralizing and organizational justice. *Journal of Organizational Behavior: The International Journal of Industrial, Occupational and Organizational Psychology and Behavior*, 23(5), 675–694.

Lim, V. K., & Chen, D. J. (2012). Cyberloafing at the workplace: gain or drain on work? *Behaviour & Information Technology*, 31(4), 343–353.

Lodahl, T. M., & Kejner, M. (1965). The definition and measurement of job involvement. *Journal of Applied Psychology*, 49, 24–33.

Mercado, B. K., Giordano, C., & Dilchert, S. (2017). A meta-analytic investigation of cyberloafing. *Career Development International*, 22(5), 546–564.

Niaei, M., Peidaei, M. M., & Nasiripour, A. A. (2014). The relation between staff cyberloafing and organizational commitment in organization of environmental protection. *Kuwait Chapter of the Arabian Journal of Business and Management Review*, 3(7), 59.

Ramayah, T. (2010). Personal web usage and work inefficiency. *Business Strategy Series*, 11(5), 295–301.

Schaufeli, W. B., & Bakker, A. B. (2004). Job demands, job resources, and their relationship with burnout and engagement: A multi-sample study. *Journal of Organizational Behavior: The International Journal of Industrial, Occupational and Organizational Psychology and Behavior*, 25(3), 293–315.

Stanton, J. M., 2002. Company profile of the frequent Internet user. *Communications of the ACM*, 45 (1), 55–59.

Strazdins, L., Shipley, M., & Broom, D. H. (2007). What Does Family-friendly Really Mean? Wellbeing, Time, and the Quality of Parents' Jobs. *Australian Bulletin of Labour*, 33(2), 202.

Strazdins, L., Shipley, M., Clements, M., Obrien, L. V., & Broom, D. H. (2010). Job quality and inequality: Parents' jobs and children's emotional and behavioural difficulties. *Social Science & Medicine*, 70(12), 2052–2060.

Yogun, A. E. (2015). Cyberloafing and Innovative Work Behavior Among Banking Sector Employees. *International Journal of Business and Management Review*, 3(10), 61–71.

Alptekin Develi and Ayse Gokcen Kapusuz

The Relationship Between Psychological Capital and Job Embeddedness: A Theoretical Approach

1 Introduction

In today's individual performance-oriented work environment, positive psychology has an important place to be able to consider the strengths, wellness, resiliency, and other positive characteristics of employees' behaviors. As Diener (2000) and Peterson (2000) noted that emphasizing the individual's positive sides and behaviors in workplaces by focusing on the strengths and positive outcomes is the aim of positive psychology to be able to develop wellness and personal life.

From this point of view, in recent years psychological capital which is positively related to individual performance and personal well-being has become an important tool for examining positive organizational behavior. On the other hand, the concept of job embeddedness, which expresses the wishes of the employees to stay at work, has emerged as a new subject in the literature. Factors that ensure employees do not leave their work have been tried to be identified for a long time by numerous researchers. The issue of job embeddedness has brought a different perspective for this situation. Although many studies have determined the antecedents of job embeddedness, there is no study examining the relationship between job embeddedness and psychological capital. This chapter aims to contribute to filling a gap in the field of organizational behavior by explaining the theoretical relationship between psychological capital and job embeddedness.

In the sections that follow, the concepts of psychological capital and job embeddedness are primarily explained with their components and dimensions. Afterward, the relationship between these two concepts is explained through the Field Theory and Strong Ties Approach. Finally, the anticipated relationship is discussed and recommendations are provided for managers and future researches.

2 Theoretical Framework

This part of the chapter explains the concepts of psychological capital and job embeddedness. In addition, the relationship between these concepts is discussed.

2.1 Psychological Capital

Toward the end of the 1990s, positive psychology was introduced with the help of research conducted by Prof. M. Seligman and his colleagues in the field of organizational behavior. Seligman and Csikszentmihalyi (2000) handle the subject as a science of positive individual and organizational features. After that, psychological capital was first proposed by Luthans and his colleagues. They also created a Psychological Capital Scale in 2007.

Psychological capital can be defined as positive psychological capital which refers to processes that include positive attitudes, behaviors and their feedbacks, and criticism. All of these issues contribute to the improvement and development of an individual, group, or organization. Psychological capital is one of the main topics of positive organizational behavior (Luthans & Youssef, 2004). As Keleş (2011) emphasized, psychological capital contains strengths of individual capabilities which are known as measurable, developable, and effectively controllable applications.

All these aforementioned positive sides of individuals positively affect job performance, human well-being, and motivation as well. Besides other uses of the term "*capital*", it is used to determine "*the value of human resources*" in this context. Luthans and his co-authors also noted that the context of psychological capital cannot be considered as stable because of the liveliness and variety of personality traits (Luthans, Avolio, Avey & Norman, 2007: 542).

Psychological capital positively affects individuals through the following four components. These four components of psychological capital can be developed and managed to experience success.

2.1.1 Self-Efficacy/Confidence

According to Bandura (1982), self-efficacy is expressed as an individual's cognitive evaluation or belief about their abilities and capabilities (Luthans, 2002). Bandura (1997) emphasized that the number of abilities and capabilities of a person is not as much important as what the individual can do with these capabilities and how they believe in that. Self-confident people can choose and develop methods for attaining their goals (Caprara & Cervone, 2003).

2.1.2 Hope

Hope is expected to be a significant context within entrepreneurship as setting and planning goals and future situations, dreaming different ways to be able to achieve goals (Baker & Nelson, 2005). Luthans and Youssef (2004) suggested that managers and employees should be urged to develop their hope and reach the goals they desire by this means. Several researches point out that hope is positively related to life satisfaction, work satisfaction, and performance and motivation to cope with stressful events (Valle, Huebner & Suldo, 2004; Luthans & Youssef, 2004).

2.1.3 Optimism

It is related to expectations about positive outcomes and best possible results (Carver, Scheier & Segerstrom, 2010). It can be said that optimistic people in both organizational and personal life, as opposed to pessimists, generally know how to manage experiences with different kinds of difficulties and bad situations (Scheier, Carver & Bridges, 2001).

2.1.4 Resiliency

Resiliency is about individuals' capability to succesfully cope with important risks and changes (Luthans, 2002). This dimension of psychological capital is also associated with bouncing back from bad and negative situations and experiences and adapting to changes and stressful conditions (Tugade & Fredrickson, 2004). Resilient people take lessons from adversities (Masten, 2001).

2.2 Job Embeddedness

The concept of job embeddedness, which was first proposed by Mitchell and his colleagues (2001), explains the reasons why employees want to stay in their organizations. The employee turnover from the current jobs brings significant cost to the organizations (Mitchell, Holtom, Lee, Sablynski & Erez, 2001). For this reason, as a general approach, both managers and researchers examine the factors that lead to turnover intentions. Job embeddedness, which emerges with a different approach, shows itself as a concept that addresses the direct reasons that keep employees at work. In this context, job embeddedness came to the fore in explaining the tendency of employees to continue working in the organization and the efficiency of efforts to reduce employee turnover (Zorlu, Avan & Bulut, 2016).

Job embeddedness can be defined as a degree that shows the situation extent to which employees are settled in their work and organization (Sekiguchi, Burton & Sablynski, 2008). The situation of being embedded in the work is an approach that deals with why the person wants to stay in the organization with a positive point of view. The concept is defined as the combination of forces that prevent the employee from leaving work (Halbesleben & Wheeler, 2008). The notion of job embeddedness, which brings a new point of view to the classic turnover perspective, deals with financial, psychological, and social impacts with an integrated approach that is effective for the retention of employees (Zhang, Fried & Griffeth, 2012).

Job embeddedness is different from similar concepts such as job satisfaction and organizational commitment. According to this detail, the concepts of job satisfaction and organizational commitment focus only on work-related factor. However, job embeddedness encompasses non-work issues and social topics as well as the related factors. On the other hand, job satisfaction and organizational commitment address the specific reasons that enable employees to connect to their work (nature of work, salary, promotion, managerial support, coworker support; affective commitment, continuance commitment, normative commitment). However, job embeddedness explains why people feel this way about the specific reasons and represents a general structure that assesses the scope of work, regardless of whether they are a committed or satisfied employee (Mitchell et al., 2001; Maertz & Campion, 2004; Alıcı, 2017).

In the literature, although there are many studies consider both the concept of job embeddedness as a whole and evaluate this concept through different ways, in order to better understand the job embeddedness in organizations and to explain the scope of this concept, it is useful to explain the following dimensions as follow below (Mitchell, Holtom, Lee & Erez, 2001):

2.2.1 Links

It can be expressed as a formal or an informal relationship between the employee and other people. It makes an employee dependent on a particular environment both psychologically and financially by his family, colleagues, or other people outside of work. As such connections increase for the employee, they will feel more embedded in their work. Therefore, the employee's desire to stay in the job or the organization will be much more intensive than before.

2.2.2 Fit

It is related to the harmony between the employee and their environment and how they feel themselves within this harmony. According to the job embeddedness approach, the employee's personal values, career goals, and professional knowledge and skills should be compatible with the corporate culture. A high level of compliance will increase the job embeddedness of the employees.

2.2.3 *Sacrifice*

It can be defined as the attitude of the employee to stay in the organization considering the material and psychological losses that they will have to endure if they leave their job or workplace. For example, leaving their job would make them run out of money, lose the facility of a company vehicle, be deprived of health insurance, and be separated from colleagues. Thus, the sacrifice dimension refers to the attitude of the employee to remain in the work when taking these losses into account.

2.3 The Relationship between Psychological Capital and Job Embeddedness

The relationship between psychological capital and job embeddedness can be explained by the Field Theory (Lewin, 1951), one of the most important theories of social psychology. This theory, by adapting the concept of physical space to psychology, suggests that social events and phenomena should be perceived as a whole. According to the theory, social behavior develops simultaneously with the environment. In order to analyze social behavior, the whole must first be looked at. In the Field Theory, the living space of the person is defined as the whole of the interrelated phenomena that exist at the same place and the same time for that individual. It also expresses behavior as a function of the environment. The living space encompasses all the needs of the person and the psychological environment that they perceive as to their needs. The Field Theory involves a dynamic, psychological, and holistic approach (Lewin, 1951; Burnes & Cooke, 2013).

Considering the characteristics of the Field Theory, it is seen that it is a powerful theory that explains the relationship between psychological capital and job embeddedness. Because both psychological capital and job embeddedness are the subjects covered by positive psychology and positive organizational behavior. On the other hand, the concept of job embeddedness is a holistic concept which addresses the willingness of employees to work. Besides, psychological capital is a phenomenon that strengthens human values. It is seen that there is a positive relationship between these two variables. In more detail, according to Field Theory, a change in one of the parts constituting the field also forces the whole area of change. Social behaviors of individuals are shaped within this scope (Akkoç, 2017). Thus, the phenomenon of psychological capital will enable individuals to focus on their strengths through its components, which are self-efficacy, optimism, hope, and resiliency. In this way, the employee who perceives all these via their field will exhibit job embeddedness in the same area.

The relationship between psychological capital and job embeddedness can also be explained by the Strong Ties Approach. This approach emphasizes social bonds which include closeness and cooperation among employees and individuals. These bonds are considered as a component of mutual cooperation (Bourdieu, 1986). The power of a social network is characterized as the time spending among actors, emotional sharing and intimacy, cooperation, and confidence (Leij & Goyal, 2011). This theory is known as a traditional approach which is used to understand the connections of social networks, to examine the effectiveness of social bonds among individuals, and to specify the beneficial relationship for the social actors (Coleman, 1988; Podolny, 2001; Sözen & Gürbüz, 2017). Close bonds and networks develop trust and cooperation among social groups, individuals, and organizations (Bekmezci, 2017) and reduce uncertainty (Kraats, 1998). Strong ties will create social support and improve trust in an organization (Ada & Ada, 2010), and they will also increase knowledge sharing (Sözen, 2007), social networks, and communication. From this point of view, since the psychological capital is a concept that increases the self-efficacy, hope, optimism, and resiliency levels of individuals, the positive effects of this increase will be reflected in the job embeddedness.

3 Discussion and Conclusions

In this chapter, the concepts of psychological capital and job embeddedness, which are new concepts in the management literature, were examined. Moreover, the possible relations among these concepts and their components are introduced based on both the literature and in the context of the Field Theory and Strong Ties Approach, which covered these two issues. Furthermore, suggestions were provided for managers and for future researches.

The possible relationship among these variables can be expressed in detail as follows. In general, it is predicted that psychological capital and job embeddedness are in a positive relationship because of their positive points of views, meanings, components, and emphases. For example, it is anticipated that there will be a positive relationship between self-efficacy as a component of psychological capital and link as a component of job embeddedness in which self-efficacy increases as link also increases. The level of self-efficacy will be able to determine the level of links of employees in an organization. On the other hand, a positive relationship between optimism, which is one of the components of psychological capital, and sacrifice, as one of the components of job embeddedness, can be considered as well. Optimistic individuals can easily sacrifice in workplaces to remain in their work. Their optimistic point of view will direct them to sacrifice materials or beliefs. It is projected that there is another positive association in which resiliency level increases as sacrifice also increases. Resiliency also increases work commitment, and so decreases the intensity of the desire to leave the work or job. These resilient individuals sacrifice to be able to bounce back from the stressful and negative situations in an organization. Another positive relationship between hope and fit is also considered and anticipated. Hopeful employees will try to create harmony in a work environment. This harmony will increase the positive personal relationship, cooperation, and communication among the employees of an organization.

It is possible to show evidence from empirical studies in the literature for the idea that psychological capital will positively affect job embeddedness. In this sense, the relationship between psychological capital, organizational commitment, and job satisfaction can be examined. Although they are different from the concept of job embeddedness, organizational commitment and job satisfaction are the concepts which are closest to it. From this perspective, all subdimensions of psychological capital are found to be positively related to job satisfaction (Badran & Morgan, 2015). It has also been found that psychological capital positively contributes to explaining organizational commitment (Sahoo & Sia, 2015). These empirical proofs support the study's foresight that psychological capital will be positively correlated with job embeddedness.

Based on the results of the study, it can be said that it would be a lucrative approach for managers to create an organizational culture that will positively contribute to the level of the psychological capital perception of employees. Thus, the employees will be embedded in the job and the organization and the turnover rate of the employees, which is one of the biggest problems, will decrease. Future studies can clarify these relations which are predicted theoretically by means of applied research with quantitative or qualitative research pattern.

References

Ada, S. & Ada, Ş. (2010). A meta analytic study on the importance of weak ties in organizations, *Balıkesir Üniversitesi Sosyal Bilimler Enstitüsü Dergisi*, 13(23), 115–128.

Akkoç, İ. (2017). 1. bölüm. In Ö. Turunç & H. Turgut (Eds.), *Yönetim ve strateji: 101 teori ve yaklaşım* (pp. 11–68). Ankara: Siyasal Kitabevi.

Alıcı, İ. (2017). İşe gömülmüşlük. In S. Polatcı & K. Özyer (Eds.), *21. yüzyılda örgütsel davranış* (pp. 79–94). İstanbul: Beta

Badran, M. A., & Youssef-Morgan, C. M. (2015). Psychological capital and job satisfaction in Egypt. *Journal of Managerial Psychology*, *30*(3), 354–370.

Baker, T., & Nelson, R. E. (2005). Creating something from nothing: Resource construction through entrepreneurial bricolage. *Administrative Science Quarterly*, 50(3), 329–366.

Bandura, A. (1997). *Self-efficacy: The exercise of control*. New York: W. H. Freeman

Bandura, A. (1982). Self-efficacy mechanism in human agency. *American psychologist*, 37(2), 122–147.

Bekmezci, M. (2017). 4. bölüm. In Ö. Turunç & H. Turgut (Eds.), *Yönetim ve strateji: 101 teori ve yaklaşım* (pp. 165–217). Ankara: Siyasal Kitabevi.

Bourdieu, P. (1986). The forms of capital. In J. G. Richardson (Ed.), *Handbook of theory and research for the sociology of education* (pp. 241–258). New York: Greenwood

Burnes, B., & Cooke, B. (2013). Kurt lewin's field theory: A review and re-evaluation. *International Journal of Management Reviews*, 15(4), 408–425.

Caprara, G. V., & Cervone, D. (2003). A conception of personality for a psychology of human strengths: Personality as an agentic, self-regulating system. In L. G. Aspinwall & U. M. Staudinger (Eds.), *A psychology of human strengths: Fundamental questions and future directions for a positive psychology* (pp. 61–74). Washington: American Psychological Association.

Carver, C. S., Scheier, M. F., & Segerstrom, S. C. (2010). OPTIMISM. *Clinical Psychology Review*, 30(7), 879–89.

Coleman, J. S. (1988). Social capital in the creation of human capital. *American Journal of Sociology*, *94*, 95–120.

Diener, E. (2000). Subjective well-being: The science of happiness and a proposal for a national index. *American Psychologist*, 55, 34–43.

Gargiulo, M., & Benassi, M. (2000). Trapped in your own net? Network cohesion, structural holes, and the adaptation of social capital. *Organization Science*, 11(2), 183–196.

Halbesleben, J. R., & Wheeler, A. R. (2008). The relative roles of engagement and embeddedness in predicting job performance and intention to leave. *Work & Stress 22*(3), 242–256.

Keleş, N. H. (2011). Pozitif psikolojik sermaye: Tanımı, bileşenleri ve örgüt yönetimine etkileri. *Organizasyon ve Yönetim Bilimleri Dergisi*, *3*(2), 343–350.

Kraatz, M. S. (1998). Learning by association? Interorganizational networks and adaptation to environmental change, *Academy of Management Journal*, 41(6), 621–643.

Leij, M. V. D., & Goyal, S. (2011). Strong ties in a small world. *Review of Network Economics*, 10(2), 1–20.

Lewin, K. (1951). *Field theory in social science: Selected theoretical papers*. In D. Cartwright (Ed.). Oxford, England: Harpers.

Luthans, F. (2002). The need for and meaning of positive organizational behavior. *Journal of Organizational Behavior*, 23(6), 695–706.

Luthans, F., & Youssef, C. M. (2004). Human, social, and now positive psychological capital management: Investing in people for competitive advantage. *Organizational Dynamics*, 33(2), 143–160.

Luthans, F., Avolio, B. J., Avey, J. B., & Norman, S. M. (2007). Positive psychological capital: Measurement and relationship with performance and satisfaction. *Personnel Psychology*, 60(3), 541–572.

Luthans, F., Luthans, K. W., & Luthans, B. C. (2004). Positive psychological capital: Beyond human and social capital. *Business Horizons*, 47(1), 45–50.

Maertz Jr, C. P., & Campion, M. A. (2004). Profiles in quitting: Integrating process and content turnover theory. *Academy of Management Journal*, 47(4), 566–582.

Masten, A. S. (2001). Ordinary magic: Resilience processes in development. *American Psychologist*, 56(3), 227–238.

Mitchell, T. R., Holtom, B. C., Lee, T. W., Sablynski, C. J., & Erez, M. (2001). Why people stay: Using job embeddedness to predict voluntary turnover. *Academy of Management Journal*, 44(6), 1102–1121.

Peterson, C. (2000). The future of optimism. *American Psychologist*, 55(1), 44–55.

Podolny, J. M. (2001). Networks as the pipes and prisms of the market. *American Journal of Sociology*, 107(1), 33–60.

Sahoo, B. C., & Sia, S. K. (2015). Psychological capital and organisational commitment: Nature, structure and relationship in an Indian sample. *Asia-Pacific Journal of Management Research and Innovation*, 11(3), 230–244.

Scheier, M. F., Carver, C. S., & Bridges, M. W. (2001). Optimism, pessimism, and psychological wellbeing. In E. C. Chang (Ed.), *Optimism & pessimism: Implications for theory, research, and practice* (pp. 198–216). Washington: American Psychological Association.

Seligman, M., & Csikszentmihalyi, M. (2000). Positive psychology: An introduction. *American Psychologist*, 55(1), 5–14.

Sekiguchi, T., Burton, J. P., & Sablynski, C. J. (2008). The role of job embeddedness on employee performance: The interactive effects with leader-member exchange and organization-based self- esteem. *Personnel Psychology*, 61(4), 761–792.

Sözen, H. C. (2007). Bağlam kapsamında örgütler arası ağ düzenekleri: Dayanıklı ev aletleri sektörü örneği. Unpublished doctoral dissertation, Başkent University, Institute of Social Science, Ankara/Turkey.

Sözen, H. C., & Gürbüz, S. (2017). Örgütsel ağlar. In H. C. Sözen & N. Basım (Eds.), Örgüt kuramları (pp. 317–341). İstanbul: Beta

Tugade, M. M., & Fredrickson, B. L. (2004). Resilient individuals use positive emotions to bounce back from negative emotional experiences. *Journal of Personality & Social Psychology*, 86(2), 320–333.

Valle, M. F., Huebner, E. S., & Suldo, S. M. (2004). Further evaluation of the children's hope scale. *Journal of Psychoeducational Assessment*, 22(4), 320–337.

Zhang, M., Fried, D. D., & Griffeth, R. W. (2012). A review of job embeddedness: Conceptual, measurement issues, and directions for future research. *Human Resource Management Review*, 22(3), 220–231.

Zorlu, Ö., Avan A. & Bulut, Ş. (2016). Otel işletmelerinde işe bağlılık düzeyinin arttırılması: İşgören fedakârlık tutumunun rolü. *ÇATALHÖYÜK International Journal of Tourism and Social Research*, 16, 1–16.

Güller Banu Karaman Menemencioğlu

Work Alienation[1]

1 Introduction

Work alienation is a fact that work-related issues are meaningless due to organizational and environmental conditions and the employee feels ineffective and powerless, abstains himself from his workplace and colleagues and develops negative attitudes towards work (Seeman, 1959).

Work alienation reflects the individual's sense of frustration regarding the position in the workplace. It shows that the professional development goals and career expectations of the employee and the goals and expectations of the organization do not match (Hoy, Blazovsky & Newland, 1983). Work alienation comes from many reasons such as the individual characteristics of the employee, role-related stressors, leadership styles, characteristics of the work, and the content of the work. It is a negative emotion that occurs as a result of workplace events and behaviors that the employee perceives as negative. The sense of work alienation affects the positive and negative behaviors, health and performance-based outcomes of employees (Chiaburu, Thundiyil & Wang, 2014). In this part of the book, the concepts of alienation and work alienation, their development, dimensions, antecedents and the outputs of work alienation are discussed in depth.

2 Concept of Alienation

The English term "*alienation*" comes from the Latin word "*alienatio*". The word "*alienatio*" is derived from the Latin verb "*alienare*," which means to estrange or become estranged. The meaning of the word "*alienation,*" which comes from these Latin origins, is "*causing separation*" (Kanungo, 1982, p. 9). The concept is that an individual intensely abstains himself primarily from objects in the world, secondly from humans, and finally from other people's thoughts about the world (Horowitz, 1966, p. 231).

---

1 This study is derived from the thesis titled: "**The Effect of Employees' of Their Own Values and Their Managers' Values on Their Work Alienation: The Mediating Role of Organizational Climate,** İstanbul Ticaret University, Business Administration Department, Doctoral Dissertation, İstanbul, 2018.

Work alienation is related to the working conditions that disengage employees from work and work activities (Cheung, 2008, p. 171). Employees feel that the factors that significantly affect their work and work activities are out of their control (Pearlin, 1962). Hirschfeld and Feild define work alienation as lack of interest one feels towards one's work (2000, p. 790).

Employees are irrelevant and indifferent to the objectives of the organization, the rules and principles of their work and their colleagues. Work alienation reflects the disappointment of not fulfilling the professional requirements as well as the disappointment of career and professional development (Aiken & Hage, 1966, p. 497).

3 Historical Development of Alienation

The concept of alienation has an earlier history than the term "*alienation*". It has a large and complex structure with a long history. It has been examined from the Bible to literary works and forms of studies on law, economics and philosophy (Mészáros, 2006, p. 2).

Although Hegel is known as the first user of the concept of alienation in the field of philosophy, Plotinus, one of the most important figures of Ancient Greek philosophy, formed the basis of the "*self-alienation*" concept in the field of philosophy. The hierarchy of existence in the doctrine of Plotinos is in three stages. In the first stage, it goes from the One to the multitude. In the second stage, there is the Soul, and the last stage is the Intellect. There has been a fall from one to another, and the concept of alienation appears at this point. In summary, the ongoing process of One to the multitude is alienation (Overend, 1975, p. 305; Aydogan, 2015, p. 274). Hegel is the name that emerged at the starting point of the concept of alienation in the history of philosophy. After Hegel, the important people who worked on this subject were Feuerbach and Marx.

According to Hegel, the alienation of man is the same as human history. What the mind is really dealing with is the realization of its own idea. But in doing so, he is hiding it from himself and is being proud and happy because of the alienation which is created from this secret (Fromm, 2004, p. 47). In Hegel's philosophy, Spirit is becoming another entity in nature. Nature has emerged as a result of the externalization of the Spirit. Later, it is understood that nature is not an entity outside of itself and is free from alienation. As a result, the concept of alienation in Hegel's philosophy encompasses the process of breaking down the essence of the Spirit and returning to its essence. In his approach, alienation is seen as a positive experience because it is the path to return (Salihoglu, 2014, p. 2, 3).

Ludwig Andreas Feuerbach, in his study on the concept of alienation, was interested in the religious side of alienation, although he was influenced by Hegel. In his work "The Essence of Christianity," he stated that human essence, which is the source of alienation, is the same as religion (Ergil, 1978, p. 95). According to him, religion is the cause of alienation as it entails the reunification of the human essence (Overend, 1975, p. 307).

Marx's theory of alienation was directly influenced by Hegel, Feuerbach and the British political economy in the process of formation.

According to Marx, the concept of the productive man who comprehends the objective world with his own power cannot be fully understood without the concept of lack of productivity (alienation). For Marx, human history is the history of human development and at the same time the increase of alienation. The concept of socialism is liberation from alienation, the return of man to himself and self-realization. Marx defines alienation as the individual sees himself as a passive subject separated from the object (Fromm, 2004, p. 37).

In contrast to Feuerbach, Marx assigns a broader meaning to alienation. The worker produces from nature and with nature (Marx, 1844, p. 76). Alienated labor alienates man (1) from nature and (2) himself while alienating himself from his active functions, from his life activity. This second type of alienation is presented in two types: alienation of man from his own products and alienation of man from other people (Marx, 1844, pp. 80 - 83). In short, Marx's concept of alienated worker has four dimensions. These dimensions have been named alienation from their product, alienation resulting from economic activities, alienation from their species-essence and alienation originating from other individuals (Christ, 2015, p. 555). Marx studied alienation with an approach that has social, cultural and economic dimensions. He explained this approach in the production–labor relationship.

4 Dimensions of Alienation

The concept of alienation was seen as a one-dimensional concept initially characterized by powerlessness or lack of control over work. Since the late 1950s, the other dimensions of the concept have been greatly enhanced by the work of Seeman. Seeman stated that there are five dimensions of alienation: powerlessness, meaninglessness, isolation, normlessness and self-estrangement (1959).

Powerlessness refers to a person's perceived lack of control over important events that affect his life. It is related to how people feel they have failed to control their own destiny (Seeman, 1959; Kanungo, 1979). This type of alienation can be defined as the failure of the individual's self-realization, if described in psychological terms. The individual feels that the need for respect is not met (Nelson & O'Donohue, 2006, p. 10). Powerlessness means the feeling of lack of personal success (Kohn, 1976, p. 115).

The powerlessness dimension of alienation negatively affects the quality and productivity of the employees' working life. The consequences of this negativity cause damage to both individual employees and the organization. Looking at the results of longer term, other stakeholders, customers, and society will be adversely affected (Kanungo, 1992).

Meaninglessness is that the individual cannot understand the situation because of the lack of clear information in the decision-making process and cannot make a definite decision about what to do (Seeman, 1959, p. 786). An individual who has meaninglessness has difficulty in understanding the consequences of his own behavior. Similarly, he cannot make sense of the behavior of others in society. In short, meaninglessness is the inability to predict the consequences of behaviors or to make adequate predictions (Sarfraz, 1997). At the same time, when the expectations about the results are worse than the predictions, a sense of meaninglessness can be seen (Seeman, 1959).

Meaninglessness occurs when employees feel that they participate little in the overall production process, and therefore when they consider their roles insignificant (Mottaz, 1981). When the division of labor is increased and work is divided into simple, small tasks and these tasks do not require a responsibility and decision making, the employee feels worthless; the employee moves away from the desire to work for organizational purposes. The employee now thinks that his work has no importance in achieving the objectives of the organization. His work becomes meaningless to the employee (Shepard 1971).

There are links between the dimensions of meaninglessness and powerlessness of alienation. Both seem to be the main reason for the lack of control and freedom in the way Marxism put forward. In some cases, the meaninglessness dimension may be a priority for the dimension of powerlessness. For example, the complexity of complex works can lead to high levels of control, and failure to meet this can lead to a sense of powerlessness (Kanungo, 1979; Seeman 1959).

Isolation refers to the isolation of the individual from society. If the individual cannot communicate and establish relations with other people in society and has accepted this situation, then isolation (social isolation) has taken place. The individual now feels alone, outside the society (Seeman, 1959). According to the theories of social interaction, each individual, as a member of a group, meets the need to belong, being loved and love others. It has been suggested that this sense of belonging is a source of motivation because it provides an identity and increases self-esteem (Tajfel, Billig, Bundy & Flament, 1971; Turner, Brown &

Tajfel, 1979). For the continuity of this feeling, the individual must remain a member of the group. To remain a member of the group, an individual must adherence to group norms and behave accordingly. If the group norms conflict with the individual's own rules and behaviors, the individual does not feel that he belongs to the group and consequently he feels isolated (Sarfraz, 1997). The individual has been mentally separated from the popular cultural rules of society. Isolation, and hence the feeling of loneliness, leads to anxiety, weakens the sense of belonging and prevents the happiness of the individual. Although the individual feels mentally separate, he remains in conflict with the necessity of being in a relationship with others (Nelson & O'Donohue, 2006).

Isolation refers to the lack of identification with the organization, the organization's objectives, or other employees (Mottaz, 1981). Miller (1975) stated that the individuals' sense of isolation in organizations is effective when communicating with four different groups in life levels. These groups are (p. 263) people in the position of official authority in the organization, people holding actual control over the activities of the organization, the most respected colleagues in the organization and other colleagues within the organization.

The *normlessness* dimension of alienation is derived from Durkheim's concept of "*anomie*" (Dean, 1961). Anomie is a condition in which the common values and common meanings of the social system regulating behaviors are no longer understood and accepted and the meaning of the new values has not yet been developed. (https://www.britannica. com/topic/anomie).

It is observed that there are two types of normlessness. The first of these is called *aimlessness*. Aimlessness is defined as the lack of values that can be or maybe the purpose of life, the loss of internal and socialized values, the feeling of distrust by a loss. The second subtype of normlessness can be called a *conflict of norms*—conflicts such as individuals' freedom to respond to social restrictions in behavior and the desire for individuality against sociality (Dean, 1961).

In defining the dimension of normlessness, Seeman's definition is similar to the definition of aimlessness. Normlessness is the use of ways that are not socially acceptable in determining the way of behavior in order to reach a certain purpose (Seeman, 1959). The idea that doing anything is considered moral while staying out of trouble, justifying the idea of doing business by taking advantage of the deficits of the law, and if things are going well, it is not important whether the work is right or wrong, are the indicators of normlessness (Kohn, 1976).

Self-estrangement is defined as the inability of the individual to enjoy life, the difficulty of being socialized, and, as a result, to become estranged from self-esteem. Self-estrangement emerges as the inability of the employees to stand out themselves in the organization and not to make sense of the work they do. As a result of self-estrangement, the employee is more concerned with external factors such as money and security. The employee who is estranged from the goals of the organization and the internal factors, such as success, does not satisfy with his work (Seeman, 1959).

Self-estrangement in the workplace is caused by job tasks with limited job requirements and an acceptable level of job satisfaction and, therefore, no commitment to work (Sarros, Tanewski, Winter, Santora & Densten, 2002).

5 Antecedents of Work Alienation

Individual characteristics, role-related stressors, leadership styles, characteristics of work and content of work are listed as the main reasons of work alienation.

Although work alienation is revealed by organizational and work-related variables, it is a phenomenon the individual lives within. Therefore, it is predicted that there is an interaction between individual characteristics and the sense of alienation. Two individual features stand out: success needs and the locus of control. The need for success is defined as the willingness of a person to achieve the goal. There is an inverse relationship between the need for success and alienation (Chiaburu et al., 2014). Individuals with an internal locus of control think they have control over everything and there is a negative relationship between internal locus of control and alienation with work (Banai, Reisel and Probst, 2004).

The variables that stand out as role-related stressors are role ambiguity and role conflict. Role ambiguity is defined as lack of knowledge about expectations for an organizational role, methods of fulfilling expectations or what the performance results from the role should be (Rizzo, House & Lirtzman, 1970). The individual with a high perception of role ambiguity may have difficulty in understanding the meaning and importance of his work for the organization. This situation causes the job to be meaningless for the individual (Atay and Gerçek, 2017, p. 328). Uncertainty may occur at both individual and team level. Increasing uncertainty about the future will increase stress and work alienation (Zeffane, 1993).

According to the human role theory, a social individual exhibits different behaviors that can be predicted according to their social identity or situation. Role conflict occurs when there are two or more incompatible behaviors in a person's behaviors (Biddle, 1986). Stress caused by role ambiguity or emergence of role conflict may cause psychological disturbances. These psychological problems and the sense of dissatisfaction are predicted to lead to work alienation (Michaels, Cron, Dubinsky & Joachimsthaler, 1988).

Leadership styles play a crucial role in managerial processes and forms of organizational communication. The supporting leadership style, encouraging employees' participation in decisions and providing freedom to them seems to reduce work alienation (Boerner, 1998; Banai & Reisel, 2007). The transformational leadership style, which leads, inspires and understands the needs of employees, decreases work alienation (Sarros et al., 2002; Babadağ and Iscan, 2017). Leader behavior that encourages employee participation and eliminates conflicts and uncertainties can reduce employee ambiguity and provide emotional support, thus reducing the alienation of employees (Michaels et al., 1988).

The style of autocratic leadership, in other words, limiting participation in decision making and limiting their freedom in duties may lead to more alienation (Allen & LaFollette, 1977; Kanten & Ülker, 2014). Managers who have punishment methods, communication-based belittling and arbitrary behaviors that leave employees in difficult positions are called as small tyrants. These small tyrants cause an increase in the unpredictability and conflicts in the working environment. This environment weakens the employee's commitment to work and the organization and increases work alienation (Ashforth, 1997, Akhtar & Shaukat, 2016).

Work characteristics such as diversity of duties, feedback, autonomy and importance of the task are related to work alienation (Chiaburu et al., 2014). The diversification of tasks gives employees a chance to use their skills and abilities while doing their work. This makes the work meaningful and important for employees (Hackman & Lawler, 1971). Work that people find meaningful and important will reduce their alienation. On the other hand, those who work in repetitive and unimportant tasks are more likely to become alienated from work (Shantz, Alfes, Bailey & Soane, 2015).

Employees need to know what they have achieved to be motivated. It is important to provide feedback to the employee in a credible manner and thus to satisfy his needs. (Hackman & Lawler, 1971). With work-related feedback, work alienation is reduced (Banai, 2004; Banai & Reisel, 2007).

Seeman (1959) stated that alienation is the result of a person's powerlessness and negative emotions felt by the need for autonomy. The fact that highly centralized enterprises have very little autonomy due to the tasks assigned to them and little participation in institution-wide decisions shows that they are likely to have high levels of work alienation (Aiken & Hage, 1966).

Meaninglessness, which is one of the dimensions of alienation, exists when the employees feel that they contribute very little to the general production process and thus their roles are insignificant (Mottaz, 1981). Banai et al. (2004),

Banai and Reisel (2007) and Chiaburu et al. (2014) stated that there is a negative relationship between the importance of the task and alienation.

Seeman (1959) stated that individuals were alienated when they could not see the whole system, processes and the relationship between them. Employees' one-dimensional vision decreases their identification and thus increases their alienation.

In addition to individual factors and business characteristics, there are constraints arising from the organizational structure that may affect alienation in workplaces. Among these constraints are formalization, bureaucratization, centralization, authority hierarchy, participation in decision-making process and organizational support (Chiaburu et al., 2014).

Formalization is defining and governing work facilities by administrative rules, policies, and procedures. (Ford & Slocum, 1977). It therefore acts as a guide for employees and reduces role ambiguity. This type of formalization reduces work alienation (Podsakoff, Williams & Todor, 1986; Michaels et al., 1988; Michaels et al., 1996). From another aspect of formalization, high levels of formalization expect the superiors to adhere to established work routines rather than allowing them to decide how to do the work. This can serve as a limiting force for the feeling of the employee that he is free in the way he does the work and has the utmost control over it. (Greene, 1978; DeHart-Davis & Pandey, 2005). When perceived this way, it will contribute to the increase of work alienation (Greene, 1978; Aiken & Hage, 1966). Strict procedures arising from bureaucratization, increased rules and limitations, increased authority and controls cause work alienation (Bonjean & Grimes, 1970).

In centralization, planning and decision-making activities are concentrated in a particular group. Increased centralization leads to increased alienation (Aiken & Hage, 1966; DeHart-Davis and Pandey, 2005).

In authority hierarchy power is not evenly distributed. As the authority becomes centralized, alienation increases. Participation in the decision-making process provides voice feedback. It gives employees the opportunity to own the work they do, which increases their commitment to the organization and their duties, and ultimately leads to less alienation (Chiaburu et al., 2014).

Increased organizational support will provide cognitive, emotional and physical resources for an employee and will decrease alienation (Shantz et al., 2015). When work-based organizational support is provided, isolation decreases (Marshall, Michaels & Mulki, 2007; Taştan et al., 2014).

6 Outputs of Work Alienation

Work alienation is a negative effect occuring as a result of the events and behaviors employees perceive as negative towards the organization. It affects the positive and negative behaviors, health and performance-based outputs of employees experiencing the sense of alienation.

6.1 Work Alienation and Positive Behavior Outputs

Alienation has an inverse relationship with career satisfaction. As alienation occurs due to the problems stemming from both the business and the organization, employees experiencing work alienation have also dissatisfaction towards their career (Chiaburu et al., 2013). One dimension of alienation, workplace isolation, has an adverse effect on job satisfaction, job involvement and organizational commitment. (Marshall et al., 2007). As studies have shown, alienated employees have lower job satisfaction, job involvement, job identification and commitment. (Chiaburu et al., 2014). There is an inverse relationship between powerlessness, meaninglessness and self-alienation dimensions of alienation and organizational citizenship behavior (Jesús Suárez-Mendoza and Zoghbi-Manrique-de-Lara, 2008).

6.2 Work Alienation and Negative Behavior Outputs

The sense of alienation contains the feeling of powerlessness, meaninglessness, isolation, and separation. For employees who find their job meaningless and experience work alienataion, reduced willingness to work and hence increase in work absence is foreseeable (Chiaburu et al., 2014). Similarly, alienated employees have less reason to continue to work in the workplace as they do not feel a sense of belonging to the organization (Tuna ve Yeşiltaş, 2015; Chiaburu et al., 2014; Kurtulmuş ve Yiğit, 2016).

There are similarities between factors leading to alienation and burnout (Karger, 1981). The democratic or autocratic management style, the degree of participation in the decision-making process and the characteristics of the work affect the employees positively or negatively. These factors cause both alienation and burnout syndrome. The burnout syndrome is a result of alienation, that is to say, alienation is a symptom of burnout syndrome (Özler ve Dirican, 2014).

6.3 Other Outputs of Work Alienation

Alienation can also cause health problems. In addition to psychological health problems, it can cause muscle tension, headaches and chest pain (Chiaburu et al., 2014, s. 28).The sense of powerlessness can cause depression (Hagan & Kay, 2007).

One of the other consequences of alienation is the smoking and alcohol problem. It is known that, in relation to employee behavior, work stress increases smoking and alcohol consumption. In the framework of alienation, the alcohol problem has been associated with particular dimensions of powerlessness and isolation. It was found that the employee used alcohol to feel stronger and more valuable. Besides, it is also known that self-estranged employees increase the consumption of alcohol in order to get the feeling of false happiness thanks to the effect of alcohol (Seeman & Anderson, 1983; Greenberg & Grunberg, 1995).

References

Aiken, M., & Hage, J. (1966). Organizational alienation: A comparative analysis. *American Sociological Review, 31*(4), 497–507.

Akhtar, S., & Shaukat, K. (2016). Impact of petty tyranny on alienation from work: Role of self-esteem and power-distance. *Global Journal of Flexible Systems Management, 17*(3), 275–285.

Allen, B. H., & LaFollette, W. R. (1977). Perceived organizational structure and alienation among management trainees. *Academy of Management Journal, 20*(2), 334–341.

Ashforth, B. E. (1997). Petty tyranny in organizations: A preliminary examination of antecedents and consequences. *Canadian Journal of Administrative Sciences/Revue Canadienne des Sciences de l'Administration, 14*(2), 126–140.

Atay Elmas, S., ve Gerçek, M. (2017). Algılanan rol belirsizliğinin işe yabancılaşma üzerindeki etkisinin ve demografik değişkenlere göre farklılıklarının incelenmesi. *Sosyal Bilimler Arastirmalari Dergisi, 7*(2), 321–332.

Aydoğan, E. (2015). Marx ve öncüllerinde yabancılaşma kavramı. *Atatürk Üniversitesi Sosyal Bilimler Dergisi*, (54), 273–282.

Babadağ, Ö. G. D. M., & İşcan, Ö. F. (2017). Dönüştürücü liderlik ile işe yabancılaşma arasındaki ilişkide algılanan etik iklimin aracı rolü. *Manas Sosyal Araştırmalar Dergisi, 6*(4), 399–428.

Banai, M., & Reisel, W. D. (2007). The influence of supportive leadership and job characteristics on work alienation: A six-country investigation. *Journal of World Business, 42*(4), 463–476.

Banai, M., Reisel, W. D., & Probst, T. M. (2004). A managerial and personal control model: Predictions of work alienation and organizational commitment in Hungary. *Journal of International Management, 10*(3), 375–392.

Biddle, B.J. (1986). Recent development in role theory. *Annual Review of Sociology*, (12), 67–92.

Boerner, S. (1998). Work alienation and continuous improvement: The effects of leadership style. In Harry Boer (eds)., *Proceedings of the 2nd International*

EuroCINet Conference on Continuous Improvement: from idea to reality. (pp. 63–75). Enschede, The Netherlands: Twente University Press, 14–15 September.

Bonjean, C. M., & Grimes, M. D. (1970). Bureaucracy and alienation: A dimensional approach. *Social Forces, 48*(3), 365–373.

Cheung, C. K. (2008). Lagged harm of work restructuring and work alienation to work commitment. *International Journal of Employment Studies, 16*(2), 170–207.

Chiaburu, D. S., Thundiyil, T., & Wang, J. (2014). Alienation and its correlates: A meta-analysis. *European Management Journal, 32*(1), 24–36.

Christ, O. (2015). The concept of alienatıon in the early works of Karl Marx. *European Scientific Journal, 11*(7), 551–563.

Dean, D. G. (1961). Alienation: Its meaning and measurement. *American sociological review, 26*(5), 753–758.

DeHart-Davis, L., & Pandey, S. K. (2005). Red tape and public employees: Does perceived rule dysfunction alienate managers? *Journal of Public Administration Research and Theory, 15*(1), 133–148.

Ergil, D. (1978). Yabancılaşma kuramına ilk katkılar. *Ankara Üniversitesi SBF Dergisi, 33*(03), 93–107.

Ford, J. D., & Slocum Jr, J. W. (1977). Size, technology, environment and the structure of organizations. *Academy of Management Review, 2*(4), 561–575.

Fromm, E. (2004). *Marx's Concept of Man.* Wiltshire: Continuum.

Greenberg, E. S., & Grunberg, L. (1995). Work alienation and problem alcohol behavior. *Journal of Health and Social Behavior, 36*(1), 83–102.

Greene, C. N. (1978). Identification modes of professionals: Relationship with formalization, role strain, and alienation. *Academy of Management Journal, 21*(3), 486–492.

Hackman, J. R., & Lawler, E. E. (1971). Employee reactions to job characteristics. *Journal of Applied Psychology, 55*(3), 259–286.

Hagan, J., & Kay, F. (2007). Even lawyers get the blues: gender, depression, and job satisfaction in legal practice. *Law & Society Review, 41*(1), 51–78.

Hirschfeld, R. R., & Feild, H. S. (2000). Work centrality and work alienation: Distinct aspects of a general commitment to work. *Journal of Organizational Behavior,* 21(7) 789–800.

Horowitz, I. L. (1966). On alienation and the social order. *Philosophy and Phenomenological Research, 27*(2), 230–237.

Hoy, W. K., Blazovsky, R., & Newland, W. (1983). Bureaucracy and alienation: A comparative analysis. *Journal of Educational Administration, 21*(2), 109–120.

Jesús Suárez-Mendoza, M., & Zoghbi-Manrique-de-Lara, P. (2008). The impact of work alienation on organizational citizenship behavior in the Canary Islands. *International Journal of Organizational Analysis*, *15*(1), 56–76.

Kanten, P., ve Ülker, F. (2014). Yönetim tarzinin üretkenlik karşiti iş davranişlarina etkisinde işe yabancilaşmanin aracilik rolü. *Sosyal ve Beşeri Bilimler Araştırmaları Dergisi*, (32), 16–40.

Kanungo, R. N. (1979). The concepts of alienation and involvement revisited. *Psychological bulletin*, *86*(1), 119–138.

Kanungo, R. N. (1982). *Work Alienation: An Integrative Approach*. New York: Praeger Publishers.

Kanungo, R. N. (1992). Alienation and empowerment: Some ethical imperatives in business. *Journal of Business Ethics*, *11*(5–6), 413–422.

Karger, H. J. (1981). Burnout as alienation. *Social Service Review*, *55*(2), 270–283.

Kohn, M. L. (1976). Occupational structure and alienation. *American Journal of Sociology*, *82*(1), 111–130.

Kurtulmuş, M., ve Yiğit, B. (2016). İşe Yabancılaşmanın Öğretmenlerin İşten Ayrılma Niyetine Etkisi. *Mersin Üniversitesi Eğitim Fakültesi Dergisi*, *12*(3).860–871.

Marshall, G. W., Michaels, C. E., & Mulki, J. P. (2007). Workplace isolation: Exploring the construct and its measurement. *Psychology & Marketing*, *24*(3), 195–223.

Marx, K. (1844). *El yazmaları* (Çev. Murat Belge), 11. Baskı, Birikim Yayınları, İstanbul.

Mészáros, I. (2006). *Marx's theory of alienation*. Aakar Books, New Delhi.

Michaels, R. E., Cron, W. L., Dubinsky, A. J., & Joachimsthaler, E. A. (1988). Influence of formalization on the organizational commitment and work alienation of salespeople and industrial buyers. *Journal of Marketing Research*, *25*(4), 376–383.

Michaels, R. E., Dubinsky, A. J., Kotabe, M., & Un Lim, C. (1996). The effects of organizational formalization on organizational commitment and work alienation in US, Japanese and Korean industrial salesforces. *European Journal of Marketing*, *30*(7), 8–24.

Miller, J. (1975). Isolation in organizations: Alienation from Authority, Control, and Expressive Relations. *Adminisrative Science Quarterly*, *20*(2), 260–271.

Mottaz, C. J. (1981). Some determinants of work alienation. *The Sociological Quarterly*, *22*(4), 515–529.

Nelson, L. & O'Donohue, W. (2006). Alienation, psychology and human resource management. Proceedings of the 2nd Australian Centre for Research in Employment and Work (ACREW) Conference. 1-4 July, Prato, Italy.

Overend, T. (1975). Alienation: A conceptual analysis. *Philosophy and Phenomenological Research*, *35*(3), 301–322.

Özler, N. D. E., & Dirican, M. Ö. (2015). Örgütlerde yabancılaşma ile tükenmişlik sendromu arasındaki ilişkiyi belirlemeye yönelik bir araştırma. *Dumlupınar Üniversitesi Sosyal Bilimler Dergisi*, (39). 291–309.

Pearlin, L. I. (1962). Alienation from work: A study of nursing personnel. *American Sociological Review*, *27*(3). 314–326.

Podsakoff, P. M., Williams, L. J., & Todor, W. D. (1986). Effects of organizational formalization on alienation among professionals and nonprofessionals. *Academy of Management Journal*, *29*(4), 820–831.

Rizzo, J. R., House, R. J., & Lirtzman, S. I. (1970). Role conflict and ambiguity in complex organizations. *Administrative Science Quarterly*, 15(2), 150–163.

Salihoğlu, G. H. (2014). Örgütsel yabancilaşma. *Organizasyon ve Yönetim Bilimleri Dergisi*, *6*(2), 1–11.

Sarfraz, H. (1997). Alienation: A theoretical overview. *Pakistan Journal of Psychological Research*, *12*(1–2), 45–60.

Sarros, J. C., Tanewski, G. A., Winter, R. P., Santora, J. C., & Densten, I. L. (2002). Work alienation and organizational leadership. *British Journal of Management*, *13*(4), 285–304.

Seeman, M. (1959). On the meaning of alienation. *American Sociological Review*, 24(6), 783–791.

Seeman, M., & Anderson, C. S. (1983). Alienation and alcohol: The role of work, mastery, and community in drinking behavior. *American Sociological Review*, 48(1), 60–77.

Shantz, A., Alfes, K., Bailey, C., & Soane, E. (2015). Drivers and outcomes of work alienation: reviving a concept. *Journal of Management Inquiry*, *24*(4), 382–393.

Shepard, J. M. (1971). *Automation and alienation: A study of office and factory workers*. The MIT Press: Cambridge.

Tajfel, H., Billig, M. G., Bundy, R. P., & Flament, C. (1971). Social categorization and intergroup behaviour. *European Journal of Social Psychology*, *1*(2), 149–178.

Taştan, S., İşçi, E., ve Arslan, B. (2014). Örgütsel destek algısının işe yabancılaşma ve örgütsel bağlılığa etkisinin incelenmesi: istanbul özel hastanelerinde bir çalışma. *Pamukkale University Journal of Social Sciences Institute/Pamukkale Üniversitesi Sosyal Bilimler Enstitüsü Dergisi*, (19). 121–138.

Tuna, M., ve Yeşiltaş, M. (2015). Etik iklim, işe yabancılaşma ve örgütsel özdeşleşmenin işten ayrılma niyeti üzerindeki etkisi: Otel işletmelerinde bir araştırma. *Anatolia: Turizm Araştırmaları Dergisi*, *25*(1), 105–117.

Turner, J. C., Brown, R. J., & Tajfel, H. (1979). Social comparison and group interest in ingroup favouritism. *European Journal of Social Psychology*, *9*(2), 187–204.

Zeffane, R. (1993). Uncertainty, participation and alienation: Lessons for workplace restructuring. *International Journal of Sociology and Social Policy*, *13*(5/6), 22–52.

https://www.britannica.com/topic/anomie

Basak Dogan

On the Way to Sustainability: Organizational DNA

1 Introduction

In today's business world, one of the most important problems of organizations that produce various goods or services to meet people's desires and needs is to ensure sustainability. Along with the globalization phenomenon, the borders in commercial and social activities have begun to disappear, and the organizations keeping the market boundaries in a narrow scope have had the opportunity to expand to wider markets. The fact that information and communication technologies, and especially the technologies that have increased the production efficiency in recent years, have begun to be used extensively in organizations has had an increasing impact on this opportunity. Therefore, the competition between organizations to take advantage of these opportunities has gradually increased, and the organizations found themselves trying to sustain their existence in a highly variable and challenging competition environment.

The organizations' ability to sustain their existence in the aforementioned variable and challenging competition environment depends on the fact that they make correct decisions and apply the right strategies. In this context, the information that will form a basis for decision-making and strategy-making processes should reach the organization accurately and should be permanent in the organization.

Nowadays, organizations are regarded as "organic assets", in other words "living organisms". It is also stated that it is more suitable for organizations with variable environmental conditions to have an organic structure with respect to sustaining their existence (Koçel, 2015, 358). In various studies in the organization literature (Porter, 2006), it is indicated that living organisms should adapt to the environment to sustain their existence (Ülgen and Mirze, 2013, 80) and should evolve the characteristics they have in case of necessity (in the mechanism of coevolution) to ensure this adaptation.

It is beneficial for the organization to know its own characteristics with respect to adaptation to the environment. Thus, adaptation to the environment can be achieved without damaging the organizational texture. Here, the concept of organizational DNA emerges as a contemporary concept developed to analyze and understand the characteristics of the organization.

2 Organizational DNA

DNA is expressed as a nucleic acid that has the hereditary information necessary for the functions and biological developments of all living things. This structure, that consists of two molecular chains next to each other in theoretically infinite length and coiled with each other, contains the information of all kinds of characteristics that a living organism has (Çetin, 2014, 23). The information that living beings need for the realization of all activities that constitute their lives from fetus to death is stored in their DNA (Onay and Ergüden, 2012, 204).

The DNA that living beings carry in each part of their bodies is identical, which adds the feature of being unique to the living being (Çetin, 2014, 24) and also means that the whole information contained in DNA reaches all the elements of the living being (Çandır, 2005, 39). Therefore, the basic function of DNA as a constituent containing the hereditary characteristics of living organisms is that it is an information store for living beings.

The characteristics that the organizations, that are considered to be living organisms, have since their establishment and that direct their activities throughout their lives are contained in their DNA. Each organization is accepted to have its own DNA (Çetin and Döş, 2014, 562). Organizational DNA is distinctive like fingerprinting in an organization, and each member of the organization has the DNA of the organization to which they belong (Döş, 2013, 9). The structure, decision rights, incentive systems and information flow functions of the organizations form the DNA of an organization when they are interconnected in numerous ways (Dehoff, Jaruzelski and Kronenberg, 2005).

Organizational DNA is a metaphor trying to explain the distinctive features of an organization (Neilson, Pasternack and Mendes, 2004a). Morgan has defined organizational DNA as the vision, values and the sense of aiming at the objective that enable employees to understand and adopt the mission and power of the organization and that keep the organization together (cited in Nart, 2018, 233). Baskin defines organizational DNA as all structural and procedural information of an organization accessible by everyone (cited in Çetin, 2014, 24). According to Baskin, organizational DNA has two important information; organizational identity (infrastructure, values and norms, vision and mission of the organization, etc.) and procedural opinions (the compliance of the part to the whole, the adaptation of a person to the organization where he/she works, etc.) (cited in Çetin, 2014, 24).

When the studies on the determination of organizational DNA are examined, it is seen that there are three different points of view on organizational DNA, as stated in the study of Çandır (2005, 39). From the first point of view, organizational

DNA is considered as a database in which structural and procedural information is brought together and made available to everyone, but according to the second point of view, organizational DNA consists of basic relationships. The third point of view considers organizational DNA as a whole composed of four basic building blocks including structure, decision-making, motivators and information.

Neilson, Pasternack and Mendes (2004b), determine seven types of organizational "species" on the basis of DNA as summarized below:

- *The Resilient Organization.* This organization is flexible enough to adapt quickly to external market shifts; yet, it remains steadfastly focused on and aligned with a coherent business strategy. This forward-looking organization anticipates changes routinely and addresses them proactively.
- *The Military Organization.* Often driven by a small, hands-on senior management team, this organization succeeds through sheer force of will, the will of its top executives. It can conceive and execute brilliant strategies, but its middle-management bench can be shallow and short lived.
- *The Just-in-Time Organization.* Although not always proactive in preparing for impending changes, this organization has demonstrated an ability to "turn on a dime" when necessary, without losing sight of the big picture. Although it manages to hold on to good people and performs well financially, it has not made the leap from good to great.
- *The Fits-and-Starts Organization.* Scores of smart, motivated and talented people populate this organization, but they do not often pull in the same direction at the same time. When they do, they can execute brilliant, breakout strategic moves, but the organization typically lacks the discipline and coordination to repeat these successes on a consistent basis.
- *The Outgrown Organization.* This firm has outgrown its organizational model; it is bursting at the seams. Too large and complex to be effectively controlled anymore by a small team of top executives, it has yet to "democratize" decision-making authority. Consequently, much of the organization's potential remains untapped.
- *The Overmanaged Organization.* Burdened with multiple layers of management, this organization tends to suffer from "analysis paralysis." When it does move, it moves slowly and reactively, often pursuing opportunities later or less vigorously than its competitors do.
- *The Passive-Aggressive Organization.* So congenial that it seems conflict free, and this is the "everyone agrees but nothing changes" organization. Building a consensus to make major changes is no problem; implementing them is what proves difficult.

The resilient organization, the military organization and the just-in-time organization are characterized as healthy species; nevertheless, the fits-and-starts organization, the outgrown organization, the overmanaged organization and the passive-aggressive organization are characterized as unhealthy species (Onay and Ergüden, 2012, 209; Bostancı, Çelik and Kahraman, 2017, 141). An organization's tendency toward sustainability is a result of its DNA (Crittenden et. al, 2011, 75), and it is very likely that the healthy species are competitive and sustainable.

By analyzing the genetic material of an organization, in other words, the organizational DNA, the underlying reasons for organizational problems can be revealed and "gene therapies" (solutions to organizational problems) can be developed. In this context, the main purpose of analyzing organizational DNA is to determine in what way the critical interventions that will extend the survival time of organizations, that have a certain lifetime like all living beings, can be performed (Çandır, 2005, 123). Therefore, the concept of organizational DNA is closely associated with sustainability.

3 Sustainability

Sustainability refers to the capacity to maintain a situation or process during an undetermined period of time (Yavuz, 2010, 64). The concept of sustainability has been identified with the concepts such as values, governance, transparency, diversity, ethical principles, social responsibility, defending human and employee rights, protecting the environment and providing benefit to the society (Kesen, 2016, 555). Therefore, it is one of the most discussed concepts not only specifically to organizations but also throughout the society.

In the most general sense, sustainability is defined as meeting today's requirements without endangering the ability of future generations to meet their own requirements (Porter and Kramer, 2006). The sustainability phenomenon has gained its contemporary meaning along with the concept of sustainable development which was first defined as "ensuring economic development by using the resources without violating the right to life of future generations" (Günel, 2017, 40) in the Brundtland Report prepared by the World Commission on Environment and Development in 1987 (Mısırdalı Yangil, 2016, 132). Sustainability, which includes environmental and social concerns as well as economic welfare, refers to keeping all long-term interests between man and nature at a constant balance throughout the society (Garvare and Johansson, 2010, 737).

In organizational literature, sustainability can be expressed as a management mentality that aims to transfer the organization to the future in a healthy way (Kuşat, 2012, 229). In management science, it is seen that this mentality is defined by two interrelated different points of view that are mentioned as creating a permanent competitive advantage in the long term to ensure continuity of organizations and the fulfillment of responsibilities regarding the sustainable development goal of the society in which it functions (Kesen, 2016, 555).

Sustainability, which is a modern management paradigm, has been proposed as an alternative to the preventive effect of economic-benefit–based production processes starting with the industrial revolution on social-benefit–based environmental and social development in the long term (Akgül, 2010; Tokgöz and Önce, 2009; Kuşat, 2012; Mucan et al., 2016, 59). The defenders of sustainability indicate that businesses' business models based on traditional methods have lost their validity. To be a new business model and the need for investment in the future are the two main characteristics of sustainability (Tokgöz and Önce, 2009).

It is stated that the problems that the organizations have with respect to sustainability are due to the presence of unskilled employees in the organization, inefficient usage of limited organizational resources, weak management structure, lack of accurate determination of organizational goals, and insufficient communication and coordination (Kuşat, 2012, 238).

4 The Importance of Organizational DNA for Organizational Sustainability

Sustainability in organizations can be evaluated within the context of various internal factors including organizational knowledge management and transfer, organizational learning, organizational value, organizational happiness, organizational citizenship, organizational reputation, organizational social responsibility, institutional management and organizational social capital (Kuşat, 2012, 230). It can be said that organizational knowledge management and transfer from among these factors are closely associated with the concept of organizational DNA. Ultimately, organizational DNA has a function that allows the storage and transfer of knowledge in the organization.

When organizational DNA is destroyed, each organizational unit carrying the organizational DNA is also destroyed, and problems arise in the processes and activities in time. The organization becomes increasingly less productive, the costs are increased, organizational culture is damaged and "early ageing" occurs in the organization (Çandır, 2005); and this situation puts the existence of the organization in danger. Therefore, the sustainability of the organization is adversely affected when organizational DNA begins to lose its function.

For a healthy sustainability practice in organizations, economic, social and environmental parameters should be included in all basic, strategic and operational processes and decision-making mechanisms of organizations (Öztel et al., 2012, 33–34). At this point, the inclusion of these parameters in the DNA of the organization will have an effect that will facilitate the sustainability practices.

In order to create an organizational DNA that will contribute to sustainability, attention should be paid to the following issues by considering the structure and properties of biological DNA (Çandır, 2005, 49):

- *Starting from simple:* DNA consists of only four symbols. It is important to write out the functioning of the organization in the form of simple instructions that everyone can understand in the organization.
- *Grouping:* It is necessary to combine simple instructions into relatively small groups, which represent individual parts of more complex procedures, such as the merger of the cornerstones of DNA in columns.
- *Collecting:* Organizational columns, like our genes, should be collected in larger instruction groups that define the relevant procedural groups.
- *Compressing:* It is stated that it is necessary to compress the procedures together as far as possible when needed, so that they can be small/collected and easily accessible. It is like collecting all procedures in a database that everyone can access.

It is also important that all information about the organization is easily accessible in the public records of an organization's DNA. It is foreseen that any organization that has not made information easily accessible will lose customers in today's competition environment (Çandır, 2005, 52). This situation may also lead to consequences that will negatively affect sustainability in the long term.

To explore organizational DNA, that creates a difference for the organization, triggers success and leads to value creation, and to exhibit an effective management approach that will enable it to achieve superiority by using these characteristics (Aydın, 2016, 30) will make positive contributions to the continuity of the organization.

5 Conclusion

Ensuring the sustainability of organizations has been an important problem since organizations have started to exist. Although the life of organizations is assumed to be unlimited, many organizations lose their sustainability and terminate their existence in time.

Organizational DNA is one of the concepts associated with sustainability in the organization literature. Organizational DNA can be defined as a structure that contains the information about the distinctive features of the organization and provides the transfer of this information to the elements in the organization and to the future. Therefore, the information contained in the organizational DNA is important with respect to ensuring sustainability.

The information on the methods of how to develop applications and strategies for the non-occurrence of the problems that the organizations have with respect to sustainability, such as the presence of unskilled employees, inefficient usage of limited organizational resources, weak management structure, the lack of accurate determination of organizational goals, and insufficient communication and coordination, is included in organizational DNA that will make positive contributions to the organization's functioning and ability to sustain its existence as it should be.

Organizations are regarded as living organisms. The fact that these living organisms have healthy DNA will help them to accurately direct their activities so that a significant step will be taken toward sustainability. In order to create a healthy organizational DNA, it will be useful that organization managers determine simple and clear procedures and implement the applications that will enable these procedures to reach everyone.

References

Akgül, U. (2010). "Sürdürülebilir Kalkınma: Uygulamalı Antropolojinin Eylem Alanı", *Ankara Üniversitesi Dil Tarih ve Coğrafya Fakültesi Antropoloji Dergisi*, 24: 133–164.

Aydın, E. (2016). "Yönetimde Sürdürebilirlik Sorunsallığı, Paradokslar ve Yeni Paradigmalar", ÇOMÜ Girişimcilik ve Kalkınma Dergisi, 11 (2): 25–35.

Bostancı, A., Çelik, K., Kahraman, Ü. (2017). "Okulların DNA Profilleri ile Öğretmenlerin Psikolojik Sermayeleri Arasındaki İlişki", Adnan Menderes Üniversitesi Eğitim Fakültesi Eğitim Bilimleri Dergisi, 8 (2): 140–156.

Çandır, E. (2005). Örgütsel DNA ve Bir Uygulama. (Basılmamış Yüksek Lisans Tezi). Bursa: Uludağ Üniversitesi Sosyal Bilimler Enstitüsü.

Çetin, R. B., DÖŞ, İ. (2014). "Örgüt DNA'sı Ölçeğinin Geliştirilmesi ve MEB Üzerine Bir Tarama Çalışması", Uluslararası Sosyal Araştırmalar Dergisi, 7 (31): 560–575.

Çetin, R. B. (2014). Okul DNA'sı Metaforunun Çeşitli Değişkenlere Göre İncelenmesi. (Basılmamış Yüksek Lisans Tezi). Kahramanmaraş: Kahramanmaraş Sütçü İmam Üniversitesi Sosyal Bilimler Enstitüsü.

Crittenden, V. L., Crittenden, W. F., Ferrell, L. K., Ferrell, O. C., Pinney, C. C. (2011). "Market-Oriented Sustainability: A Conceptual Framework and Propositions", Journal of the Academy of Marketing Science, 39 (1): 71–85.

Dehoff, K., Jaruzelski, B., Kronenberg, E. (2005), "Innovation's OrgDNA". Accessed: 06.11.2018, https://www.strategyand.pwc.com/media/uploads/InnovationsOrgDNA.pdf

Döş, İ. (2013). "School DNA and Its Transfer", American Journal of Human Ecology, 2 (1): 7–15.

Garvare, R., Johansson, P. (2010). "Management for Sustainability: A Stakeholder Theory", Total Quality Management, 21 (7): 737–744.

Günel, T. (2017). Kurumsal Kuram Perspektifinden Kurumsal Sürdürülebilirlik: İşletmelerin Kurumsal Sürdürülebilirlik Raporlamaları Üzerine Bir Uygulama. (Basılmamış Yüksek Lisans Tezi). Ankara: Başkent Üniversitesi Sosyal Bilimler Enstitüsü.

Kesen, M. (2016). "İşletme Yönetiminde Sürdürülebilir İnsan Kaynakları Yönetiminin Yeri ve Önemi", İnsan ve Toplum Bilimleri Araştırmaları Dergisi, 5 (3): 554–573.

Koçel, T. (2015). İşletme Yöneticiliği, İstanbul: Beta.

Kuşat, N. (2012). "Sürdürülebilir İşletmeler İçin Kurumsal Sürdürülebilirlik ve İçsel Unsurları", Afyon Kocatepe Üniversitesi İİBF Dergisi, 14 (2): 227–242.

Mısırdalı Yangil, F. (2016). "Bilgi Toplumunda Liderlik: Sürdürülebilir Liderlik", Sosyal Bilimler Dergisi, 48: 128–143.

Mucan, B., Kayabaşı., Madran, C. (2016). "Yöneticilerde Sürdürülebilirlik Algısı ve Firma Uygulamalarına Yönelik Değerlendirme", Ekonomik ve Sosyal Araştırmalar Dergisi, 12 (2): 57–72.

Nart, S. (2018). Dijital Dönüşüm Sürecinde Örgütsel DNA: Meritokrasi Üzerinden Bir Değerlendirme, ICOPEC 2018 Bildiriler Kitabı (10 Years After the Great Recession: Orthodox versus Heterodox Economics), ed. Halit Sağlam ve Mehmet Emin Kenanoğlu, Londra: IJOPEC Publication Limited, 231–237.

Neilson, G., Pasternack, B. A., Mendes, D. (2004a). "The Four Bases of Organizational DNA", Booz-Allen-Hamilton's Organizational DNA Reading Materials. Accessed: 04.11.2018, https://www.orgdna.com/orgdna_readingstoolkit.pdf

Neilson, G., Pasternack, B. A., Mendes, D. (2004b). "The Seven Types of Organizational DNA", Strategy and Business, 35. Accessed: 04.11.2018, https://www.strategy-business.com/article/04210?pg=0

Onay, M., Ergüden, S. (2012). "Yeni Bir Metafor: Kurum DNA'sı", Sosyal ve Beşeri Bilimler Dergisi, 4 (1): 203–212.

Öztel, A., Köse, M. S., Aytekin, İ. (2012). "Kurumsal Sürdürülebilirlik Performansının Ölçümü İçin Çok Kriterli Bir Çerçeve: Henkel Örneği", Tarih Kültür ve Sanat Araştırmaları Dergisi, (Special Issue: Tüketim Toplumu ve Çevre), 1 (4): 32–44.

Porter, T. B. (2006). "Coevolution As a Research Framework For Organizations and The Natural Environment", Organization and Environment, 19 (4): 479–504.

Porter, M., Kramer, M.R. (2006). "Strategy And Society: The Link Between Competitive Advantage And Corporate Social Responsibility", Harvard Business Review. Accessed: 25.10.2018, https://hbr.org/2006/12/strategy-and-society-the-link-between-competitive-advantage-and-corporate-social-responsibility

Tokgöz, N., Önce, S. (2009). "Şirket Sürdürülebilirliği: Geleneksel Yönetim Anlayışına Alternatif", Afyon Kocatepe Üniversitesi İİBF Dergisi, 11 (1): 249–275.

Ülgen, H., Mirze, K. (2013). İşletmelerde Stratejik Yönetim, İstanbul: Beta.

Yavuz, V. A. (2010). "Sürdürülebilirlik Kavramı ve İşletmeler Açısından Sürdürülebilir Üretim Stratejileri", Mustafa Kemal Üniversitesi Sosyal Bilimler Enstitüsü Dergisi, 7 (14): 63–86.

Bilâl Ezilmez

Emotional Labor and New Approaches

1 Introduction

Emotion can be defined as personal feelings peculiar and special for a person. Therefore, as a reality, employees reflect their feelings to their business lives. More or less, some level of emotions are reflected in various conditions according to the works done; that is, to some extent labor is spent in the representation of emotions. Even though this labor is more mental, it can sometimes be physical. Another definition of labor spent in this framework is emotional labor (EL). The concept of EL is defined as the effort, planning and control necessary to reflect the feelings that the organization expects in interpersonal work processes.

The phenomenon of emotion can generally be defined as one's subjective feeling state. It can also be stated that the phenomenon of emotion is related to having something and pointing out at something. So, it may be suggested that the phenomenon of emotion might contain the following four components (Seçer, 2005):

- Evaluation of a situational stimulus or environment,
- Changes in physiological or bodily sensations,
- Significant or limited representation of meaningful hand, arm and face movements,
- The combination of one or more of above components can also be called as emotion.

Emotions occupy an important place in human life and become the cornerstone of man's psychological state and behavior. Although their knowledge was as old as the history of mankind, it took a long time for them to be considered important for daily life and especially for the business world. The prejudice that emotions are against the mind and listening to emotions will make people unhappy and unsuccessful has played an important role in this. However, today there are plenty of debates and approaches in the related literature on positive emotions and their favorable contributions to cognitive processes and rational decision-making (Çukur, 2012).

When a person does business, he cannot behave as if he has no feelings. Emotion is the general name of short responses to a given stimulus, and emotions are factors that help people to adapt to the environment. There are also environmental, cultural and individual differences in the interpretation and management of emotions. The situation called emotion regulation or emotion management is that a certain emotion is controlled by the person who is living with it and projected and conveyed accordingly. This situation is made by paying a fee when it is called EL (Seçer, 2005; Hochschild, 1983).

2 What Is Emotional Labor?

In the last 20–25 years, one of the subjects that attracted most attention and focused on organizational behavior was workplace feelings. However, expression of EL is relatively new as a concept and came to mind in 1983 with the book "*The Managed Heart: The Commercialization of Human Feeling*" by Arlie Russell Hochschild. Although it is relatively new as a concept, its historical background is based on old times. EL has started when people control their emotions in their social lives (Hochschild, 1983). Emotion regulation, emotion work, emotional contagion, EL and emotional intelligence are all emotion-related concepts that find place in organizational labor studies.

So, when and how does EL occur? When an employee manipulates his or her feelings in order to display the proper emotion in context with display rules or occupational norms then EL occurs (Chu, 2002). This means that in order to provide social norms, the person's suppression of some emotions in order to make him comfortable is awakening some of the other emotions, which is also defined as emotion regulation. This is essential in the service sector to please the customer and to work in his or her favor.

When a person changes his or her emotions such as outward feelings, actions and body language to perform a job, all this is reflected differently. Since these behaviours are integral parts of the human behavior, it is important to examine people's EL demonstrations in more depth. It is a feature of the business role that is now underway to ensure that a certain emotional message is conveyed to the other person with the behaviors that a person performs while doing one's job. Consequently, this kind of work, which is dealt with in the dimension of making a certain emotional expression and reflecting this feeling of expression to the other side (usually customers), is called EL (Seçer, 2005).

2.1 Dimensions of Emotional Labor

A variety of dimensions have been put forward in researches on EL. Knowing, defining and managing the concept of emotion is the basis of the concept of EL in general. The main dimensions of EL in terms of demonstration are the emotions to be shown, how to show them, and the frequency and duration of display to from the employee towards the customer under the control of the display rules by the employer (Grandey, 2000; Hochschild, 1983; Morris and Feldman, 1996; Ashfort and Humprey, 1993). In addition to these, some certain strategies (like deep, surface and genuine acting) to put the feelings into practice are also important components of this process for managing and regulating emotions as a part of the employees' job.

2.2 Antecedents of Emotional Labor

In terms of EL demonstration, it is necessary to know which emotions will be shown for which purpose as a part of work. As stated in most of today's studies, it is more important to show expected emotions in the service sector. In this case, the expectations of customers who are served are seen as the most important components in terms of EL demonstration. It is important what emotion to be displayed by the employee towards the clients; and of course, the range of interaction, the duration of interaction, the frequency of interaction and the interaction routines affect the results. Briefly, in some service delivery work, EL is the product itself and many examples of EL can be provided (Steinberg and Figart, 1999).

Furthermore, factors such as gender, age and culture are also the subject of many researches as the main premises of EL demonstration (Steinberg and Figart, 1999). In some studies, EL and the behaviors that occur at work are evaluated in terms of only female and male employees. It is stated that gender-specific roles, expectations and EL create and nourish female–male work stratification and wage difference (Özkaplan, 2009).

Structural factors are divided into three groups: individual factors, organizational factors and interaction characteristics. In such approaches, gender, affect, empathy, self-adaptation and emotional intelligence are considered as individual factors; emotional behavior rules are independence (autonomy) and social support are organizational factors (Köse, 2009). The duration, frequency and variety of the emotions to be exhibited are evaluated as interaction characteristics.

Personality and personal traits are also important factors, and individual and demographic characteristics, such as personality, are frequently investigated in research as independent variables predicting EL. It is a fact that outward personalities use more EL (Basım et al., 2013).

2.3 Emotional Labor Strategies and Display Rules

Hochschild (1983) describes emotional behavior in two dimensions: surface acting behavior and deep acting behavior. Surface acting behavior expresses a certain emotion without expressing reality and acting as a role. This kind of EL is the most frequently seen and studied EL demonstration in the workplace. In many respects, it is considered important because it leads to negative results.

In general, surface acting behavior is a kind of masking of negative emotions. These negative emotions are feelings of anger, disgust and unhappiness and are masked by emotions such as happiness, care and excitement. The second type, deep acting labor behavior, emerges as two types of EL. The first is to show the sense of real feeling. The other is the behavior of the correct method. It is the use of past emotional experiences by the employee who feels otherwise and knows that one should not show them. EL exhibited in deep acting behavior is often referred to as methodological behavior (Ashfort and Humprey; 1993).

EL of employees to their customers is generally examined in three ways: Surface Behavior, Deep Behavior and Genuine Behavior. Surface acting behavior can be defined as the way the employees behave in accordance with expectations by controlling their emotions although they do not change their true feelings (Grandey, 2003). Deep acting behavior occurs when the employee tries to harmonize his or her real feelings with the expected behavior (Grandey, 2003). Genuine EL strategy is the type of behavior that occurs when the employees are already feeling the feelings that they have to reflect (Ashfort and Humprey, 1993).

In examining the causes and consequences of these three types of EL demonstrations, the support provided by the supervisor and the support provided by the employee's colleagues influence the outcome of the *EL process*. If these two supports are positive, they can make positive contributions to the results if they support the expectations of the employees (Hochschild, 1983; Grandey, 1999, 2000).

In order to understand properly what EL is we should be able to be aware and determine the right responses in a certain situation at work. What is the rule or rules that the desired emotion is to be directed, how and for what to manage? According to these rules, people exhibit the correct EL behavior that is desired by showing the correct EL. These rules are like written rules describing what is right at a workplace. They can be part of a business education, or they define the desired styles (Hochschild, 1979; 1983). *EL* means control of emotions in order to provide social norms. This situation is necessary in social and business life, so it is necessary to know the social conditions and environmental conditions and how to provide them (Öz, 2007).

In addition, it is another remarkable factor that the expected sensation is positive EL or negative EL, which is desired to be exhibited to the service area during the demonstration of EL behavior (Grandey, 2000). In some cases, negative emotions are also expected. It is expected that the judges who judge the criminals in the court will carry out their work by showing negative emotions to the police who are investigating the criminals in the security center. On the other hand, it is known that health personnel, ground and air hostesses and teachers perform their duties by showing positive emotions.

2.4 Results of Emotional Labor Display

As a result of EL demonstration behaviors, the following negative results are observed: emotional dissonance (Hochscild, 1983), the sense of burnout and the intention to quit work (Grandey, 2000). In surface acting emotional strategy, there may be some health and psychological consequences. Sometimes employees and organizations prioritize customer expectations and trigger emotional dissonance and self-alienation if they are not met (Ashfort and Humprey; 1993).

In some studies, the consequences of *EL* behavior process are examined in two groups as positive and negative results. The negative results shown in such studies are: loss of self-esteem, emotional conflict, job-related stress, increased intention to quit, decrease in burnout and job satisfaction. As for the results of the EL behavior process that are considered positive; increase in individual performance, increase in self-efficacy, financial benefit, customer satisfaction and the performance increase of the organization (Köksel, 2009). Emotional commitment to go to work and job satisfaction are positive results for the employees with improvements in customer service (Morris and Feldman, 1996).

EL can provide good results for business. Deep acting behavior leads to more positive service than surface acting behavior, but both relate to burnout, dissolution and negative work attitudes in some ways (Grandey, 2000).

On the other hand, the results of some other research show that EL behaviors are thought to be necessary behaviors with emotion display and of course, this is positive in terms of job commitment and job satisfaction. The acceptance of the EL behavior involved in the work is high in terms of job loyalty and job satisfaction according to the ones who think that such behaviors are extra except for the job. In this respect, it is inevitable for organizations to show more respect to the rules of emotional impression (Diefendorff et al.; HYPERLINK \l "2006).

Data from some studies have shown that positive emotions are expressed or reflected differently when negative emotions are masked. (Glaso and Einarsen, 2008).

3 Main Approaches for Emotional Labor

Hocschild (1983) was not only the first person to bring the concept of EL to literature, but also made important contributions by grouping the professions in the field of EL:

- In busy jobs, employees are communicating with their stakeholders face-to-face or on the phone, verbally or non-verbally.
- Employees affect the feelings, attitudes and behaviors of the stakeholders.
- In the organizations where they are located, managers have the right to control and control the emotions of the employees. There are rules determined in this direction.
- Only surface acting and deep acting were considered by her as EL display strategies.
- The consequences focused on are emotional dissonance,

Emotion management work is applied in many professions. Funeral services, courts, policemen and health workers feel the necessity of showing different emotions because of their different situations (Hochschild 1979). In this case, there are rules for displaying EL behavior, which can change from sector to sector and from business to business. According to the researcher, it is a kind of necessity to ask people from different classes, genders, ethnic and religious groups to show the feelings that are presumed to be true in a particular situation (Hochschild, 1979).

According to another main EL approach considering the social identity theory, it is proposed that some of the effects of the EL phenomenon are softened by the social and individual identities of the person and that the employees are warned by the pressure of EL to show the service role. In this context, the results of research on macro, micro and meso levels are discussed and genuine (natural) acting strategy was contributed to the literature (Ashfort and Humprey, 1993). The content, density, diversity and consistency of the emotions of the members of the EL organization are taken into consideration as a part of the approach. The weak side of this approach is that there is no strong survey to measure the performance of EL.

In Morris and Feldman's approach (1996), the structure of EL is conceptualized in four dimensions: the frequency of the right emotional display, the attention to the rules of choice, the diversity of the emotions to be shown, and the emotional dissonance that arises as a result of the emotion that the organization wants, not the reality. In this framework, the organization has been discussed in terms of business and individual. The consequences stressed are emotional exhaustion and low satisfaction.

When recruiting employees, organizations can assist individuals in the sense that they meet the demands of their behavior patterns by pre-empting the conditions of EL in the workplace (Morris and Feldman, 1996). Many studies have examined the negative effects of EL and its employees. However, the study

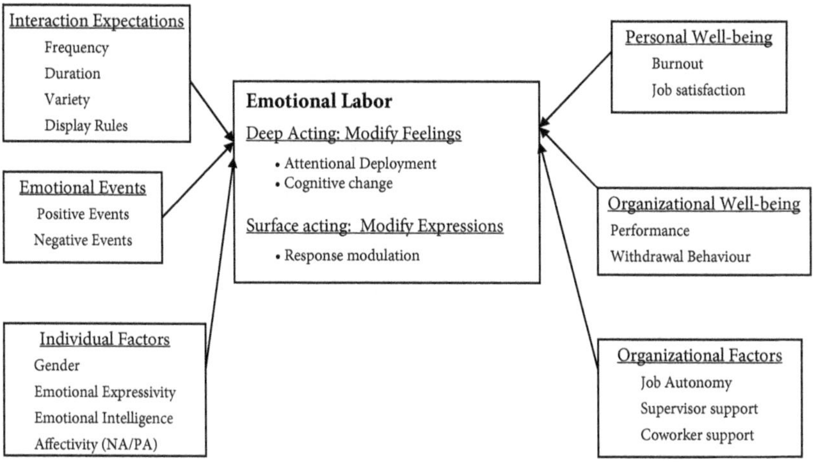

Fig. 1: Grandey's Model for Emotional Labor. **Source:** Grandey, A. A. (2000). Emotion Regulation in the Workplace: A New Way to Conceptualize Emotional Labor. Journal of Occupational Health Psychology, 5(1), 95–110.

states that the multi-dimensional concept of EL does not uniformly erode all employees (Morris and Feldman, 1996).

In Grandey's approach EL was studied from the point of the tension in the management of emotions when one's job role demanded certain expressions to be shown to the client. Basically, it reviewed and compared the EL angles of existing studies in order to define these angles. For this, it is discussed from the perspective of individual differences, such as emotional intelligence, and organizational factors, such as support for the superior (Grandey, 2000). In the following model (Fig. 1) all the variables studied and analyzed by Grandey (2000) are seen in details. Individual and organizational factors are together studied here without ignoring employees for the sake of the organization.

3.1 Emotional Labor and Management

The most important challenge facing public managers is to make their work more efficient. It is concluded that what is needed is not only to care for more people, but to pay attention to the emotional state of the employees (Newman et al., 2009). In order to influence the motivation and mood of the subordinates, leaders show EL. EL leaders can better express feelings and become better communicators. Communication skills can help them to be perceived as transformational leaders (Humphrey et al., 2008).

In the nature of management, three EL display strategies are also important for leaders. It is suggested that the individual differences that determine the responses to the leader emotion representations in important events are skills such as emotional intelligence, self-control and political skills. Key outcomes are the trust of the followers and the welfare of the leader. The EL demonstration of the leader is also affected by the circumstances (Gardner et al., 2009).

On the whole, it is said that if managers are for effective democratic administration, they develop emotional and cognitive value of the employees and the company. Such concepts only contribute positively to EL in the work place (Kiel and Watson, 2009). In general, the degree of emotion regulation is higher in the leader than in the followers. Instead of masking and suppressing the viewers, the leader shows their feelings at a high level (Glaso and Einarsen, 2008).

4 Recent Studies New Approaches

According to a recent study, the link between emotion regulation and EL has considerable importance; hence, this link should not be ignored or weakened in the future studies, and also laboratory and field studies are needed to test the relationships between EL and its agents (Grandey et al., 2015).

Grandey and Gabriel (2015) emphasize that in order to develop the future of EL studies in a healthy way, researchers and scholars will discuss the concept of EL in all dimensions. They also suggest the necessity of testing the factors such as the complexity of structure and measurement, and the limitations of understanding of the premises for healthy and good results. Deep EL behavior is positively associated with some personality traits, and in this case, the desired effective service delivery can be achieved. On the other hand, surface acting EL behavior, as well as personality traits such as honesty and emotional stability, can be positively related to undermining of the service provided (Chi and Grandey, 2016).

In a study in 2017, it is suggested that the concept of spiritual labor can be included in the EL studies by discussing the phenomenon of workplace spirituality and spirituality (Gungor-Delen, 2017).

5 Conclusion

Since there is no common definition and a relatively fixed standard survey, EL can bring some positive results for organizations. For example, exhibiting the correct behavior towards customers through emotional behavior rules can reduce the problems that may arise between the employee and the client and increase his or her individual performance. In practice inevitably individual differences can emerge as employees use EL. Similarly organizational differences will also be possible. Surely, the performance of EL can positively contribute to job satisfaction and the pride in work for employees.

Despite the existence of positive sides, EL can bring some negative consequences for employees. The characteristics of the work, personal characteristics of the employee and EL depending on the expectations of the organization; job satisfaction, burnout, alienation and stress related to work can lead to some important negativity.

Despite the fact of all the negative appearances, an offer can be made: when organizations abandon the strict emotional display rules by developing the positive working climate and positive workforce, employees can realize these humanitarian practices and then being more motivated their EL efforts will be more effective. It is clear that we have much more to learn about emotion work and EL.

References

Ashforth, B. E. and Humphrey, R. H. (1993). Emotional Labor in Service Roles: The Influence of Identity, *Academy of Management Review*, 18, 1, 88–115.

Basım, H. N., Beğenirbaş, M. ve Yalçın, R. C. (2013). "Öğretmenlerde Kişilik Özelliklerinin Duygusal Tükenmeye Etkisi: Duygusal Emeğin Aracılık Rolü", *Kuram ve Uygulamada Eğitim Bilimleri*. 13. 3. 1477–1496.

Chi, N. and Grandey, A.A. (2016). Emotional Labor Predicts Service Performance Depending on Activation and Inhibition Regulatory Fit. *Journal of Management*. Volume 45 issue 2, p. 673–700.

Chu, H. K. (2002). *The Effects of Emotinal Labor on Employee Work Outcomes* (Yayımlanmamış Doktora Tezi). Virginia Polytechnic Institute and State University.

Çukur, Cem Şafak; (2012); "Duygusal Düzenleme ve Duygusal İşçilik" konulu konferans; Atılım Üniversitesi. 13. 04. 2012; Ankara.

Diefendorff, J. M.; Richard, E. M. ve Croyle, M. H. (2006). Are emotional display rules formal job requirements? Examination of employee and supervisor perceptions, *Journal of Occupational and Organizational Psychology*, 79, 273–298.

Gardner, W. L.; Fischer, D.; ve Hunt; J. G. (2009). Emotional Labor and Leadership: A threat to authenticity? *The Leadership Quarterly*, 20, 466–482.

Glaso, L. ve Einersen, S. (2008). Emotion Regulation in Leader–Follower Relationships, *European Journal of Work and Organizational Psychological*, 17, 4, 482–500.

Grandey, Alicia A. (1999). "The effects of emotional labor; Employee attitudes, stres and performance", (Unpublished PhD Thesis)". Colorado State University.

Grandey, A. A. (2000). Emotion Regulation in the Workplace: A New Way to Conceptualize Emotional Labor, *Journal of Occupational Health Psychology*. 5, 1, 95–110.

Grandey, A. A. (2015). Smiling for a Wage: What Emotional Labor Teaches Us About Emotion Regulation. *Psychological Inquiry*. 26. 1. 54–60.

Grandey, Alicia A.; Allison Gabriel. A. (2015). Emotional Labor at a Crossroads: Where Do We Go from Here? *Annual Review of Organizational Psychology and Organizational Behavior*, 2. 323–349.

Grandey, A. A.; Rupp, D. and Brice, W. N. (2015). Emotional Labor Threatens Decent Work: A Proposal to Eradicate Emotional Display Rules. *Journal of Organizational Behaviour*, 36. 770–785.

Grandey, A. A. Fisk, G. M. Mattila, A. S. Jansen, K. J. Sideman, L. A. (2005). Is "service with a smile" Enough? Authenticity of Positive Displays during Service Encounters, *Organizational Behavior and Human Decision Processes*. 96, 38–55.

Grandey, A. A.; (2003) When "The Show Must Go On": Surface Acting and Deep Acting As Determinants of Emotional Exhaustion and Peer-Rated Service Delivery, Academy of Management Journal, 2003, v. 46, No. 1, 86–96.

Güngör-Delen, M. (2017) "Emek Sürecinde Son Nokta: Duygusal Emek & Tinsel Emek.", Türkmen Kitabevi. İstanbul.

Hochschild, Arlie R. (1979). "Emotion Work, Feeling Rules, and Social Structure", *American Journal of Sociology*. 85, 3, 551–575.

Hochschild, Arlie Russell; (1983). "The Managed Heart: The Commercialization of Human Feeling". Berkeley and Los Angeles: University of California Press.

Humphrey, R. H.; Pollack, J. M. ve Hawver, T. (2008). Leading with Emotional Labor, *Journal of Managerial Psychology*. 23. 2. 151–168.

Kiel, L. D. and Watson, D. J. (2009); Affective Leadership and Emotional Labor: A View from the Local Level, *Public Administration Review*. January–February.

Köksel, L. (2009). İş Yaşamında Duygusal Emek ve Ampirik Bir Çalışma (Yayınlanmamış Manisa: Yüksek lisans tezi) Celal Bayar Üniversitesi, Sosyal bilimler Enstitüsü.

Morris, J. A. ve Feldman, D. C. (1996). The Dimensions, Antecedents and Consequences of Emotıonal Labor, *Academy ot Management Review*, 21, 4, 986–1010.

Newman, M. A.; Guy, M. E. and Mastracci, S. H. (2009) Beyond Cognition: Affective Leadership and Emotional Labor. *Public Administration Review*. January -February.

Öz, E. Ü. (2007). Duygusal Emek Davranışlarının Çalışanların İş Sonuçlarına Etkisi. İstanbul: Beta.

Özkaplan, Nurcan; (2009); Duygusal Emek ve Kadın İşi/Erkek İşi; *Çalışma ve Toplum, 2009/2.*

Seçer, Ş. H. (2005); *Çalışma Yaşamında Duygular ve Duygusal Emek: Sosyoloji, Psikoloji ve Örgüt Teorisi Açısından Bir Değerlendirme*, Sosyal Siyaset Konferansları Dergisi "Prof. Dr. Nevzat Yalçıntaş'a Armağan Özel Sayısı", Sayı. 50; www.iudergi.com.

Steinberg, R.J. and Figart, D. M. (1999). Emotional Demands at Work: A Job Content Analysis, Annals of the American Academy of Political and Social Science, 561, Emotional Labor in the Service Economy (January), 177–119.

Ezgi Dede, Burcak Vatansever Durmaz, and Canan Cetin

Responsible Leadership

1 Introduction

The subject of responsible leadership has begun to take place in the literature and attract attention in the business world. There are basically two reasons for this interest and increased attention. First one is that with increasing complexity and connectedness in society, workers, clients, suppliers, public entities, environmental institutions, and citizens in the organizations are seen as an independent piece of puzzle in social life. Second reason is that there is an increase in awareness, public interest and intervention in financial crises, layoffs, downsizings, environmental problems, corporate scandals and unethical behaviors in business environment. For these reasons, the responsibility of the leaders and the managers and the compliance of their behaviors with the code of ethics have been a focus of high interest (Marques et al, 2018, p. 3). Leadership is defined as "the process (act) of influencing the activities of an organized group in its efforts toward goal setting and goal achievement" (Stogdill, 1950, p. 3). In leadership definitions, the word "influence" is mostly used because in a leadership process there is a relational part and the leader should exert some kind of inducement over another party. The other definition of leadership is made by Yukl in 2006. Yukl sees leadership as a process in which individuals in the group understand what is to be done to achieve common goals, and that leaders influence them around the common purpose and facilitate individual and group efforts to achieve these goals. While responsible leadership leads to the development of leadership definitions, it emphasizes how the leaders use the power they have. Leaders in responsible leadership use their power to improve the lives of people, not to lose the value of their careers, economy or society. From this point of view, responsible leaders do not only influence employees but they also influence internal and external stakeholders (Marques et al, 2018, p. 3).

2 Definitions of Responsible Leadership and the Roles of Responsible Leaders

While the definitions of responsible leadership are mostly considered within the concept of stakeholder theory, there are also some differences between these definitions. One definition is that responsible leadership is "a relationship between leaders and stakeholders through value-oriented and ethical principles" (Pless, 2007, p. 438). According to Maak and Pless's definition, responsible leadership is a process based on relational and ethical relationships where there is a social interaction with all stakeholders (Maak and Pless, 2006; Maak, 2007). Voegtlin states what responsible leaders should do in this process: First, leaders need to think about how one person's behavior can have consequences for all stakeholders and how these results will have an impact. Second, they use their impacts in order to provide an environment for the resolution of conflicts and invite the affected stakeholders to this environment. Finally, they try to weigh the arguments made to provide consensus and to balance the interests of the stakeholder claims (Voegtlin, et al, 2012; Voegtlin, 2011). According to responsible leadership, leaders want to open up a broader target audience (stakeholders) in order to secure the legitimacy of the organization within the society and to establish mutually beneficial stakeholder relations and maintain this established relationship (Voegtlin, et al, 2012, p. 8). For a better understanding of responsible leadership, Maak and Pless have developed a model to explain how responsible leadership takes on different roles and fulfills corporate social responsibility (CSR). What is meant by corporate social responsibility is an external necessity that extends from the leader–audience relationship to the leader–stakeholder relationship and ensures the fulfillment of social responsibility (Shi & Ye, 2016). For good corporate social responsibility practices, leaders should be role models and try to foster an ethical culture; at the same time, they should encourage employees for the necessity of CSR and about the significance of the organization's social responsibility activities (Voegtlin, et al, 2012, p. 12). The roles of responsible leadership do not mean different persons, and the integration of these roles is a leader. Leaders are around a stakeholder relations (employees' direct reports, customers, suppliers, peers, family, other stakeholders, etc.). In order to gather and mobilize stakeholders with different backgrounds, values or conflicting demands around a common vision, leaders must display certain roles: the role of being a steward which is meant as a custodian of values and resources; a good citizen role which is active and cares for member of communities; a servant role and a visionary role which provides inspiration and perspective with respect to a desired future. The roles within the circle are keywords for the self-image and self-understanding of a responsible leader. In addition to these roles, there are some that are connected with them and are more "operational" such as being the architect of inclusive systems, being a change agent and transforming, coaching by supporting followers and storyteller and meaning enabler of shared systems of meaning. It should be underlined again that all roles are related to each other, and these roles take into account specific responsibilities or activities in relational processes in organizations. Even if the meaning and the temporal significance differ, they are integrated to each other in a holistic way (Maak and Pless, 2006, p. 107).

3 Structure of Responsible Leadership

Responsible leadership is thought as a construction of multi-dimension structure by most of the scholars. For example, Doh and Stumpf indicate that responsible leadership has three dimensions which are named as values-based leadership, ethical decision-making and quality stakeholder relationships. Likewise, Lynham and Chermack argue that responsible leadership consists of ethics, effectiveness and endurance dimensions. In addition to this, Doh and colleagues suggest that responsible leadership is a composition of stakeholder culture, resource management practices and managerial support dimensions. Another scholar who looks at responsible leadership from the behavioral perspective claims that it has two dimensions. First one is "do good behaviors" and the second one is "avoid harm behaviors". The dimensions are conceptually different from one another. Avoid harm behaviors are the behaviors in which managers avoid harmful outcomes for stakeholders and the larger society. For example ensuring product safety, avoiding discrimination in hiring practices, limiting corruption and avoiding environmental pollution are such behaviors that are supported by managers. Another dimension is to do good behaviors and they refer to behaviors such as engaging in philanthropy, broadening access to products, designing employees-friendly workplaces and supporting development (Stahl & De Luque, 2014, p. 238).

4 Difference Between Responsible Leadership and Other Leadership Types

In general, responsible leadership is *"a values-based and through ethical principles driven relationship between leaders and stakeholders who are connected through a shared sense of meaning and purpose through which they raise one another to higher levels of motivation and commitment for achieving sustainable values creation and social change" (Pless,2007, p. 438).* Relationship between other types of leadership and responsible leadership such as ethical, authentic, servant and transformational leadership styles, which are the value-centered leadership styles, are investigated. Ethical leaders try to influence followers by demonstrating ethical behaviors. In ethical leadership, the relationship between the leader and the subordinates is gaining importance, whereas in responsible leadership, the leader and the stakeholder relations come to the fore. Furthermore, in ethical leadership, the outcomes which seem at micro-level perspective (e.g., leader effectiveness, employee job satisfaction and dedication) are considered. On the other hand, responsible leadership uses this micro-level perspective to achieve multi-level outcomes (Pless & Maak, 2011, p. 6).

In servant leadership, the character of the leader and the way to serve other people is important (Parris & Peachey, 2013, p. 5). Servant leaders serve the organization and the members of the organization. Leaders first and foremost think their constituencies' interests rather than their interests. These leaders have service-oriented attitude. There are some similarities between servant leadership and responsible leadership. They share the idea that leadership must serve the needs and legitimate interests of followers or stakeholders (Pless & Maak, 2011, p. 6–7). Furthermore, leaders and followers must support each other through a high level of motivation and high moral values. The difference between responsible leadership and servant leadership is that although responsible leadership cares the interests of constituencies beyond self-interest the responsible leader does not think that he or she should pursue "self-sacrificial servanthood" just for the sake of developing his or her own good and serving followers. The basic motivation source is not serving the others, instead responding to followers at the same time outside stakeholders and society. In addition to this, within the context of responsible leadership theory, leaders do not limit their followers as stakeholders only in workplace, but also perceive them as stakeholders both inside and outside the organization (Pless & Maak, 2011, p. 7).

Authentic leadership theory focuses on the factors such as high moral standards, honesty and accuracy, and it leads the others by these factors. According to Avolio et al, 2004, p. 4 authentic leaders are aware of themselves, their behaviors and their thoughts and other people perceive them as confident, hopeful, optimistic, resilient and of high moral character (Avolio & Gardner, 2005, p. 321). Authentic leadership process often centers at the individual level. Authentic leaders influence their followers by some important mechanisms. These are, for example, self-awareness which is a deep sense of self that provides knowledge about one's values, identity, emotions and aims or the self-regulatory processes that take control and evaluate one's own intentions and behavior. The components of authentic leadership are also included in responsible leadership, but it goes further in responsible leadership. Responsible leaders should understand the sense of others' emotions and values, reflect on the adequacy of their own emotions and values, and evaluate them according to general standards and local needs. Similar to authentic leadership, responsible leadership also tries for the positive outcomes in the organization, but in responsible leadership theory there are not only traditional economic outcome variables, but it also has value on social capital by stakeholders (Pless & Maak, 2011, p. 7).

Transformational leadership is primarily the process of creating commitment to organizational goals and then encouraging viewers to achieve these goals. Transformational leaders establish a climate of trust by creating a common vision with their followers, and they transform the personal values of followers to support the vision and goals of the organization. Transformational leadership is also an individual-level phenomenon, and it builds an organizational commitment and empowerment among followers to fulfill organizational goals (Stone et al.2004, p. 350). Transformational leadership consists of some contextual factors like country culture or organizational culture, but it does not consider leadership in the context of stakeholder theory (Bass and Steidlmeier 1999, p. 200). Responsible leadership considers the followers as stakeholders within and outside the organization, which is a broader point of view than the transformational leadership. Besides, this change and transformation terms are important for both of them. However, while responsible leaders use change to achieve a higher social goal, the goals of transformational leaders are not so high (Pless & Maak, 2011, p. 7).

5 Antecedents of Responsible Leadership

The antecedents of responsible leadership can be categorized as personal and situational factors. Responsible leadership behaviors are affected by some personal factors such as personality traits, relational intelligence, empathy, cognitive moral development and machiavellianism. Personality traits such as "big five factors" (neuroticism, extraversion, openness, agreeableness and conscientiousness) have a considerable effect on the emergence of responsible leadership. Personality traits also include values and beliefs, cognitive processes, generalized expectancies and affective states. Most of the studies suggest that managers who pursue their own interests engage in actions that put the stakeholders at risk or loss. On the other hand, managers who embrace self-transcendent values care for others and are more likely to work for the benefit of the society (Stahl & De Luque, 2014, p. 241). One of the special personal traits is machiavellianism, and it is emphasized that it has a negative effect on responsible leadership. Leaders with machiavellianism do not trust others and want to control them. At the same time, such leaders tend to neglect ethical rules (Shi & Ye, 2016, p. 880). Also relational intelligence which includes both emotional intelligence and ethical intelligence is important for demonstrating responsible leadership behaviors for leaders. Leaders should build and maintain a trustful relationship with stakeholders. There are many stakeholders with very different characteristics in a stakeholder society because of the globalization. Leaders must have strong social skills to establish good relationships with these stakeholders. High emotional intelligence which is the first dimension of relational intelligence makes leaders control and use their own emotion and understand others' emotion successfully; in addition to this, they deal with complex relationships effectively. Ethical intelligence which is the second dimension of the relational intelligence makes leaders manage with integrity and make "profits with principles". In short, the relational intelligence is a necessary ability for leading responsibly (Shi & Ye, 2016, p. 879). Empathy is defined as an ability to experience and understand others' emotion from the point of view of others. Leaders with empathy are more concerned with their stakeholders. It is emphasized that the empathy of the leader affects whether a leader is a responsible leader or not. Responsible leaders particularly concern about interests and needs of stakeholders and what can be done to meet their demands (Shi & Ye, 2016, p. 879). According to the cognitive moral development theory, with the development of cognitive morality, a person develops the ability to make moral judgment and decision (Shi & Ye, 2016, p. 879). It is generally about how ethical dilemmas are considered by the organization members which means that how they determine what is right or wrong in a certain statement (Trevino, 1986, p. 604). Within the scope of this theory, leaders with high cognitive moral development find ethical solutions to their problems with all their stakeholders. In the case of conflicting interests of different stakeholders, the responsible leaders are able to make ethical decisions (Shi & Ye, 2016, p. 879).

Situational factors as well as personal factors have important implications for responsible leadership. Situational factors include moral intensity, cultural value orientations, institutional context and media. Moral intensity focuses on the importance of adhering to ethical rules when deciding on the situations faced by leaders. The term "moral intensity" determines the extent of issue-related moral imperative in a situation, and it means that the leaders behave responsibly in some situations but they behave irresponsibly in other situations (Stahl & De Luque, 2014, p. 242). "The degree of badness of an act" is defined as moral intensity, and it has six dimensions which are concentration of effect, probability of effect, proximity, social consensus, temporal immediacy and magnitude of consequence. These dimensions have an impact on the leaders' every step of decision-making process (Carlson et al, 2002, p. 17). Cultural value orientations can shape beliefs about the leaders' behaviors, styles, skills and personality traits. Effective leaders should understand and manage the culturally diverse workforce, and leaders should be aware of how leadership behaviors interact with followers' affective, cognitive and behavioral outcomes by the cultural value orientations (Kirkman et al, 2009, p. 744). The institutional context is of great importance for responsible leadership behaviors. For example, if the corruption is approved in the leader's country, the leader may take part in some corruptions even if he/she does not personally approve it. However, if the leader is in a country where corruption is banned and unapproved, the leader can then move away from unethical behavior by following the institutional system (Shi & Ye, 2016, p. 880). With the popularization of the media, people are easily and quickly informed about the companies. In the event of corporate scandals, the public will be aware of this situation quickly and this damages the corporate reputation immediately. For this reason, in order to build trust and gain respect, leaders must be accountable to stakeholders inside and outside the organization. Especially in an environment where the media follows everything, the responsibility of the leaders increases. Through media, leaders tend to behave responsibly (Shi & Ye, 2016, p. 880).

6 The Consequences of Responsible Leadership

The consequences of responsible leadership are divided into two categories as the consequences of individual level and organizational level. The consequences of individual level include turnover intention, job satisfaction, organizational commitment, unethical behaviors and work performance. If an individual feels dissatisfied because of the job, characteristics of job or the leader, then the thought of quitting arises which means turnover intention (Nadiri & Tanova, 2010, p. 34). According to Doh et al, 2011, employees' perceptions of responsible leadership were grouped in three groups: low, moderate and high. It is determined that 36.8 % of those who have low level of responsible leadership perception left their jobs within one year. A positive emotional attitude which comes after the evaluation of one's work is called job satisfaction (Voegtlin, 2011, p. 61). Employees with high job satisfaction feel relaxed and happy in their work environment, and this results desirable outcomes for the organization. Responsible leaders take care of their employees, create a working environment where their ideas are heard and cared about, and ensure that their employees are satisfied with their jobs (Voegtlin, 2011, p. 61). Employees who feel that they are participants in the decisions and they are important for their supervisors are committed to the organization they are working (Voegtlin et al,2012, p. 12). Responsible leaders play an important part in organizations as role models and ensure employees take an active role in decision-making processes. As a result of this, employees who follow the responsible leaders have high level of organizational commitment

(Doh & Quigley, 2014, p258). If the employees are strongly affiliated to an organization with a higher level of commitment, they will try to achieve organizational goals without thinking of an opportunity for personal interest (Dhar, 2015, p. 420). Behaviors that are morally unacceptable by the public is called unethical behaviors (Kaptein, M., 2008, p. 980). Responsible leaders can influence employees to reduce their unethical behavior (Voegtlin, 2011). Employees in organizations often perceive leaders as role models, and employees will act according to ethical principles when responsible leaders demonstrate ethical behavior. Responsible leaders have a positive effect on work performance of their followers (Shi & Ye, 2016). Also with the perspective of stakeholders, if they trust the leader, they feel committed to what the organization is trying to achieve and is more motivated on their job; as a result, their work performance increases (Doh & Quigley, 2014).

The consequences of organizational level consist of organizational performance, legitimacy of the organization and corporate social responsibility. According to Doh and Quigley, 2014, responsible leaders can influence organizational performance through two specific pathways including a psychological pathway and a knowledge-based pathway. In the first pathway which is called psychological, it is determined that responsible leadership theory is a stakeholder-oriented approach and in this approach employees are psychologically motivated and influenced by their leaders. Employee motivation also positively affects the performance of the organization. Legitimacy of the Organization: "*Legitimacy is a generalized perception or assumption that the actions of an entity are desirable, proper, or appropriate within some socially constructed system of norms, values, beliefs, and definitions*" (Suchman, 1995, p. 574). There are three types of legitimacy. First one is pragmatic legitimacy which is based on the self- interested calculations of the closest target group of an organization. The second one is moral legitimacy and it rests on a positive normative evaluation of the organization and its activities. The main difference between them is that moral legitimacy is "sociotropic". In other words pragmatic legitimacy rests on judgments about whether a given activity benefits the evaluator or not. On the other hand, moral legitimacy rests on judgments about whether the activity is "the right thing to do" (Suchman, 1995). Third one is cognitive legitimacy and it refers to "knowledge about the new activity and what is needed to succeed in an industry". In conclusion, responsible leadership can provide legitimacy to the organization (Shi & Ye, 2016, p. 881). What organizations do within the framework of social responsibility is generally considered as corporate social responsibility. Corporate social responsibility is required for responsible leaders. Responsible leaders are expected to deal with scandals occurring in the institution and fulfill their social responsibilities. Responsible leaders participate in many social responsibility activities. Some of these include providing a comfortable working environment for employees, producing healthy and safe food for customers, cooperating with partners in a fair and honest manner, protecting resources and the environment, and so on (Shi & Ye, 2016, p. 882).

References

Avolio, B. J., & Gardner, W. L. (2005). Authentic leadership development: Getting to the root of positive forms of leadership. The Leadership Quarterly, 16(3), 315–338.

Bass, B. M., & Steidlmeier, P. (1999). Ethics, character, and authentic transformational leadership behavior. The Leadership Quarterly, 10(2), 181–217.

Carlson, D. S., Kacmar, K. M., & Wadsworth, L. L. (2002). The impact of moral intensity dimensions on ethical decision making: Assessing the relevance of orientation. Journal of Managerial Issues, 14(1), 15–30.

Dhar, R. L. (2015). Service quality and the training of employees: The mediating role of organizational commitment. Tourism Management, 46, 419–430.

Doh, J. P., & Quigley, N. R. (2014). Responsible leadership and stakeholder management: Influence pathways and organizational outcomes. Academy of Management Perspectives, 28(3), 255–274.

Doh, J. P., Stumpf, S. A., & Tymon, W. G. (2011). Responsible leadership helps retain talent in India. In Responsible Leadership, Journal of Business Ethics, 98 (pp. 85–100). Springer, Dordrecht.

Kaptein, M. (2008). Developing a measure of unethical behavior in the workplace: A stakeholder perspective. Journal of Management, 34(5), 978–1008.

Kirkman, B. L., Chen, G., Farh, J. L., Chen, Z. X., & Lowe, K. B. (2009). Individual power distance orientation and follower reactions to transformational leaders: A cross-level, cross-cultural examination. Academy of Management Journal, 52(4), 744–764.

Maak, T. (2007) Responsible Leadership, Stakeholder Engagement and the Emergence of Social Capital. Journal of Business Ethics, 74, 329–343.

Maak, Th. and Pless, N.M. (2006) Responsible Leadership in a Stakeholder Society—A Relational Perspective. Journal of Business Ethics, 66, 99–115.

Marques, T., Reis, N., & Gomes, J. F. (2018). Responsible Leadership Research: A Bibliometric Review. BAR-Brazilian Administration Review, 15(1), p. 2–25.

Nadiri, H., & Tanova, C. (2010). An investigation of the role of justice in turnover intentions, job satisfaction, and organizational citizenship behavior in hospitality industry. International journal of hospitality management, 29(1), 33–41.

Parris, D. L., & Peachey, J. W. (2013). A systematic literature review of servant leadership theory in organizational contexts. Journal of business ethics, 113(3), 377–393.

Pless, N. M. (2007). Understanding responsible leadership: Role identity and motivational drivers. Journal of Business Ethics, 74(4), 437–456.

Pless, N. M., & Maak, T. (2011). Responsible leadership: Pathways to the future. In Responsible Leadership Journal of Business Ethics, 98 (pp. 3–13). Springer, Dordrecht.

Shi, Y., & Ye, M. (2016). Responsible leadership: review and prospects. American Journal of Industrial and Business Management, 6(8), 877–884.

Stahl, G. K., & Sully de Luque, M. (2014). Antecedents of responsible leader behavior: A research synthesis, conceptual framework, and agenda for future research. Academy of Management Perspectives, 28(3), 235–254.

Stogdill, R. M. (1950). Leadership, membership and organization. Psychological bulletin, 47(1), 1.

Trevino, L. K. (1986). Ethical decision making in organizations: A person-situation interactionist model. Academy of management Review, 11(3), 601–617.

Voegtlin, C. (2011) Development of a Scale Measuring Discursive Responsible Leadership. Journal of Business Ethics,98, 57–73.

Voegtlin, C., Patzer, M., & Scherer, A. G. (2012). Responsible leadership in global business: A new approach to leadership and its multi-level outcomes. Journal of Business Ethics, 105(1), 1–16.

Fahri Erenel

On Duties and Responsibilities of Human Resources Management

1 Technology and Working Life

Based on Greek mythology, Plato states that technology seeps into our lives, making humanity feel dependent on it to a large extent (Chaharbaghi and Willis, **2000**, p. 394). When we elaborate on this statement aoristically, it is possible to say that technology has made great changes not only in our daily lives but also in our professional lives.

It is clearly seen that every society has attributed a different meaning to the verb "to work". The verb "to travail" refers to "to work" in Western languages, however it is derived from Latin "tripalium" that means "instrument of torture". Moreover, the Romans use the term "labour" as the equivalence of "work", whereas the very same term is also associated with "toil, exertion, hardship, pain, fatigue". In Azerbaijani, people use the verb "işlemek" and in Kyrgyz, people use the verb "emgeg" – which both mean "to operate, to perform" – as the equivalence of "to work". As an attempt to change the nature, meaning of the term "work" (or the verb "to work") can change depending on social conditions and perception of societies. All in all, it can be defined in broad strokes as "all sorts of activities holding value of use and providing goods or services" (Istanbul University, School of Open and Distance Education, Sociology Course Book, **2017**, p. 55–56).

It is seen that machine power has started to replace man power with Industry 4.0. Industry 4.0 is a generic statement that covers modern automatization, data interchange and production industry (Kozanoğlu, **2016**, p. 18). It is the situation that machine power can manage the production stages autonomously by replacing man power. New industrial revolution has showed up when the developments in computer and internet technologies have enabled to guard machines. With this new age that can be defined as "internet of objects", production has changed dimension and it has been aimed to pass on to more advanced technology (Bulut and Akçacı, **2017**, p. 7:53).

Nowadays, the statement that "Machine is an important tool that increases the productivity of workers", which is one of the most significant assumptions about technology with the replacement of workers with the machines, should be questioned (Ford, **2015**:12). A research done in General Electric firm demonstrates that productivity has increased by 40 % after they have passed on to automatization from traditional production. It has been detected that a workload that can be done in 16 days with 86 workers in traditional production system can be done in a shorter time period like 16 hours (AUZEF Industry Sociology Course Book, **2017**, p. 177–178).

In addition to the fact that new technologies create new jobs, their destructive effects are mathematically shown by Wassiliy Leontief, an economist with a Nobel Prize. According to Leontief's application to the economy of Australia, it has been demonstrated that there is about 50 % decrease in white collar jobs and 75 % decrease in blue collar jobs. In a study conducted on the use of robots in Germany, 6 employees were hired against 4 skilled workers who left the work while only 1 new worker was hired against 28 unqualified workers that had to leave their jobs after the use of robots (AUZEF Coursebook of Industrial Sociology, **2017**, p. 180–181).

The effects of industrial transformation on working life have started to be felt recently. States, educational institutions, employers and, most importantly, employees should be prepared for this process and should be able to react rapidly by following the developments closely. It is envisaged that there will be huge differences not only in job descriptions and requirements but also in qualitative and quantitative competences of employees with the labour-intensive manufacturing technologies giving their way to automatization. It is very important to manage this concept appropriately, which is thought to have a great effect on human labour, not only for the institutions but also for the employees. Such studies as previously encountered in the process of agriculture and mechanization will be able to provide support to the process in order to overcome it with as little damage as possible.

2 Technology and Organizational Structure

To understand how the organizations structured, we should know how they work. An organizational structure can be described as the total ways that labours are divided into different roles and coordination of these roles.

There are 5 coordination mechanisms to control the organization works: Mutual harmony, direct supervision, standardization of products and standardization of worker skills. These are the main components of the structure and can be considered as a glue that hold the structure altogether. Other all topics follow these.

Every organization has a founding purpose. When we think an organization as a logo, we can see that there is the production of goods and services department at the bottom. When you go above, there is administrative component including three parts. On the top, strategic top management takes place with its own staff. Below them, middle level management, which connects strategic top management and the production of goods and services department with chain of command, on the left technical structure and on the right support staff take place. Support staff supports the work of production of goods and services department indirectly apart from basic goods and services process.

Quick and sudden technological and social changes led to a world which is more connected to each other, uncontrolled and complicated. Organization and government systems which were effective a couple of years ago were abandoned and made invalid. Serieyx (1993) calls this an organizational blast (Bing Bang) (Bolman and Deal, **2013**, p. 31).

Industry has placed the autonomous decision making of physical processes by being followed via ciber-physical systems at smart factories which can be changed according to user desires and communicating objects with both themselves and people on 4.0 focal point. This era which break out with this new system is called 'Smart Factory Era' and 'Smart Production Era' (Soyak, **2017**, p. 74).

Another aspect of Industry 4.0 considered to affect the work life is 'dark factories' approach. It is aimed with dark factories to increase the quality of service and fast and limitless mass production. Although the system is stated to darken the factories, it is thought to contribute to production a lot. Even though it is supposed that human effort will be devalorised in this system, on the contrary, it is considered that a new social sub-structure will be established from employers' aspect and a work structure considering individual differences will be provided (Alçın, **2016**, p. 21).

3 Technology and Management of Human Resources

Organizations value division of labour in order to increase productivity or prefer to be specialized in the work. Management of human resources is significant among the structures of organizations in terms of creating the structure and designing the positions.

In each organization, at least a part of activities related to management of human resources are definitely administered. However, the appearance of human resources as a unit or branch depends on the time having passed since the establishment of the organization and its size. As long as a company gets bigger, the main purpose of human rights remain unchanged, the approaches in realizing the goals differentiate (Bingöl, **2003**, p. 33–34).

The role of Human Resources Management (Mcentire, **2006**, p. 311) which has two main purposes as enhancing the productivity and providing a competitive advantage by improving the quality of work life is being questioned with a wider perspective nowadays.

Authority which is the key element of all positions and includes guiding and coordinating others' actions has three types: executive, planner and operational. Human resources management has all these three powers. Depending on the size of the organization, human resources can consist of only one person or a large group. Thus, a human resources manager should not only have the ability to convince but also the ability to manage and a big knowledge about behavioural sciences and social psychology (Palmer and Winters, **1993**, p. 27–28).

Human resources management is a business function that contributes to organizational goals. In addition to its traditional duties such as recruitment, dismissal and salary payments, human resources management has undertaken the task of providing new technologies to the organization, redesigning jobs, career planning for employees and training the future managers (Özgen et al, **2002**, p. 9). The concept of Human Resources includes everyone from the top-level managers to the low-level employees, as well as the potential workforce outside the organization (Kaynak et al, **1998**, p. 15).

Human resources management, which can also be defined as the whole of practices and functions that enable human resources to be managed efficiently and legally by being beneficial for the organization, individuals or environment in any organizational or peripheral environment, carries out the functions of planning, staff management, assessment, promotion, development, conservation and industrial relations (Uyargil et al, **2008**, p. 3–10).

These functions appear under different titles in various studies. In a study, these functions have been stated as job design and analysis, workforce planning, human resources supply and selection, evaluation and management of success, education and development, career management, job evaluation, salary and wage management, establishment and execution of collective contracts, health and security, promotion, research and statistics, communication within and outside the organization (Temir, **2002**, p. 19–20).

Keçecioğlu named the term human resources as "Integrated Human Resources Management" because of its duties and significance in strategical management. And, he stated the responsibilities as follows: choosing staff, organization, job evaluation, assessment, career and succession planning, developing, wage management, workplace relationships, worker health and safety, company culture and change management (Keçecioğlu, **2006**, p. 30–36). These responsibilities are parallel to the ones stated above. Also, Keçecioğlu stated that if there are no administrative affairs, environmental health and public relations departments, human resources department takes on the responsibility of managing relationships with external establishments (Keçecioğlu, **2006**, p. 34–35).

Keçecioğlu named the term human resources as "Integrated Human Resources Management" because of its duties and significance in strategical management. And, he stated the responsibilities as follows: choosing staff, organization, job evaluation, assessment, career and succession planning, developing, wage management, workplace relationships, worker health and safety, company culture and change management (Keçecioğlu, **2006**, p. 30–36). These responsibilities are parallel to the ones stated above. Also, Keçecioğlu stated that if there are no administrative affairs, environmental health and public relations departments, human resources department takes on the responsibility of managing relationships with external establishments (Keçecioğlu, **2006**, p. 34–35).

Human resources manager is a consultant who assists managers at all levels for the solution of arising problems about the staff. S/he does this in the fields of diagnosing employees' problems of motivation and efficiency and handling these problems, evaluating employees and helping them make progress, getting involved in the formation of management philosophy and business strategies of the organization. Intercorporate relations and communication with employees rank among the mentioned goal-directed operations (Palmer & Winters, **1993**, p. 29).

Human resources management has to play various roles in order to ensure that the ethical rules, ethics education, ethic corporate culture, ethical decision-making, strategic management can be carried out successfully and brought into the organizational structure. Depending on the ethical codes, harmonization of culture with ethical codes, teaching and adopting ethical codes to employees are some of the important duties that human resources management will fulfil. At the same time, human resources management needs to take an active role in processes such as building the structure of ethical decision-making processes and controlling and rewarding ethical behaviours.

Ethics and fair code of conduct towards employees play an important role in human resources management. The main activities related to ethics in human resources management can be considering ethical rules in the employment and selection of the personnel, in the evaluation of the personnel, in the reward and punishment system and in cases where it is possible to see aggression and violence in the workplace (Dessler, **2000**, p. 524–528).

In another source, quality management is also listed as one of the functions of human resources management. It is stated that quality management and total quality management include issues related to human resources; in organizations where there is no quality assurance system, activities about establishment and management of the quality assurance system should usually be supervised by human resources departments (Tahiroğlu, **2002**, p. 32).

Human resources management plays an important role from the recruitment of people to the retirement phase and develops and applies contemporary methods to enable them to work effectively and efficiently (Özgen et al., **2002**, p. 8–9).

That is where human resources management steps in. Some plans and methods should be prepared to minimize possible negativity in layoffs and to ensure that those who are dismissed can easily adapt to the new environment and quickly find a new satisfactory job (Feldman & Leana, **1994**, p. 252).

Human Resources Management also deals with corporate social responsibility. Corporate social responsibility is defined as creating awareness of the positive change, occurring in employees' daily life, in their immediate circle and in the society in which they live, for all the employees in a corporation. Corporate social responsibility must be integrated into a corporation's working principles. This concept can guide the Human Resources in terms of preparing long-term plans. (Görpe, **2007**, p. 169–173).

It makes human resources strategically important for information management since human recourses management and information management has a wide range of common interests and fields, and human resources workers are much closer to the formation which is required by information management when compared to other workers. Human resources management especially has an active role in forming an information map which constitutes the base for information gain and aims to detect lacks of an organization. Additionally, human resources management has an indirect impact on the efforts and attempts of information management, rather than a direct one on information management (Soliman and Spooner, **2000**, p. 340).

While facing with the problems like uncertainty, anxiety, stress as other workers do, workers of human resources department in amalgamation and purchasing undertake heavy-duties such as informing the other workers about amalgamation of business, keeping up the commitment and motivation of the workers, helping determine to dismiss someone from employment, designating vacancies and the ones to whom be assigned, specifying new compensation and education policies, determining new policies of new human resources if a changeover comes into question, and doing all of these co-ordinately with the integration team. (Bernhut, **2000**, p. 53–54).

Today's rapidly changing, highly competitive global business environment has created a strategic need for international assignments. As global companies compete for new markets, technologies, products, investors and best talents, the demand for short- or long-term assignments has increased (Bennett at al., **2000**, p. 239). As a result of globalization and many enterprises gaining multinational structure, local human resources management covering individuals working within a single country is called international human resources management, which is the management of policies and practices related to the procurement, selection, evaluation, development and rewarding of individuals with different cultures who have the potential to work in different countries.

Human resources management does not only attract attention with the increasing costs in the budgets of a lot of managements but also constitute the biggest expenditure for some managements. The responsibility of human resources management and its managers among important functions of management which has a broad application area is getting gradually harder. Human resources management needs to show top managers that it is properly managed and also its applications are measurable. Briefly, to enable new programs to be accepted only if they will yield profit to the management by measuring the contributions of that function to the management and to enable marginal/pure programs to be adapted to the management by deactivating or reviewing them again take an important place among the main functions of human resources managers. Drucer tried to guide about the mission of human resources management in the future by saying "First of all, stuff departments (HR, Purchasing Department, etc.) should set their goals on employees' profits rather than their costs". The transition of human resources departments from the image of a unit creating costs to the image of a unit making contributions will be possible only with the fact that the contributions are measured and shared (Tüzüner, **2000**, p. 30–31).

Human resources specialists and managers are required to know the attitude and behaviours of the employees in the company and their potential for creativity beforehand. Therefore, these managers are required to help protect the general functioning of the company by eliminating the problems that would be originated from the behaviours of their current employees in a systematic way.

Nowadays, many companies are developing methods to attract and develop human capital. Google may be the foremost one among these companies. Although it is stated that starting to work at Google is more difficult than starting to work at Harvard, Google has continued to grow by prioritizing the idea that it is more difficult to keep the people who are smart and have high energy in the work than employing them. Google, except from the high price, has tried to match the needs of their employees and save them from wasting time by distracting them and by providing the social rights and the opportunity to work in their own projects. It seems that only a few companies develop various ways like Google. These companies see talent and motivation as the necessity of work. Most of them continue to follow an old idea which is mentioned as "everything given to the employees syphon all the money at the balance-sheet", "being stolen money from one's pocket or being emptied one's bank account" (Bolman and Deal, **2013**, p. 165).

Why do managers follow less efficient strategies while there are better ones? One of the reasons is that managers following an X theory fear that they will lose control, or their employers will get spoiled. Second, investing in people requires time and resistance, which is necessary for receiving feedback. The managers who encounter a pressure of expecting a relentlessly immediate result, usually decide on decreasing the cost, changing the strategy or reorganization which may give a quicker result. (Bolman and Deal, **2013**, p. 167) Most of the human resource managers do not have the necessary "know-how" and research results that guide implementations. Due to lack of expertise, many organizations have been getting help from insufficient consulting companies and/or heading towards comparisons of human resources in national and international platforms. The result is relatively efficient human resources systems imported from sources outside the company. Many organizations indicate that these systems do not meet their needs (Aycan, **2001**, p. 258).

4 Results

Most of the competences that a Human Resources Specialist must have are actually western originated concepts. Sargut believes that since the human itself is the main issue when it comes to organization and administration, therefore, it is nothing but a vain dream trying to solve the local organization's problems by specialists who are incognizant to the local people of that society. The ones who comprehend both universal and contemporary knowledge with the local information together will solve the organizational and administrative problems in Turkey much easier (Sargut, **2001**, p. 2).

Today, businesses have begun to place more importance on human resources policies and applications in order to gain sustainable competitive advantage and high performance. The present human resources employees serve the purposes such as organization-related competition, ethics, union and technology (Vardarlıer, **2016**, p. 465). Technological innovation, as one of the purposes of human resources in the organization, is especially prominent as one of the most important organizational strategies in today's competitive environment. In our age of global world, the change is inevitable, and it is mostly seen that the organizations which cannot adapt to those changes come to a standstill in sustainability. In this sense, it must be known well in what areas the technology is going to put earnings to the organization.

This concept, which starts to lead to radical change on the way of labour use on production systems, affects many areas especially the Human Resources. This concept affects the human resources in many different ways and continues to do so. It is suggested that this concept will cause radical changes on labour force. Frase (**2017**, p. 15) stated that the effect of this radical change on labour from the perspective of human resources would lead to different and new professions.

In conclusion, it is predicted that the industry 4.0 starts to be effective in many areas of human resources and its effects will increasingly continue. Labour will cause major changes both on the job description and requirements and on the qualifications and quantity of the workers due to the fact that automation replaces production technologies. This concept which is especially predicted to affect human labour is to be managed truly by the management and the workers.

References

Alçın, S. (2016). "Üretim İçin Yeni Bir İzlek: Sanayi 4.0", *Journal of Life Economics*, pp. 19–30.

Aycan, Z. (2001). "Human Resources Management in Turkey. Current Issues and Challenges", *International Journal of Manpower*, 22 (3), pp. 252–260.

Bennett,R.J. and Payne, D.A. (2000). *Local and Regional Economic Development: Renegotiating Power under Labour*. Ashgate Publishers, Aldershot.

Bernhut, S. (2000). Corporate Social Responsibility Interview with Pratima Bansal. *Ivey Business Journal*.

Bingöl, D. (2003). *İnsan Kaynakları Yönetimi*. Beta Basım Yayın Dağıtım, İstanbul.

Bolman L.G. ve Deal T.E. (2013). *Organizasyonları Yeniden Yapılandırmak*. Çev:Ahmet Aypay ve Abdurrahman Tanrıöğen, Seçkin Yayıncılık, Ankara.

Bulut, E., Akçacı, T. (2017). "Endüstri 4.0 ve İnovasyon Göstergeleri Kapsamında Türkiye Analizi", *ASSAM Uluslararası Hakemli Dergi (ASSAM – UHAD) ASSAM International Refereed Journal*, 7, pp. 50–72.

Chaharbaghi, K. and Willis, R. (2000). "The Technology, Mythology and Economy of Technology", *Management Decision*, 38(6), 2000, pp. 394–402.

Dessler, G. (2000). *Human Resource Management*. Prentice Hall, New Jersey.

Ford, M. (2015). *Robotların Yükselişi*. Çev: Cem Duran, Kronik Kitap, İstanbul.

Frase, P. (2017). *Dört Gelecek. Kapitalizmden Sonra Hayat*. Koç Üniversitesi Yayınları, İstanbul.

Görpe, S. (2007). *Halkla İlişkiler Rolleri ve Yansımaları*, Yıldız Dilek Ertürk (ed.), Halkla İlişkiler Alanına Örgütsel Davranış Yansımaları. Nobel Yayın Dağıtım, Ankara.

İstanbul Üniversitesi Açık ve Uzaktan Eğitim Fakültesi (AUZEF). (2017). Sosyoloji Lisans Programı Yayını, Endüstri Sosyolojisi Ders Kitabı, İstanbul.

Kaynak, T. etc. (1998). *İnsan Kaynakları Yönetimi*. İ.Ü. İşletme Fakültesi Yayınları, İstanbul.

Keçecioğlu, T. (2006). *Stratejik İnsan Kaynakları Yönetimi*. Sistem Yayıncılık, İstanbul.

Kozanoğlu H. (2016). "Endüstri 4.0 İnsan Emeği ve Mühendis", *Elektrik Mühendisliği Dergisi*, 459, pp. 18–19.

Leana, C. R. and Feldman, D. C. (1994). Collective Job Creation Strategies for Laid-off Workers. In: London, M. (Ed.) *Employee Development and Job Creation: Human Resource Strategies for Organizational Growth*. Society for Industrial and Organizational Psychology, Practice Series, Vol. 5, Greenwich

McEntire, David A. (2006). *Disaster Response and Recovery: Strategies and Tactics for Resilience*. Wiley, New York.

Özgen, H., Öztürk, A. ve Yalçın, A. (2002). *İnsan Kaynakları Yönetimi*. Nobel Kitabevi, Adana.

Palmer, M. ve Winters, K. (1993). *İnsan Kaynakları*. Rota Yayınları, İstanbul.

Sargut, S. (2001). *Kültürler Arası Farklılaşma ve Yönetim*. İmge Kitapevi, Ankara.

Soliman, F & Spooner, K. (2000) "Strategies for Implementing Knowledge Management: Role of Human Resources Management", *Journal of Knowledge Management*, 4, pp. 337–345.

Soyak, A. (2017), "Teknolojiye Dayalı Sanayileşme: Sanayi 4.0 ve Türkiye Üzerine Düşünceler", *Marmara Sosyal Araştırmalar Dergisi*, vol. 11, pp. 68–83.

Tahiroğlu, F. (2002). *Düşünceden Sonuca İnsan Kaynakları*. Hayat Yayıncılık, İstanbul.

Temir, A. (2002). *İnsan Kaynakları Yönetimi*. Kara Harp Okulu Basımevi, Ankara.

Tüz, M. V. (2001). *Kriz ve İşletme Yönetimi*. Alfa Basım Dağıtım, İstanbul.

Tüzüner, L. (2000). *İnsan Kaynakları Yönetiminde Ölçme ve Değerlendirme*. Beta Basım Yayım, İstanbul.

Uyargil, C. etc. (2008). *İnsan Kaynakları Yönetimi*. Beta Basın Yayım, İstanbul.

Vardarlıer, P. (2016). "Strategic Approach to Human Resources Management during Crisis", *Procedia – Social and Behavioral Sciences*, vol. 235, pp. 463–472.

Gaye Özçelik

The Rise of the Crowd Work under the Gig Economy: Implications for Human Resource Management

1 Introduction

The so-called gig-economy, where flexible, independent employment patterns prevail in contrast to permanent jobs, has been growing tremendously and globally in recent years – mainly rising in the USA and also crossing the Atlantic Ocean to Europe and other overseas regions. According to Mc Kinsey Global Institute 20 to 30 percent of the working-age population in the United States and Europe participate in some form of independent work today. Gig economy refers to the collection of markets which link workers to consumers for completion of a gig or a task. It is symbolized by online platforms, where individuals engage in formal agreements with client organizations to provide services to the organisations' end-customers. Due to the exponential growth of technological progress and digitalisation, more and more workers, who are called "crowd workers" – a population of workers, who are located in different parts of the world to undertake independent, short, simple, and mostly clerical tasks and are compensated on the basis of tasks completed (Berg et al, 2018; Cantarella and Strozzi; 2018) – are participating in this 'gig', 'on-demand', or 'platform-based' economy, all of which have been contributing to the transforming nature of work in diverse ways.

There are divergent views put forward by scholars, practitioners, and consulting companies (Steward and Stanford, 2017; Kuhn; 2016) as to whether the gig economy has generated both opportunities and challenges for employment. Looking on the bright side, the rise of the gig economy has benefited both the economy and workforce in terms of endorsing job growth and flexible working patterns by facilitating temporary or contractual employment generating supplementary income as an amendment to the post-Great Recession period (Dokko et al., 2015). On the other hand, the gig economy has raised some concerns as it gives rise to precarious working conditions and stands in contrast to traditional employment, which provides what are considered to be decent jobs to employees in the form of such as a fair income, assurances, protection and security in the workplace, as well as opportunities for personal development (Berg et al, 2018; Kuhn, 2016; Dokko et al., 2015).

The transformation along with the extension of the labour markets into non-traditional forms of employment and problems accompanying it has become a critical challenge for the Human Resource Management (HRM) field. As gig workers have no or a very limited contact with the organisations that they work for (Harvey et al., 2018), it has been argued that there may well be a compelling argument for them to have a sense of organisational support (Harvey et al., 2018). The theory of organisational support – employees' general perception regarding the extent to which the organisation values their contributions and how favourable it treats them – holds that employees with positive perceptions of their organisations are more likely to reciprocate with positive attitudes and favourable work behaviours, thereby helping them to reach their objectives (Eisenberger et al, 1986; Eisenberger et al, 2002). This view can be predicated on the social exchange theory of Blau (1964) – a process of interactive exchanges between parties that may result in economic and social outcomes – and Gouldner's (1960) the norm of reciprocity – the moral obligation to respond positively to supportive behaviour. It has been noted in the literature that the role of human resources management (HRM) in cultivating positive relationships between organisations and their workforce reinforces the latter's perceptions of organisational support (Tremblay et al., 2010; Becker and Gerhart, 1996), thus leading to a positive HRM-organisational performance link. That is, human resource practices constitute a sign of how workers are treated by companies (Mitlacher, 2008). Hence, it has become paramount for HRM to conceptualize clearly and embrace this new form of employment, i.e. "crowd working". HRM functions need to be focused on finding alternative ways to implement their practices so as to take into account this new work paradigm.

By drawing on and organisational support theory, the aim in this chapter is to address the key challenges and drawbacks crowd workers have to face, whilst also proposing some ways by which HR policies and practices should be implemented in the gig economy. First, there is examination of the literature on the gig economy and crowd working in terms of their impact regarding issues of organisational support that might guide how these workers consider treating their tasks and organisations. Subsequently, there is consideration of ways that HR practices could be organised for this unconventional form of work.

2 The 'Gig Economy' and Crowd Work Defined

There has as yet been no single agreed-upon definition of the 'gig economy', but a couple of descriptions have been developed with regards to the term. Not only that, different terms are also voiced to have gig economy go along with other non-traditional economic activities, such as the 'sharing economy', 'peer-to-peer economy', 'collaborative economy' (Selloni, 2017; Steward and Stanford, 2017), or 'platform economy', all of which are part of a transforming cultural, technological business environment. Before proceeding towards clarification of the definition of the 'gig economy' itself, it is considered appropriate to provide descriptions of those non-conventional forms of arrangements that are not deemed synonymous, but share important overlapping features. The sharing economy, also known as the collaborative economy or peer economy, involves generating money on a digital platform to offer or receive services, such as letting out or renting assets, i.e. rooms on the AirBnB platform (Ainsworth, 2017). It represents a marketplace where transactions take place between consumers on a peer-to-peer basis, instead of companies, to meet their wants and requirements (Selloni, 2017). The platform economy refers to the enablement of information technologies (IT) services to facilitate and encourage opportunities for gig work (Ainsworth, 2017).

The gig economy, about which multiple descriptions exist, is often used to address a "crowd" labour market defined as businesses and workers, who do not develop a traditional, long-term full-time employee-employer relationship, but rather, search for alternative short-term working arrangements, which broadly include independent contractors as well as on call workers, online platform workers and temporary workers (Gallup, 2018; Ainsworth, 2017; Sundararajan, 2016; Dokko et al., 2015), who are called "crowd workers" (Cantarella and Strozzi, 2018). The so-called crowd work is an employment form that uses an online platform to enable organizations or individuals to access an indefinite and unknown group of other organisations or individuals to solve specific problems or to provide specific services or products in exchange for payment (Cantarella and Strozzi, 2018). Work outsourced to crowds can vary from transportation services offered in the physical world (e.g. Uber, Lyft) to tasks that are completed and delivered online (Ellmer and Reichel, 2018).

Looking at the operational network of gig work, Steward and Stanford (2017) discuss the triangular link between the worker, who performs the service, the intermediary firm or 'interactive online platform' (Ellmer and Reichel, 2018) or client organisation, which conventionally used to be the employer in the typical working relationship and the end-user of the service, namely an individual or a business customer. Interactive online platforms, by communicating open calls towards the crowd as tasks to be completed over a predefined period of time, serve as infrastructure to invite its workers to engage in these tasks. Platforms either take a certain proportion of the remuneration that the crowd worker receives, after completing the task or charge a fee to him or her, for its assuming an intermediary role of providing support or supervision services. In this sense, a reciprocal exchange pattern is developed between the online platforms, with organisations and crowd workers as independent contractors (Ellmer and Reichel, 2018). These exchange patterns that are shaped by the governance mechanisms – being structures of roles and responsibilities, feedback mechanisms, monetary or non-monetary incentive structures to motivate the crowd to fulfil tasks (Zogaj and Bretschneider, 2014) – are built on institution-based trust and enable productive processes among the involved parties (Ellmer and Reichel, 2018; Kuhn and Maleki, 2017).

It is also necessary to distinguish and define the roles and responsibilities assumed especially by workers and the client organisations. These workers can be employed for low wage tasks that do not require high level of skills such as personal care attendants, drivers or for higher wage tasks, where more elaborate skill levels are expected such as editors, lawyers, and consultants. The benefits of enhanced flexibility are exchanged for insecurity and lack of protections such as minimum wage, the right to organise, the opportunities to develop skills, and civil rights protections, which are provided to typical employees by labour laws (Steward and Stanford, 2017; Dokko et al., 2015). In the meantime, though the intermediary companies may assume roles of monitoring, supervising, and guiding the worker for effective platform use (Steward and Stanford, 2017), some responsibilities seems to be blurred as they take the advantage of classifying these workers as independent contractors rather than employees, which in this case would be incurred additional costs.

3 Crowd Work Characteristics: Organisational Challenges

3.1 Issues Regarding Organisational Support

When considering the nature of relationship between crowd workers and organisations, there are some specific crowd work characteristics representing what these crowd workers do and how they work, thus influencing their feelings of organisational support. In this section, organisational support theory as well as social exchange theory are drawn upon to explain the social-exchange nature of the crowd worker-organisation dyad and the feelings of organisational support, as perceived by the worker (Harvey et al., 2018).

Organisational support theory (OST) concerns the degree to which employees have faith in their work organisation valuing their contributions and taking care of their wellbeing – perceived organisational support (POS) (Eisenberger et al. 1986; Rhoades and Eisenberger, 2002). Where this perception is positive, this engenders in employees the need to develop a felt obligation to help the organisation and to engage in greater work-related efforts, thereby eliciting the norm of reciprocity. That is, there is an exchange relationship between the organisation and employees, such that the latter perform their tasks to reciprocate organisation as they are paid by organisation to respond for employee's efforts.

Regarding organisational support, HR practices constitute an important variable to be related to POS. Research has demonstrated that HR practices, especially those that recognise employee contributions, act as antecedents to the degree to which employees perceive support from their organisations (Allen et al., 2003). Approaching the issue from strategic HRM (SHRM) perspective (Armstrong, 2016), formulating HR policies and programs, which result into better POS will help achieve the goal of SHRM – ensuring that a firm's human capital contributes to the achievement of its objectives. The presence of proper HRM practices, i.e. fairness of rewards/recognition, and learning and growth opportunities in the workplace gives strong signals to employees that the organisation values and supports them, whilst also trying to establish or maintain a social exchange relationship with them (Allen et al, 2003).

Crowd workers usually perform their tasks in an irregular manner, driven by the demand fluctuations for their services (Ellmer and Reichel, 2018; Stewart and Stanford; 2017). These workers commonly perform their tasks by getting organised around a web-based platform and make their earnings on a piecework basis, where payment is tied to the completion of specific tasks (Ellmer and Reichel, 2018; Steward and Stanford, 2017; Dokko et al., 2015). Part of the resources that are provided by the company in the typical employer–employee relationship, can be offered to gig workers. These may range from provision of some or all of the tools to be used at work, such as computer equipment, Internet access, mobile phones and bicycles for food delivery services (Steward and Stanford, 2017; Cherry and Aloisi, 2017). They usually work independently with a high level of autonomy and freedom in completing their tasks (Bush and Balven, 2018). In this regard, they may have no or very little contact – only through an application on their mobile devices – with the organisation. These crowd workers do not usually engage in the typical relationship with their supervisors or other organisational members, upon which, according to Blau (1964), all social exchange relationships are based. They are less likely to receive assistance and guidance, during the times when they have to face difficult customer problems and when needing address other issues so as to complete gig work. Moreover, they do not receive explicit supervision and have contact with the organisation on an irregular basis (Bush and Balven, 2018). Hence, they are less likely to develop feelings of organisational support (Harvey et al., 2018) and have positive exchange relationships, when compared to their traditionally employed counterparts.

3.2 Implications for Human Resource Management

The issue of employing crowd workers is a matter to be considered by organisations and their HRM functions, who they may deem appropriate for some tasks. Under such circumstances, crowd work becomes a non-conventional form of labour, where there is access to a large, anonymous mass of human resources. This part of the chapter considers the HRM challenges posed by crowd work and offers some insights into how HRM practices can be organised to deliver to its workers feelings of organisational support, thus facilitating their supporting attitudes and behaviours towards their client organisations.

3.2.1 Recruitment

Recruiting workers from the crowd is very much different from doing so with full-time in-house employees. A variety of alternatives exist through which client organisations source workers from the crowd. They, themselves, may make open calls for completion of tasks to the crowds on the online platforms, from where people will make the decision as to whether or not participate. Others may utilise online platforms to access workers, such as MTurk, Upwork, or ODesk, for a fast and low-cost way of sourcing from the crowd (Bush and Balven, 2018; Ellmer and Reichel, 2018), which may limit the level of workers' experience with the organisation's operations. One viable option might be to enable these workers to understand the purpose and meaning of these called for tasks (Graham et al., 2017). For most crowd workers are kept away from accessing information about the big picture or the higher-order purpose of their tasks (Bush and Balven, 2018).

With regard to perceived organisational support (POS), it may be appropriate to look at the anticipated organisational support (AOS), which is developed prior to employment and refers to the extent to which prospective employees expect they will be cared for and valued by the organisation, if they take up a post. The candidates with high AOS before employment are likely to show high POS subsequent to their being given a job. AOS can be promoted by introducing workers to favourable HR benefits such as flexible scheduling (Eisenberger et al., 2016). In addition, making a display of their values, purpose and mission may engender workers' positive views of the organisation (Bush and Balven, 2018).

3.2.2 Training and Development

One of the implications of the gig economy is that crowd workers dealing with discrete one-off tasks are not offered properly organised training and development opportunities by online platforms or client organisations. That is, they lack the organisational support that they would be entitled to in the case of traditional employment. Hence, crowd workers themselves have to solve issues with regards to their own training and development activities (Ellmer and Reichel, 2018). The fact that digital workers are not informed about the purpose of the work they do and the extent to which it contributes to the end-clients creates information asymmetries, thus limiting their ability to upgrade their skills and capabilities. In addition, the qualifications and capacities of many crowd workers are not recognised by the client organisation, sometimes being limited to tasks only requiring a low-skill set for completion (Graham et al., 2017). It would prove beneficial for HRM practitioners to consider the characteristics of crowd tasks, such as their specific requirements, the cognitive difficulty level to complete them and the creative processes involved in performing them, where skills development would be considered as being important (Bush and Balven, 2018).

Human resource training and development are considered crucial HRM functions, being geared towards improvement of the worker's skills, knowledge, and abilities. Platforms that offer workers opportunities to develop their competencies, i.e. web programming and graphics programmes provided by Upwork (Ellmer and Reichel, 2018), can benefit workers, platforms, and end-clients. Moreover, after completing these training programs, workers' performance can be monitored and those whose overall rating is below a certain level can be given the opportunity to take on additional upskilling work.

3.2.3 Performance Management

Performance management is also another key area that needs considerably greater attention in the context of appraisals of crowd workers. One of the issues about performance is the limitation of such appraisal to just the final results. At first sight, it might seem sufficient for client organisations simply to define the expected results to be accomplished by crowd workers. However, it is equally important to assess and control how the task should be performed, especially if what is achieved does not meet the criteria of what was expected (Ellmer and Reichel, 2018). The HRM function may benefit from the revolution in computer technologies for monitoring both work processes and outcomes. For instance, Upwork has established a governance mechanism called "Freelancers Work Diary", which tries to control the work processes of workers via a screenshots system.

Another issue that researchers and practitioners recommend is the replacement of the annual rating and ranking processes with more timely captured critical incidents and instant feedback (Younger and Smallwood, 2016). This constitutes another topic for discussion, that of whether ratingless reviews would be beneficial or disadvantageous. Additionally, instead of executing just long-term reviews, ongoing regular feedback could prove more beneficial to these workers. This would seem to make sense, given that crowd workers carry out short-term specific tasks, for which giving instant feedback during their execution would be more helpful. Moreover, reputation systems – being another so-called trust-building reference for performance management – can present the past feedback workers have received with respect to the work processes and results (Ledford et al., 2016). Workers can provide feedback via social media to one another, thereby creating a web of interpersonal relationships and interactive exchanges, which would provide them with information on how to become a successful organisational member. In fact, these strong social networks may help develop POS (Eisenberger et al., 2016).

3.2.4 Careers and Retention

Given the rise of the gig economy, there is much uncertainty regarding both work roles and careers, which will be very different from the traditional organisational career. It has introduced new ways of working leading to changing career patterns on an online platform. Many individuals have already been inclined to take on multiple part-time jobs, with short-term contractual conditions. In addition, recent developments in the gig economy have given rise to independent contracting in the form of crowd-based work arrangements due partly to budget constraints and to workers' preferences for more flexibility and control over their time as well as the opportunity to select from among tasks. These new work arrangements can be considered as coming within a "portfolio career" (Nicole, 2018) – a term introduced by Handy (1994) and "protean career" (Hall, 1996). Portfolio career refers to making different contracts with different employers/clients performing a variety of and usually short-term assignments, freelancing or project-based tasks, rather than simply working for a single organisation. Such a career is actually a part of the gig economy, a career choice among crowd workers, who work on different jobs to make up one portfolio career. Similarly, a protean career is an employee-driven career based upon values of freedom and growth, where the individual reinvents one's career as the environment and one's values change. So, crowd labour's preferences are related to changes in values.

Debates on these new employment forms have given rise to positive and negative career discussions. On the plus side, these workers find the opportunity to manage their own time, develop their task portfolio, and pursue their own career paths. In addition, it allows unemployed or underemployed individuals to move on their careers (Friedman, 2014). On the down side, there are concerns about the issues of precarity and insecurity (Findlay and Thompson, 2017). As these workers generally face increasing levels of uncertainty due to the temporary nature of contracts and payment is on the basis of tasks completed (Steward and Stanford, Dokko et al., 2015), retention becomes an important consideration of crowd working for the HRM field.

The issue of how to integrate this pool of workers into organisations will become an even more pressing concern in the future. In this regard, HRM could provide ordered task activities and offer these to their most capable workers, so that they can participate in the subsequent activities and develop their skills. Secondly, HRM could develop creative compensation tools, such as bonus payments, for those workers on the basis of the number and difficulty of tasks completed as well as their prompt completion (Bush and Balven, 2018). Finally, workers could be provided with learning opportunities along with novel and varied work assignments (Hall, 2002). In parallel, Gerber et al. (2012) propose that people with different career orientations should be provided with individualised inducements and development practices by HRM functions. Learning, especially when continuously self-managed, is viewed as a key component in the retention of workers in order to develop expertise, network and reputations (Opengart and Short, 2002). Individuals who develop POS with customised inducements being offered to them in exchange more likely to develop higher felt obligations and make greater work-related effort.

4 Conclusion

The gig economy has grown at a pace in recent years, mainly due to the rise of the Internet usage online market platforms, such as Uber and Airbnb, and the improvement in people's capabilities for distant work. Organisations, acting as online platforms in the gig economy can have an impact on crowd workers' behaviours by utilising effective HRM practices and, hence, play an important role in providing organisational support for crowd workers. Particular importance should be given to the ways in which organisations support and utilise crowd workers; a rising non-negligible form of human capital.

This chapter has reviewed the literature on the rise of the crowd workers and crowd-based work arrangements under the transition to the gig economy. In addition, drawing on organisational support theory, the chapter focused on examining potential organizational challenges and proposed different ways to implement HRM practices, which can be strategically capitalized on this changing nature of work and workers, enabling organizations to achieve their business objectives. As the number of crowd workers rise and higher-level cognitive task requirements are demanded by the client organizations, it will become even more imperative to explore further the role of crowd-based work arrangements and the respective issues faced by workers and organisations in the new platform economy.

References

Ainsworth, J. (2017). "Gig Economy: Legal Status of Gig Economy Workers and Working Practices", *House of Lords Library Briefing*, https://researchbriefings.parliament.uk, 1–28. (Accessed on November 2, 2018).

Allen, D. G., Shore, L. M., Griffeth, R. W. (2003). "The Role of Perceived Organizational Support and Supportive Human Resource Practices in the Turnover Process", *Journal of Management*, 29(1), 99–118.

Armstrong, M., (2016). *Armstrong's Handbook of Strategic Human Resource Management*. 6th Edition. New Delhi: Kogan Press.

Becker, B. E., and Gerhart, B. (1996). "The Impact of Human Resource Management on Organizational Performance: Progress and Prospects". *Academy of Management Journal*, 39, 779–801.

Berg, J., Furrer, M., Harmon, E., Rani, U., Silberman, M. S. (2018). *Digital Labor Platforms and the Future of Work*, https://www.ilo.org/. Accessed on November 22, 2018, Switzerland: International Labor Organization (ILO).

Blau, P. M. (1964). *Exchange and Power in Social Life*. New York: Wiley.

Bush, J. T., Balven, R. M. (2018). "Catering to the Crowd: An HRM Perspective on Crowd Worker Engagement", *Human Resource Management Review*, http://doi.org/10.1016/j.hrmr.2018.10.003 Accessed on November 22, 2018.

Cantarella, M., Strozzi, C. (2018). *Labour Market Effects of Crowd Work in US and EU: An Empirical Investigation*, http://conference.iza.org (Accessed on November 7, 2018).

Cherry and Aloisi (2017). "Dependent Contractors in the Gig Economy: A Comparative Approach", *American University Law Review*, 66(3), Article 1, 635–689.

Dokko, J., Mumford, M., Schanzenbach, D. W. (2015). *Workers and the Online Gig Economy*. A Hamilton Project Framing Paper, Washington, USA: Brookings, http://www.hamiltonproject.org/papers/workers_and_the_online_gig_economy (Accessed on November 12, 2018).

Eisenberger, R., Huntington, R., Hutchinson, S., & Sowa, D. (1986)." Perceived Organizational Support". *Journal of Applied Psychology*, 71, 500–507.

Eisenberger, R., Stinglhamber, F., Vandenberghe, C., Sucharski, I., & Rhoades, L. (2002). "Perceived Supervisor Support: Contributions to Perceived Organizational Support and Employee Retention". *Journal of Applied Psychology*, 87, 565–573.

Eisenberger, R., Malone, G. P. and Presson, W. D. (2016) "Optimizing Perceived Organizational Support to Enhance Employee Engagement", *SHRM-SIOP Science of HR Series*, 1–22.

Ellmer, M. and Reichel, A. (2018). *Crowd Work from an HRM Perspective – Integrating Organizational Performance and Employee Welfare*. Working Paper 01, HRM Group, University of Salzburg.

Friedman, (2014). "Workers without Employers: Shadow Corporations and the Rise of the Gig Economy", *Review of Keynesian Economics*, 2(2), 171–188.

Findlay and Thompson, (2017). "Contemporary Work: Its Meanings and Demands". *Journal of Industrial Relations*, 59(2), 122–138.

GALLUP (2018). *Gallup's Perspective on the GIG Economy and Alternative Work Arrangements*. Gallup Inc., https://www.gallup.com/ (Retrieved on November 10, 2018).

Gerber, M., Grote, G., Geiser, C. and Raeder, S. (2012). "Managing Psychological Contracts in the Era of the "New" Career", *European Journal of Work and Organizational Psychology*, 21:2, 195–221.

Gouldner, A. (1960). "The Norm of Reciprocity: A Preliminary Statement". *American Sociological Review*, 25, 161–178.

Graham, M., Hjorth, I., Lehdonvirta, V. (2017). "Digital Labour and Development: Impacts of Global Digital Labour Platforms and the Gig Economy on Worker Livelihoods". *Transfer: European Review of Labour and Research*, 23(2), 135–162.

Hall, D. T.(1996). "Protean Careers of the 21st Century" *Academy of Management Executive*, 10:8–16.

Hall, D.T. (2002). Careers in and out of organizations. Thousand Oaks, CA: Sage.

Opengart, Rose & C. Short, Darren. (2002). Free agent learners: The new career model and its impact on human resource development. 21(3), 220–233.

Handy, C. (1994). *The Empty Raincoat: Making Sense of the Future*, London: Hutchinson.

Harvey, J., Bolino, M. C., Kelemen, T. K. (2018). "Organizational Citizenship Behavior in the 21st Century". (In Buckley, R. M., Wheeler, A. R, Halbesleben, J. R. B., Eds.) *Research in Personnel and Human Resource Management*, 36, UK: Emerald Publishing, 51–110.

Kuhn, K. M. (2016). *The Rise of "Gig Economy" and Implications for Understanding Work and Workers*, https://www.cambridge.org/core. (Accessed on November 12, 2018).

Kuhn, K. M. and Maleki, A. (2017). "Micro-Entrepreneurs, Dependent Contractors, and Instaserfs: Understanding Online Labor Platform Workforces", *The Academy of Management Perspectives*, 31(3), 183–200.

Ledford, G., Lawler, E., Benson, G. (2016). "A Study of Cutting-Edge Performance Management Practices: Ongoing Feedback, Ratingless Reviews and Crowd-Sourced Feedback, Center for Effective Organizations", *CEO Working Paper Series*, 1–23.

Mitlacher, L. (2008). "Job Quality and Temporary Agency Work: Challenges for Human Resource Management in Triangular Employment Relations in Germany". *International Journal of Human Resource Management*. 19(4): 446–460.

Nicole (2018) *Careers in the 21st Century: The Gig Economy and Portfolio Careers*, https://blog.ivyglobal.com (Accessed on November 22, 2018).

OECD (2017). *Future of Work and Skills*. Paper Presented at the 2nd Meeting of the G20 Employment Working Group 15-17 February 2017, Hamburg, Germany.

Rhoades, L. and Eisenberger, R. (2002). "Perceived Organizational Support: A Review of the Literature", *Journal of Applied Psychology*, 87(4), 698–714.

Selloni D. (2017). "New Forms of Economies: Sharing Economy, Collaborative Consumption, Peer-to-Peer Economy". In: *Co-Design for Public-Interest Services*. Research for Development. Springer, Cham.

Steward, A. and Stanford, J. (2017). "Regulating Work in the Gig Economy: What Are the Options?" *The Economic and Labour Relations Review*, 28(3), 420–437.

Sundararajan, A. (2016). *The Sharing Economy: The End of Employment and the Rise of Crowd-Based Capitalism*, Cambridge, MA: MIT Press.

Tremblay, M., Cloutier, J., Simard, G., Chênevert, D., Vandenberghe, C. (2010). "The Role of HRM Practices, Procedural Justice, Organizational Support and Trust in Organizational Commitment and In-Role and Extra-Role Performance", *The International Journal of Human Resource Management*, 21:3, 405–433.

Younger, J., Smallwood, N. (2016). "Performance Management in the Gig Economy", *Harvard Business Review*, https://hbr.org/, (Accessed on November 15, 2018).

Zogaj, S. and Bretschneider, U. (2014). *Analyzing Governance Mechanisms for Crowdsourcing Information Systems: A Multiple Case Analysis*. In: European Conference on Information Systems (ECIS), Tel Aviv, Israel. 1–11.

Mustafa Babadag and Gokhan Kerse

Changing the Limits of Work: Job Crafting and Its Importance

1 Introduction

In today's ambiguous and overly competitive environment, organizations are designing the work to be done as per organizational goals beforehand and present the work to their employees in a ready state in order to increase their performance. However, no matter how presenting the work in a ready state is thought to be beneficial in theory and also in the applications of the past, it is now reckoned that in today's environment it is not able to create the desired effect (Kerse, 2017: 284). The reason behind can be understood when looked into literatures of psychology, social psychology and management as individuals have different personality traits and expectations. Additionally, the feeling of work alienation, as defined in self-determination theory, shows that individuals desire to have control over the work they are doing. The ones who feel they don't have the control tend to question their work and feel alienated from their job (Babadag, 2018: 212). For this reason, presenting an already prepared and top down work to individuals may form an obstacle for the organizations in getting the desired outputs. The way to overcome this is to present an environment for the employees in which they would be able to act proactively. In other words, the employees should be able to have the initiative to change the work they are doing and its physical, temporal and cognitive boundaries (Wrzesniewski and Dutton, 2001: 179). This notion is expressed as job crafting and is a relatively new concept in the literatures of management and organization. It can be stated that studies on job crafting in Turkey is in its infancy. Thus, this concept, which is thought to be able to bring important outcomes to organizations, should be worked on more and its importance should be comprehended better. From this point of view, in this chapter, the definition, dimensions and importance of the concept of job crafting are to be touched upon.

2 Concept of Job Crafting

The concept of job crafting has been brought in the literature by Wrzesniewski and Dutton with their studies in 2001 (Wrzesniewski and Dutton, 2001). However, the concept had emerged as an idea 30 years ago in the studies of Kulik,

Oldham and Hackman (Tims, Bakker and Derks, 2012: 173). Even though there are different explanations on the definition of job crafting, generally it can be defined as the process of employees proactively changing the physical, temporal, emotional, cognitive and relational boundaries of their work (Wrzesniewski, LoBuglio, Dutton and Berg, 2013: 283). In other words, job crafting is creating or initiating change in work (Grant and Ashford, 2008: 4; Griffin, Neal and Parker, 2007: 344). In this process of creating change, employees try to make the job-related applications more relevant with their personal interests and values (Slemp and Vella-Brodrick, 2013: 126). Because as per person-job fit theory, the mismatch of an individual's skills, needs and values with the attributes of job can lead the employee to be unhappy about the job (Nielsen and Abildgaard, 2012: 366). For this reason, employees are trying to shape their jobs in accordance with their needs, values and skills and with the aim to be happy in their work. Thus, the employees tend to change the quality and resources of their work proactively to make it more meaningful, appealing and satisfying (Demerouti, 2014: 237; Wrzesniewski and Dutton, 2001: 179).

While job crafting suggests a status of employees trying to create harmony between their jobs and themselves and also trying to create happiness, it also includes the endeavour of re-conceptualizing the job, changing the way of doing the job, defining the persons to be in contact with and the frequency of that contact and changing the cognitive importance and value they attribute to their jobs (Tims and Bakker, 2010: 3). In other words, in job crafting, employees display physical, cognitive and relational changes of behaviour in their job as per their personal wishes and understanding (Wrzesnieswski and Dutton, 2001: 179–180). Wrzesnieswski and Dutton (2001) based the resource of motivation needed to create the changes which employees are performing in the job tasks as per their personal wishes upon the needs of the employees. The first of these is the need of having control over the specific angles of their work. When satisfying this need, employees are avoiding negative outcomes such as job alienation (Demerouti and Bakker, 2014: 419). Secondly, individuals desire to create and sustain a positive sense of self in the eyes of themselves and others. The pressure to create a positive image also spreads to many sides of the work activities and may lead the employees to change the tasks and relations which consist of work. Because this change may ensure a positive self-image to be manifested and to be seen by others as well. The third motivation is the need for connection, which is considered as a basic human need (Wrzesnieswski and Dutton, 2001: 181–183). As a result of these motivations employees try to change their tasks and other attributes of work with their own initiatives. This forms the basic attribute of job crafting (Tims et al. 2012: 174).

When looked into the literature, it is seen that job crafting is explained under the roof of Job Demands-Resources Model (JD-R) and Job Design Theory (Kooij, Tims and Kanfer, 2015: 147). From job design point of view, job crafting is defined as re-shaping the attributes of work-related tasks with an employee's own initiative in a way to be bottom-up in the organizational hierarchy and also evaluated as a proactive behaviour (Rudolph, Katz, Lavigne and Zacher, 2017: 112). From this view point, job crafting diverges from job design. Because contrary to job crafting, job design shows changes on the work as a whole and this change is performed with the initiative of the management/organization. Thus, in job crafting, the change is realized bottom-up, while in job design it is bottom-down (Kerse, 2017: 286).

From JD-R Model point of view, job crafting is defined as the activity of change on the job attributes performed by employees in the process of creating balance between job demands (for instance, heavy work load and time pressure) and job resources (for instance, autonomy and feedback) (Bipp and Demerouti, 2015: 632). As per the model, every work environment has its own characteristics and these characteristics are grouped as job demands and job resources (Tims and Bakker, 2010: 3). Job demands form the side of work which asks for energy and effort. And job resources help employees to cope with job demands and reach work goals. While job demands are attributed with health issues such as exhaustion and psychosomatic health complaints, job resources are attributed with work motivations such as enjoying work and participation (Wang, Demerouti and Le Blanc, 2017: 186). Job crafting decreases job demands while increasing job resources and thus tries to balance job demands and job resources. For this reason, it is considered to be an effective tool in increasing an individual's motivation and other work-related outcomes.

3 Dimensions of Job Crafting

Job crafting is the process of making the personal interests and values of the employees compatible with their jobs (Slemp and Vella-Brodrick, 2013: 126). In this process, the employee is performing some changes on the job. These changes may include physical, cognitive and relational changes (Rudolph et al., 2017). For this reason, the concept of job crafting can be handled in different types and dimensions. When literature is reviewed, it is seen that two different classifications are widely used for job crafting. One of these classifications is performed by Tims et al. (2012) and the other is performed by Slemp and Vella-Brodrick (2013). Tims et al. (2012) defined job crafting with JD-R Model and looked into the concept under 4 dimensions — increasing structural job resources, increasing social job resources, increasing challenging job demands and decreasing hindering job demands. These dimensions are as follows.

- *Increasing structural job resources:* This dimension of crafting implies that the employee is putting forward efforts to learn new things, improve competence and gain occupational skills (Tims et al., 2012: 177). In this crafting, the employee shows behaviours which aim to increase autonomy in work, variety of skills and other motivational attributes (Rudolph et al., 2017: 116).
- *Increasing social job resources:* This dimension of crafting means the development of interaction and relation between the employee and his/her co-workers and managers (Tims et al., 2012: 177). In this type of crafting, the employee asks for recommendations, support and feedback on the job he/she is doing from co-workers and managers (Rudolph et al., 2017: 116).
- *Increasing challenging job demands:* This dimension of crafting includes the employee to undertake new tasks within the job and to make the job more challenging. The employee in this dimension displays proactive behaviour for the job (Tims et al., 2012: 177).
- *Decreasing hindering job demands:* Finally, this dimension implies the employee to be proactively decreasing the requests (necessities) regarding the job (Tims et al., 2012: 177). With this crafting, the employee displays behaviours which aim to minimize physical, cognitive and emotional requirements, such as work load and work-family conflict (Rudolph et al., 2017: 116).

Another classification regarding job crafting is performed by Slemp and Vella-Brodrick (2013). The researchers handled job crafting under three dimensions which are task crafting, cognitive crafting and relational crafting. These dimensions are explained below.

- *Task crafting:* Task crafting includes physical and temporal changes and suggests that the employee adjusts the time and effort allocated to various tasks, adding tasks to the job or removing the existing tasks (Wrzesniewski et al., 2013: 283). In task crafting, by adjusting the amount or timing of the effort allocated to the task, the employee is making the job compatible with his/her personal skills and talents (Kerse, 2017). In other words, in this type of crafting, the employees are actively shaping their tasks by undertaking more or less tasks and by changing the scope and the used tools for the task (Kerse, 2018: 944; Niessen, Weseler and Kostova 2016: 1289). Preferring challenges and additional difficulties in work-related tasks, caring for the more enjoyed tasks more, increasing or decreasing the responsibilities of different tasks or embracing new tasks which exceed the work definition are some of the behaviours seen in task crafting (Slemp, 2016: 344).

- *Cognitive Crafting:* This type of crafting is related to the change of cognitive boundaries associated with the meaning or importance of work-related tasks or relations (Slemp, 2016: 344). In this type of crafting, the employee perceives and interprets the tasks, relations or work as a whole, in a way to change the importance of the job (Wrzesniewski et al., 2013: 283). In other words, the employees are changing their cognition in the work they are doing and in this way differentiating the meaning and importance they get from work-related experiences, creating a work identity conforming with their own (Slemp, 2016: 344). This way the work being done becomes more important and meaningful for the employee.
- *Relational Crafting:* This way of crafting implies the employee to be in contact with others in work and sustain this relationship, to spend more time with preferred individuals and to decrease or completely cut the communication with others (Wrzesniewski et al., 2013: 283). Therefore, this crafting includes creating and sustaining relationships with others in work or changing/ending the existing relationships. Taking steps towards creating new relationships, ending/preventing toxic interactions and relationships and strengthening positive relationships in work are all examples of relational crafting (Slemp, 2016: 344).

4 Importance of Job Crafting for Organizations

Job crafting is a proactive behaviour which expresses the changes employees do with their jobs by taking initiatives. With job crafting, employees try to create harmony between their personal skills, talents, preferences and the work they are doing. And for this reason they change tasks and relations in their job. This change may increase the meaning of the employees' work and could develop a positive work identity (Wrzesniewski and Dutton, 2001: 194).

Job crafting can be the key to work successfully in today's organizations in which tasks and roles keep changing. Hence, thanks to job crafting, employees are developing their skills to adapt to the demands of dynamic post-industrial workplaces. For this reason, employees make use of job crafting when faced with a new situation at work and this leads to easy adaptation to organizational changes (Demerouti and Bakker, 2014: 425).

Job crafting helps employees to shape their tasks and interactions in a way to enable them to express their value, motivation or beliefs better. Job crafting directly affects the positive perception of jobs by creating a feeling of harmony between the employees and the work (Wrzesniewski et al., 2013: 289). When employees are making changes in their work, they tend to find the work internally more fun and meaningful and thus get more motivated internally. These work-related changes enable the employees to have more control over their jobs and thus prevent getting alienated from work (Slemp, 2016: 346–347). On the other hand, employees can make use of different job crafting types in order to create virtuous organizational identities. Job crafting makes organization members think of what the good moral attributes are and act accordingly to eventually become more virtuous personalities/individualities/characters (Wrzesniewski et al., 2013: 293).

Changing the work as per personal skill, talent and interest brings lots of benefits to organizations, in addition to the organizational contributions explained above. With the increased number of studies seen in literature, it is seen that job satisfaction, work engagement and citizenship behaviours are also increased and job boredom and emotional exhaustion are decreased (Kerse, 2018: 945). Employees who are crafty at what they do get more attached to the goals they set in the decisions they make, in the problems they solve and in the work they do and thus get more motivated. In addition to this, crafty employees tend to make healthier decisions in their work, work more efficiently, be more productive and understand their work, work-related tasks and the relations these tasks engage in better. Therefore, these employees show higher job performances (Kooij et al., 2015: 150).

5 Conclusion

In this chapter, the concept of job crafting, which is a new one in organizational and management literature and is a new study topic in Turkey, and its importance are discussed. In conclusion, it can be stated that the concept of job crafting has its basis in JD-R Model and it is a process of employees creating changes on work boundaries with their own personal initiatives. Additionally, it can be put forward that job crafting enables employees to have more control over their jobs. This makes the job more meaningful and increases internal motivation. Except for all these positive outputs, when looked into the literature, it is seen that there are many other desired outcomes for organizations, such as job satisfaction, work engagement, organizational citizenship behaviour and job performance. These findings show how important job crafting is for both the employees and organizations. However, when literature is reviewed, it is seen that whether job crafting bears similar outcomes for different sectors and cultures is not a topic which has had adequate attention from researchers. For this reason, it can be suggested to study the premises and outcomes of job crafting in different sectors and cultural structures in the researches to come.

References

Babadağ, M. (2018). "The Effect of Work Alienation on Cyberloafing Behavior". *Balıkesir* University The Journal of Social Sciences Institute, 21(39), 207–240.

Bipp, T. and Demerouti, E. (2015). "Which Employees Craft Their Jobs and How? Basic Dimensions of Personality and Employees' Job Crafting Behaviour". Journal of Occupational and Organizational Psychology, 88(4), 631–655.

Demerouti, E. (2014). "Design Your Own Job Through Job Crafting". European Psychologist, 19(4), 237–247.

Demerouti, E. and Bakker, A. B. (2014). Job Crafting. In M.C.W. Peeters, J.D. Jonge and T.W. Taris (Eds.), An Introduction to Contemporary Work Psychology (pp. 414–433), UK: John Wiley & Sons.

Grant, A.M. and Ashford, S.J. (2008). "The Dynamics of Proactivity at Work". Research in Organizational Behavior, 28, 3–34.

Griffin, M.A., Neal, A. and Parker, S.K. (2007). "A New Model of Work Role Performance: Positive Behavior in Uncertain and Interdependent Contexts". Academy of Management Journal, 50, 327–347.

Kerse, G. (2017). "Adaptation the Turkish Language of the Job Crafting Scale and Relationship Between Job Crafting and Emotional Exhaustion". Journal of Business Research, 9(4), 283–304.

Kerse, G. (2018). "The Impact of Job Crafting on Person-Job Fit: "I am Compatible With My Work Because I Can Make Changes in My Work". Ataturk University Journal of Economics & Administrative Sciences, 32(4), 941–958.

Kooij, D.T.A.M., Tims, M. and Kanfer, R. (2015). Successful Aging at Work: The Role of Job Crafting. In P.M. Bal, D.T.A.M. Kooij and D.M. Rousseau (Eds.), Aging Workers and the Employee-Employer Relationship (pp. 145–161), Switzerland: Springer.

Nielsen, K. and Abildgaard, J.S. (2012). "The Validation of a Job Crafting Measure for Blue Collar Workers". Work & Stress, 26(4), 365–384.

Niessen, C., Weseler, D. and Kostova, P. (2016). "When and Why Do Individuals Craft Their Jobs? The Role of Individual Motivation and Work Characteristics for Job Crafting". Human Relations, 69(6), 1287–1313.

Rudolph, C.W., Katz, I.M., Lavigne, K.N. and Zacher, H. (2017). "Job Crafting: A Meta-Analysis of Relationships with Individual Differences, Job Characteristics, and Work Outcomes". Journal of Vocational Behavior, 102, 112–138.

Slemp, G.R. (2016). Job Crafting. In L.G. Oades, M.F. Steger, A.D. Faveand and J. Passmore (Eds.), The Wiley Blackwell Handbook of the Psychology of

Positivity and Strengths-Based Approaches at Work (pp. 351–365), UK: John Wiley & Sons.

Slemp, G.R. and Vella-Brodrick, D.A. (2013). "The Job Crafting Questionnaire: A New Scale To Measure The Extent To Which Employees Engage in Job Crafting". International Journal of Wellbeing, 3(2), 126–146.

Tims, M. and Bakker, A.B. (2010). "Job Crafting: Towards a New Model of Individual Job Redesign". SA Journal of Industrial Psychology, 36(2), 1–9.

Tims, M., Bakker, A.B. and Derks, D. (2012) "Development and Validation of the Job Crafting Scale". Journal of Vocational Behavior, 80, 173–186.

Wang, H.J., Demerouti, E. and Le Blanc, P. (2017). "Transformational leadership, adaptability, and job crafting: The moderating role of organizational identification". Journal of Vocational Behavior, 100, 185–195.

Wrzesniewski, A. and Dutton, J.E. (2001) "Crafting a Job: Revisioning Employees as Active Crafters of Their Work". Academy of Management Review, 26(2), 179–201.

Wrzesniewski, A., LoBuglio, N., Dutton, J.E. and Berg, J.M. (2013). "Job Crafting and Cultivating Positive Meaning and Identity in Work". Advances in Positive Organizational Psychology, 1, 281–302.

Gozde Kosa

Whistleblowing Concept and Management Process

1 Introduction

When someone in an organization or workplace sees or knows about something illegal going on there and informs the authorities, press etc., it is called whistleblowing. It is like "blowing the whistle" so that people's focus will go there, to where a bad thing was happening and was being covered up. It can be very dangerous for the person doing the whistleblowing because the organization can be powerful and the retribution can be enormous. Sometimes, death or imprisonment. This is what you will hear when you ask about what whistleblowing means to people outside the academic world. In addition to this definition when the literature is examined regarding the whistleblowing concept it is seen that the term whistleblowing is thought to originate from "to blow the whistle" in English (Aydın, 2003, 81).

It is defined as informing about the employees or persons who have been employed in an organization by illegal, immoral and unlawful acts (Keil et al., 2010). The etymological origins of this concept are not clear but have various definitions. In the origin of the statement, it is generally thought that the referee stops the football game by blowing a whistle when he faces an illegal situation or that the police alerts the public via blowing a whistle when a crime is committed (Balcı, 2016). Jubb (1999) states that the concept comes from the whistle (whistling) of an authority figure in environments such as a school yard or playground to handle a situation or draw the attention of children (as cited in Özler, Şahin and Atalay, 2010).

The person who initiates the whistleblowing process is called a whistleblower (Kılıçoğlu and Gürol, 1994: 1000). Whistleblowers are people who give signals in the organization they work in, aiming to reveal any abuse or negligence that threatens the people working there (Ray, 2006). Actions subject to whistleblowing are related to violations of human rights, mobbing, illegal transactions, violations of organizational objectives and if whistleblowing should purely be done for ethical purposes (Özler, Şahin and & Atalay, 2010).While defining whistleblowing it is necessary to emphasize some factors that reveal this behavior. First of all, it encounters or witnesses acts or actions that cannot be morally accepted within the organization. However, the whistleblower looks for a solution to stop the disturbing situation. Therefore, the whistleblower is in an effort to benefit the organization and the employees, which makes whistleblowing separate from any reporting behavior (Somers and Casal, 2011). Another factor is that whistleblowing behavior has moral and ethical foundations. It is a critical action carried out to stop a negative action (LePine and Van Dyne, 1998). Aktan (2006), who focuses on the relationship between whistleblowing and personal morality or virtue, argues that people who demonstrate this behavior react to ethical and unethical actions and practice not only within the organization but everywhere and at any time. Gundlach et al. (2003) argued that organizational development could be supported by eliminating unethical and unethical practices in the organization by prioritizing the relationship between whistleblowing and ethics or morality. As a result, whistleblowing, depending on individual ethical principles and moral development, is the action of the individual taking into account the benefit of the organization in which he/she works beyond his/her personal interests (as cited in Cemaloğlu and Akyürek, 2017).

Especially in the last two decades, after various accounting scandals in companies such as Enron, WorldCom, Parmalat etc., whistleblowing has been looked at as a popular concept by academics, researchers, media members, non-governmental organizations, auditing companies, lawyers and the public (Celep and Konaklı, 2012).

Although whistleblowing is a conscientious and humanitarian activity (Saygan and Bedük, 2013: 2–3) that should be done to eliminate or minimize improper action, in practice, this ethical behavior is sometimes attempted to be expressed in many negative-meaning words. For example, the words that are used in some languages are as follows: "spy", "informing", "agent", "delator", "trouble-maker" and "traitor."

As it can be understood from the definition, the act of whistleblowing is made in order to not harm other persons and institutions. The victim may be the person who whistleblows or anyone inside and outside the organization and it can even be the whole community. A whistleblower is generally a knowledgeable person. This person may already be working in the organization or someone who has already worked. In whistleblowing, "volunteering" is essential, not "forcing" or "obligation" (Aktan, 2006: 2–3). While organizations can see whistleblowing as a tool to control and correct corporate corruption, a whistleblower can do this also to gain attention or fame, to get promotion or a financial reward (Hwang vd., 2008: 505).

2 Historical Development of the Concept

This concept was first used in a legal document in 1963, which included the dangers that emerged due to security reasons. For this reason, it is the basis of this concept that unethical and illegal behaviors are tried to be prevented by a whistle (Hersh, 2002). The concept is used especially in the Anglo-Saxon literature to refer to the public when there is a common mistake (Aydın, 2003, 81). The first use of "reporting" in the organizational context is mentioned by Hartmann in an article written in 1971 (Hartmann, 1971, p. 34). This paper, which is the first one, contains a very negative evaluation about "reporting". The first dissenting idea was expressed by Smith (1971, p. 13). Smith pointed out aspects of whistleblowing that were not discussed before. Although he agrees with his predecessors that whistleblowing will not be the optimum solution, he opens a door to the ethically important function of whistleblowing. In organizations, deficiencies, wrongs and problems are ignored, if it is not dealt with a sense of responsibility and if it is preferred to keep it instead, it is a sign that the current course is not good (as cited in Alpaslan, 2006).

2.1 Features of the Concept

Whistleblowing is a phenomenon that can be seen and experienced in any organization: public, private, profitable or non-profit.

- Whistleblowing is done to expose unlawful, unaccepted behavior and actions that are not in accordance with ethical values. Three concepts are important in this second element:
  - Behaviors and actions in the organization are illegal.
  - Behaviors and events experienced in the organization are lawful but not in accordance with morality (professional ethics, work ethics, ethic principles etc.) or at least the perception made by the person who exposed the event is non-moral.
  - Behaviors and/or actions experienced within the organization are unacceptable (Aktan, 2006; Esen and Kaplan: 2018; Uyar and Yelgen: 2013).

3 Kinds of Whistleblowing

Actions that may be covered by information disclosure stealing the company's assets, giving or receiving bribe, cheating in the accounting records, taking the company's important data out of the company for the purpose of personal benefit, laundering money, neglecting the audit, not reporting ethical violations, wasting resources, using the position in the company for personal interests and getting gifts etc. can be examples for whistleblowing. Other examples include use of harmful substances in the products manufactured and hiding the situation despite the fact that there are deaths in operations above the normal rate, violations of human rights, crimes committed in the workplace, abuse, production in the workplace polluting water resources in the environment or hiding information about radiation (Aktan, 2006: 2; Aydın, 2002: 85–86)

Fledderman (1999?) defines the kinds of whistleblowing as follows: An insider is an employee's reporting of the ethical problem to his or her supervisor. Occasionally, employees can skip through all the management levels and go beyond the usual channels to the top manager or board of directors of the organization. In any case, the internal consignee remains in the firm or institution. On the other hand, outsourcing is the employee's notification of the ethical problem to the written or visual press or the relevant (judicial) authorities. In fact, although both species tend to be perceived as "disloyalty", it is generally considered to be more harmful to explain the problem to the outside than in the firm or institution. This is the result of the tradition of not letting it go further. In the meantime, it should be emphasized that when the identity of the whistleblower is anonymous, it is different. In the case of anonymity, the employee stands behind the accusations and is ready for any discussion of the forward versions. On the other hand, anonymous handing is the way that an employee keeps his/her identity secret. Today, electronic mail messages or websites without names are added to those phone calls made by unknown people. Similarly, the employee can make a statement to the press or media without allowing his/her name announced (Gerçek, 2005). When whistleblowing is considered in terms of people's emotions, "hope" leads people to an authority within the organization when there is something illegal going on and the feeling of "anger" leads people to an authority outside the organization (Henik, 2008, 116; Özler, Şahin and Atalay, 2010). According to the findings of a research conducted in 2012, the methods to reveal the illegal actions with its percentage are as follows: informing (43,3 %), management examinations (14,6 %), internal control (14,4 %), coincidence (7 %), accounting agreement (4,8 %), document examinations (4,1 %), independent control (3,3 %), observation (1,9 %), determining public theories (3 %), confession (1,5 %), information technology checks (1,1 %) and other (1,1 %) (Esen and Kaplan: 2018; Pehlivanlı, 2011).

4 Factors Affecting Whistleblowing

Researches on whistleblowing were based on the question "who does this behavior in organizational life and for what?" It was found that the personal characteristics of the employees, such as age, education level, managerial duties, locus of control, level of self-confidence etc., were related to their whistleblowing behaviors (Dozier and Miceli, 1985; Miceli and Near, 1992; Rehg et al., 2008). Researches on whistleblowing have addressed the five main factors that could affect whistleblowing activities (Hassink, Vries and Bolle, 2007):

Cultural/ethical factors: It can be seen that there is a difference between the perceptions of people who have a certain culture and their perception towards whistleblowing. For example, employees in Asian countries (such as Japan and China) exhibit more whistleblowing behavior than Westerners (such as America). In fact, this view shows us that whistleblowing behaviors are more common than individual culture where there is a common culture of life.

Retaliation: If an individual believes that s/he will face negative consequences (such as a harsh punishment) when s/he declares unethical behavior, s/he will stop the whistleblowing behavior.

Psychological factors: Organizational and internal commitment are among these factors. For example, an employee who is internally bound to his or her organization will report unethical practices in the organization more if it is an advantageous situation.

Structural factors: This factor includes policy and legal regulations for whistleblowing. As long as an organization acts with policies promoting whistleblowing, an employee exhibits more whistleblowing behavior. Otherwise, the employee is unlikely to do it.

Type of false/unethical practices: Whistleblowing varies depending on the type of improper/unethical practices (Cemaloğlu and Akyürek, 2017; Kozak and Şahin, 2018).

5 Risks that a Whistleblower Encounters

The person who will do the whistleblowing usually asks the following questions: Will they listen to me if I tell it? Does it have a negative impact on my professional career? Would that be a career suicide for me? How do my friends and the environment think? Would they call me a spy? To whom should I tell it? How should I tell it? The main risks that employees may face in this process are as follows (Aktan, 2006: 8; Çiğdem, 2012: 69; Hwang, Staley, Chen and Lan, 2008; Uyar and Yelgen: 2013):

- Instead of the nature of the information or the problem revealed, the attention can be drawn on the whistleblower.
- Employers or managers who make unethical practices a habit may describe the whistleblower as "a chronic problem worker".
- The whistleblower can be prevented by threats such as "you cannot work in this city or sector again".
- The whistleblower can part from his colleagues and can get far from the source of information too. In addition, employers or managers may also provide disparaging tasks to the whistleblower. Such tactics can sometimes be taken from

various positions of the whistleblower and sometimes can be prepared to put an end to his work.

- Tasks and responsibilities can be given to the whistleblower that he cannot handle. In this way, it may be desirable to prepare the ground for failure.
- The most common reprisals faced by those who whistleblow unethical issues are accusations and threats such as "you got those evidences illegally".
- The dismissal of those who whistleblow for reasons such as "they say they are restructuring and fire them" or giving them to the contrary duties, or rejecting all requests for appointment are common intimidation tactics. Sometimes, dismissal is not seen enough so they do anything so that the whistleblowers cannot find the opportunity to work again in their branches (negative references, to influence other employers etc.)

6 The Whistleblowing Process

It is possible to sort the steps in the whistleblowing process as follows (Kozak and Şahin, 2018; Near and Micelli, 1996; Özler, Şahin and Atalay, 2010; Trevino-Nelson, 2004, 80–83):

- Contacting the relevant manager,
- Discussing this with the family,
- Contacting the other authorities as a result of the related manager being insensitive to the problem,
- Establishing a relationship with the ethics-related officer or ombudsman in the organization (the office to investigate and report illegal and/or unethical claims within the organization),
- Considering contact with those outside the organization,
- Applying to any relevant person or institution outside the organization and leaving the job.

6.1 Reasons Why Whistleblowing Cannot Process Effectively

One of the many reasons why whistleblowing cannot function effectively is the fact that communication channels in the organization are closed and there is no awareness about ethical values. Therefore, it can be said that the anonymity of information is more common (Cemaloğlu and Akyürek, 2017).

These studies, which started after the 1960s abroad, were supported by public and private sector practices. However, due to the nature of whistleblowing, the difficulty of implementing the deadlock of the employees, either theoretically or only in practice in the public sector, was realized. This is due to the fact that employees in the private sector feel under pressure with various concerns (Uyar and Yelgen, 2015).

7 Applicatıons Around the World

Whistleblowing has become a phenomenon discussed all over the world. In South Africa, New Zealand, Japan, Belgium, Ireland, the Netherlands, India and Canada, attempts have also been made to legalize whistleblowing. In fact, the whole world has entered an important period in terms of this concept. But one of the absolute predictions is that each country, society and culture will approach this issue from their own perspective and produce different solutions. In fact, a fact that cannot be ignored is that the whole world cannot escape from the notion of a globally debated issue (Alpaslan, 2006).

8 Sample Cases

The most important problems in the rapidly globalizing world today are accounting for fraud and scandals. The most recent and important example was Time magazine's three women in the first issue of the year 2003, who whistleblowed, and were chosen as the women of the year. Sherron Watkins, one of the people of the year, noticed the company's accounting corruption and reported it to the CEO of the company. When he was appointed to a passive duty, she informed the relevant authorities of corruption at the workplace and resigned from the work and thus the collapse process of Enron began. Coleen Rowley, the person of the year and FBI agent, revealed that the FBI had already known about the September 11 attacks and reported that some months ago, from September 11, some suspicious people had taken flying lessons in the United States, and that even Moussaoui was an important suspect. She wrote a 13-page report to the members of the Senate Intelligence Committee about the attack. Despite many pressures and discriminatory treatment, Rowley continues to serve in the FBI.

The reason why Cynthia Cooper was chosen as the person of the year emerged by the end of the process as a financial auditor and vice president at the world famous WorldCom. Cooper identified $ 9 billion of corruption in the company's accounts and reported it to the auditor, Arthur Andersen. When the audit company ignored the incident, she reported the issues to the government, and revealed corruption. As a result of the incident, WorldCom Finance Manager was sentenced to 65 years of imprisonment while COOPER was promoted and her salary was doubled. The common ground for all three women was to expose important corruption by applying to the "whistleblowing" way, which has become increasingly important in work life in recent years (Aydın, 2003).

In a further denunciation, police officer Toshira Semba was rumored to be emotionally unstable and then lowered to the position of dispatcher. It was revealed that his superiors used public funds for personal purposes and wrote false reports for years to protect themselves. In Japan, the court stated that what had been done to Semba was unjustified as it revealed corruption. Traditionally, in Japan, those who leak information inside the organization are seen as traitors and are considered to be punished for betraying their superiors. However, perception in this direction is changing due to unethical, legal practices in the workplace and people like Semba who reveal the corruption (Rothwell and Baldwin, 2008; Robbins and Judge, 2015:).

9 Conclusion

A Whistleblower should always be taken as a good citizen and a human being. It is really wrong to call those people who do the whistleblowing with good intentions such names as spy or traitor (Bouville, 2008) since whistleblowing contributes to the development of the organization and increases its productivity.

The whistleblower is not that person who stands in opposition to the organization but is its very manifestation. In retaliating against the whistleblower, the organization (uselessly) retaliates against itself. The whistleblower becomes the *ethical* boundary of the organization, forcing the organization to keep the demarcation of its boundaries flexible, thus staying relationally responsive to its stakeholders (Andrade, 2015). The fact remains that although instances of wrongdoing are common in organizations today, we know little about how people make the decision to engage in whistleblowing and their reasons for doing so, and the models proposed to date explain only a small amount of variance in the whistleblowing behaviour (Edwards, 2008).

By encouraging individuals to engage in open and, if necessary, critical discussion about the group's collective interests, those who observe organizational wrongdoing may no longer feel they are sacrificing group loyalty for justice in reporting wrongdoing. Instead, in a culture of constructive dissent, people might come to view whistleblowing as an essential part of what it means to be a loyal and productive group member with an eye toward advancing collective goals to act appropriately and ethically and to follow broader societal norms (Dungan, Waytz and Young, 2015). Whistleblowing would be a much more important tool in fighting organizational wrongdoing.

Whistleblowing is critical to the exchange of information because it promotes a well-informed society. The well-informed society requires diverse information or knowledge to assure the safety of transaction and make economic conduct more efficient. Whistleblowers not only bring organizations "misconduct, which spoils stockholders'" investments and damages the public stock market, to light, but also act as competent informants providing the knowledge that an ordinary citizen finds difficult to gain (Dworkin and Baucus, 1998, as cited in Miller, 2013)

Although whistleblowing can be a difficult and arduous task, it is an essential tool in minimizing the volume and extent of misconducts that occur every day. Part of having good internal controls in an organization requires that employees have a way to report misconducts in the organization. It is essential to find ways to encourage individuals to speak out about wrongdoings so that they can be mitigated and fixed to improve the future

Researches need to be done on the effectiveness of the existing legislation and policies to better determine what works, how workers and the general society feel towards whistleblowing laws and what measures can be taken to improve the culture of openness (Banisar, 2011).

References

Alpaslan, S. (2006). Sosyal Bir Sorumluluk Olarak İhbarcılık. İngiltere: Ashgate Publishing.

Andrade, J.A. (2015). Reconceptualising whistleblowing in a complex world. *J. Bus Ethics*, 128, 321–325

Aydın, U. (2003). İş hukuku açısından işçinin bilgi uçurması. *Anadolu Üniversitesi Sosyal Bilimler Dergisi*, 2(2),79–100.

Balcı, A. (2016). *Açıklamalı eğitim yönetimi sözlüğü*. Ankara: Pegem Publications.

Banisar, D. (2011). Whistleblowing: International Standards and Developments. Corruptıon and transparency: debatıng the frontıers between state, market and socıety, World Bank-Institute for Social Research. Washington, D.C: UNAM. Available at SSRN: https://ssrn.com/abstract=1753180, Accessed on 22.11.2018.

Bouville, M. (2008). Whistle-blowing and Morality. *Journal of Business Ethics*, 81, 579–585.

Celep, C., and Konaklı, T. (2012). Bilgi ifşası: eğitim örgütlerinde etik ve kural dişi uygulamalara yönelik bir tepki. *E-International Journal of Educational Research*, 3(4), 65–88.

Cemaloğlu, N., and Akyürek, M. (2017). Örgütlerde whistleblowing (Bilgi Uçurma). *Turkish Journal of Educational Studies*, 4(3), 123–142.

Dozier, J., and Miceli, M. (1985). Potential predictors of whistle-blowing: A prosocial behavior perspective. *Academy of Management Review*, 10(4), 823–836.

Dungan, J., Waytz, A., and Young, L. (2015). The psychology of whistleblowing. *Current Opinion in Psychology*, 6, 129–133.

Dworkin, T. M., and Baucus, M. S. (1998). Internal vs. external whistleblowers: A comparison of whistleblowering processes. *Journal of Business Ethics*, 17(12), 1281–1298.

Edwards, M. (2008). The conceptualisation and measurement of whistle-blowing: A new way forward', in *22nd ANZAM Conference*, 1–15.

Fleddermann, C. (1999). Engineering Ethics. Englewood Cliffs, NJ: Prentice Hall. Retrieved from http://mathieu.bouville.name/education-ethics/Bouville-whistle-blowing.pdf, Accessed on 17.11.2018.

Gerçek, H. (2005). Mühendislikte etik sorunların ele verilmesi. *Madencilik*, 44(4), 29–38.

Gundlach, M.I., Douglas, S.C., and Martinko, M.J. (2003). The decision to blow the whistle: A social information processing framework. *Academy of Management Review*, 28(1), 107–123.

Hartmann, D. (1971). On whistle blowing. *Computer*, 4(4), 34.

Hassink, H., Vries, M., and Bollen, L. (2007). A content analysis of whistleblowing policies of leading European companies. *Journal of Business Ethics*, 75, 25–44.

Henik, E. (2008). Mad as hell or ecared stiff? The effects of value conflict and emotions on potential whistle-blowers. *Journal of Business Ethics*, 80, 111–119.

Hersh, M.A. (2002). Whistleblowers–heroes or traitors? İndividual and collective responsibility for ethical behaviour. *Annual Reviews in Control*, 26, 243–262.

Hwang, D., Staley, B., Chen, Y.T., and Lan, J.S. (2008). Confucian culture and whistle-blowing by professional accountants: An exploratory study. *Managerial Auditing Journal*, 23(5), 504–526.

Jubb, P.B. (1999). Whistleblowing: A restrictive definition and interpretation. *Journal of Business Ethics*, 21(1), 77–94.

Keil, M., Tiwana, A., Sainsbury, R., and Sneha, S. (2010). Toward a theory of whistleblowing intentions: A benefit-to-cost differential perspective. *Decision Sciences*, 41(4): 787–812.

Kılıçoğlu, A. and Gürol, E. (1994). *İş dünyasi sözlüğü*. İstanbul: Cem Yayınları.

Kozak, M.A., and Şahin, S. (2018). Bilgi İfşası (Whistleblowing) ve Etik İkilem Üzerine Çıkarımlar, inferences on whistleblowing and ethical dilemmas. *Anatolia: Turizm Araştırmaları Dergisi*, 29(1), 31 – 38.

LePine, Jeffrey A., Van Dyne, Linnand (1998). Predicting voice behavior in work groups. *Journal of Applied Psychology*, 83(6), 853–868.

Miceli, M.P., and Near, J.P. (1992). Blowing the whistle: The organizational&legal implications for companies and employees. New York: Lexington Books

Miller, A. (2013). Would You Blow-the-Whistle on a Friend? Phd. Thesis. Baylor University,https://baylor-ir.tdl.org/bitstream/handle/2104/8887/Whistleblower%20Thesis.pdf?sequence=1&isAllowed=y, Accessed on 15.11.2018.

Near, J, and Miceli, M. (1996). Whistle-blowing: myth and reality. *Journal of Management*, 22(3), 507–526.

Özler, D., Dil Şahin, M., ve Giderler Atalay, C. (2010). Teorik bir çerçevede whistleblowing-etik ilişkisi. *Eskişehir Osmangazi Üniversitesi Sosyal Bilimler Dergisi*, 11(2), 169–194.

Pehlivanlı, D. (2011). Türkiye'de suistimal, etik kurallara uyumsuzluklar. Retrieved from http://www.asildenetim.com/images2/etik kurallara uyumsuzluklarTurkiyede suiistimal.pdf. Accessed on 21.11.2018.

Rehg, M.T., Micelli, M.P., Near, J.P., and Van Scotter, J.R. (2008). Antecedents and outcomes of retaliation against whistleblowers: gender differences and power relationships. *Organization Science*, 19(2): 221–240.

Robbins, S.P., and Judge, T. A. (2015).*Örgütsel Davranış-Organizational Behavior* (İ. Erdem, Çev. Ed.). Ankara: Nobel.

Rothwell, G.R., and Baldwin, N.J. (2006). Ethical climate theory, whistleblowing, and the code of silence in police agencies in the state of Georgia. *Journal of Business Ethics*, 70, 341–361.

Saygan, S., and Bedük, A. (2013). Ahlaki Olmayan Davranışların Duyurulması (Whistleblowing) ve Etik İklimi İlişkisi Üzerine Bir Uygulama. *DokuzEylül Üniversitesi İktisadi ve İdari Bilimler Fakültesi Dergisi*, 28(1), 1–23.

Smith, J.M. (1971). More on whistle blowing. *Computer*, 4(6), 13.

Somers, M., and Casal, J.C. (2011). Type of wrongdoing and whistle-blowing: further evidence that type of wrongdoing affects the whistle-blowing process. *Public Personnel Management*, 40(2): 151–163.

Trevino, K.L., and Nelson, A.K. (2004). Managing Business Ethics. America: John Wiley & Sons.

Uyar, S., and Yelgen, E. (2015). Bilgi ifşası (whıstleblowıng) ve denetim. Yönetim *ve Ekonomi Araştırmaları Dergisi*, 13(1), 85–105.

Hakan Aslan and Burcak Vatansever Durmaz

Digital Transformation vs. Managerial Transformation

1 Introduction

The social, economic and environmental changes experienced in the world in the international sense, the intense competition in the markets, brought the necessity to keep up with these rapid changes to the countries and companies. Therefore, in general terms, there has been a need to develop various strategies in order to be able to stand one or several steps ahead of its competitors in this competitive environment, whether from countries or companies. At this point, the digital transformation in the industry has gained importance and the revolution of Industry 4.0 has begun to affect the whole world. At this stage, it is evident that the companies that are integrated with the Industry 4.0 concept will be more prominent in the international markets than their competitors. In this respect, especially in developing countries, the effective and rational use of limited resources is also one of the main factors in the solution of economic problems. At this point, in the difficult competition of digital transformation, those who care about the human factor, which is the most important of the endangered resources, touch people, keep up with the change and lead the change will survive.

All these developments have brought about a great debate. The fact that mechanization or technological developments, which we frequently encounter during every transformation, will leave the people unemployed is the beginning of the problems encountered during the digital transformation period. The technological developments within the scope of digital transformation destroy many business lines, but also reveal many new business lines. According to the research data of Yüksekbilgili (2013), by 2020, the amount of work to be done by technology will be 5 million. In other words, 5 million people will be unemployed. People who do things and work quickly become digital.

However, in the light of recent developments, we see that it has brought new opportunities along with the threat of unemployment, especially during the period of industrial revolutions, and that these opportunities are instrumental in the transformation of people. Every development has led to the emergence of new business lines, the development of new business practices and the introduction of new management approaches. From this perspective, industrial fractures did not destroy the phenomenon of human resources, but rather transformed and developed (Sobel, 1978).

2 Industrial Revolutions

It is seen that the first of the social revolutions took place in the agricultural fields in the history processes. The formation of societies in the settled life and the agricultural society is the first social revolution realized. If we look at our more recent history, the industrial revolution reappears. The industrial revolution has emerged as three major changes. The name of the process, which started in the 18th century and is called the First Industrial Revolution, is also the Age of Steam. The reason why it is called the steam age is the acceptance of James Watt's steam engine as the beginning of the period. In this period, the textile industry developed and material science changed. Shipbuilding and railway transportation became developed industries with the increase in steel production (Bulut and Akçacı, 2017).

With the technological developments, there has been dramatic increases in industrial efficiency since the beginning of the industrial revolution. At the end of the eighteenth century, the steam engine–driven machines found their way into the factories, which enabled them to realize production at a speed that manpower could not reach. The beginning of band production with the help of electricity at the beginning of the twentieth century has reduced the costs especially in the automotive sector. Similarly, many products in the manufacturing industry became more and more produced in series and quantity on tapes. Mass production was followed by automation-supported production technologies. With automation support, the machines could be programmed and controlled more. In this way, works that could be done with manpower was transferred to machines, robots and automation systems. The development of robots with automation systems made a huge decrease in production times and dramatic improvements in quality. However, in the following decades, industrial technological developments have been continuously increasing especially in the fields of mobile communication and electronic commerce (Rüßmann et al., 2015). With these technologies, developments in the electronic communication industry made cyber-physical systems possible.

Since the beginning of the 1700s, steam power has been used. The First Industrial Revolution was initiated by integrating water and steam power into the weaving loom based on mechanical foundation. The use of steam power in the textile sector revolutionized production. However, this increase in production has led to a capacity fullness in another area of the chain. In this period, their carrying capacity was insufficient due to more production than before. At this point, steam power began to be utilized in the railway.

With the invention of electricity in the 19th century, mechanization was replaced by mass production of more than one machine. The first example of mass production, as well as the Second Industrial Revolution, began in Cincinnati Slaughterhouses. Since the machines were working individually, the efficiency was calculated singularly. At this point, it was easy to comment on the system because it was based on machinery. Due to the lack of more than one machine, the efficiency was directly proportional to the power of the machine. The system used in the Cincinati Slaughterhouses was mainly the transport system. The carriage process was carried out with the carriage mounted to the ceiling in order to keep the carcass meat in the plant and to keep it in the proper position for the operations. This process, which was carried out by means of different tools, was started with the help of conveyor belt. A movement that has not added value to production, such as transport, has been initiated by the machine and has created a perspective change (Jensen, 1993).

In the Second Industrial Revolution, Frederick Winslow Taylor made a difference in tape production and business processes by interpreting the business processes scientifically with his work of "Scientific Management Principles" (Taylor, 1911). Taylorism has been applied by Henry Ford, the automotive manufacturer in America. Based on Taylorism, Ford was one of the first companies to use tape-type production. With this type of production, the average production time per car decreased from 12.5 hours to 1.5 hours without making any changes in the number of workers (Eraydın, 1992, Görçün, 2017). After the emergence of Taylorism, a different perspective emerged with the interpretation and implementation of this process by Henry Ford. This perspective is called Fordism. Fordism seemed to be advantageous when it first appeared. In existing production, productivity was increased without any increase in production resources (machinery and people). This idea seems to be applicable in the facilities of companies with few products in the product range. But the disadvantages of Fordism began to be understood later. Due to the standardization on the basis of it, the requests from the customer could not be provided with fast and in-place returns. While the fast and on-the-spot returns to the requests did not affect production efficiency, it caused a decrease in sales orders due to customer satisfaction, which was the trigger of the process. This could only be considered as one of the main items of the Fourth Industrial Revolution.

The Third Industrial Revolution began to sprout in the mid-1900s. Since semiconductors, hosts, personal computers developed in Internet catalysis, they are often referred to as computer revolution. During this period, the processes carried out by people in previous periods are gradually replaced by computers. The fact that developing technology and people leave their place in business processes to computers has created leverage effect for companies that can activate these processes quickly. It has enabled companies to show their way in the global arena rather than the production approach that countries have taken the lead. With the increase in raw material trade, the expansion of technological developments and the transfer of production technology, companies with these components spread their production all over the world (Jensen, 1993).

In the Third Industrial Revolution, developments that support the meaning of the word "revolution" have been experienced in many areas. Supply chain structure that has changed in the First and Second Industrial Revolutions has also changed in the Third Industrial Revolution. Technological developments have also created an environment for the change of Information Technology. Thanks to the developing Internet technology, computers' easier communication with each other supported new business models and E-commerce concept emerged in this period (Turkoglu, 2018).

Klaus Schwab compared the Silicon Valley of 2014 with Detroit of the 1990s. The market value of Detroit's three largest companies in 1990 was $ 36 billion, the number of employees was 1.2 million and the total revenue was $ 250 billion. The three largest companies in Silicon Valley in 2014 were the size of 1.09 trillion dollars, the income was 250 billion dollars and the number of employees was 120,000. The point of view under this is the transition from the focussed production to the idea-oriented production (Schwab, 2016).

The spread of the First Industrial Revolution outside Europe took 120 years. In contrast, the spread of the Internet lasted less than 10 years. As time progressed, the advancement of technology, the expansion of telecommunication and communication network, the increase of communication channels and the awareness of the people working on the world have accelerated (Drath and Horch, 2014).

The concept of Industry 4.0 was first introduced in a fair in 2011 in Hannover. It is the incubation period of the idea of Industry 4.0 between 2011 and 2013. Germany's current production (in factories and service sectors) has emerged as a more efficient and desirable target concept to be developed by supporting production steps with more integrated and new technologies.

The main reason for Industry 4.0 was to ensure that production could be met quickly and accurately to variable customer demands. Previously, the producers were producing by ignoring the demands of the market. As consumers' incomes increased and their education level increased, their demands began to vary. This caused the producers to meet the demands of the consumers to make money. In other words, it was not the products produced by the producers that gave direction to the market, but the demands of the consumers. For this reason, manufacturers started to make changes to meet demands, including production systems. Such a radical change took place in world history for the 4th time and created a revolutionary effect. Therefore, this process of change is called the Fourth Industrial Revolution. In this process of change, the focus was not only on production. Hybrid products combined with high service have also emerged. By making production possible in more favorable conditions and the emergence of cyber-physical factories, smart factories enable the Fourth Industrial Revolution and the virtual and physical manufacturing systems to cooperate with each other in a flexible way. In this way, it is possible to completely customize the products, meet the autonomous demands and create new business models.

Another reason for the emergence of Industry 4.0 is because they think of the development of Western countries that think that the East could be under developing technology and an opportunity that Eastern countries would be able to re-enter.

3 Industry 4.0

Industry 4.0 is the fourth industrial revolution. All units that are directly or indirectly related to production are planned to be jointly working with each other and digital data requires software and information technologies to be integrated with each other (Schuh et al., 2014).

Sener and Elevli defined Industry 4.0 as follows: "The revolution of creating value added by automating jobs requiring unskilled labour" (Senerand Elevli, 2017).

The basis of Industry 4.0 consists of 3 components. These are speed, flexibility and efficiency (Ersoy, 2017). Topics under Industry 4.0 are for the development of these 3 components. New business models are emerging to bring more flexibility and speed to business processes. For example, in the field of tourism, Airbnb company emerged as an initiative that could provide facilities and services to its customers even though there is no facility to offer any hotel, house or accommodation within its structure. Another example is the Uber company, which started its activities with the mission of delivering transportation to everyone and everywhere, although it does not have a taxi or vehicle in its structure. The entrepreneurship of these two firms, which emerged from just an idea, grew rapidly in the world and experienced growth by demand. In the sectors, changes in the business model which they are involved in, Industry 4.0's speed, flexibility and efficiency of the business processes that blend the development and changes (Steel, 2018).

Industry 4.0 is the concept of the Fourth Industrial Revolution and revolutions involve change. TDK defines the revolution as a rapid, radical and qualified change in a certain area (TDK, 2006). So the revolution involves change. The change in Industry 4.0 is the change of many points, processes, business models, job descriptions and methodology of firms.

In this transformation, sensors, machines, workpieces and information technology systems will come to the fore as interrelated systems across a value chain beyond a single enterprise. These interconnected systems (also called cyber-physical systems) interact with each other using standard internet-based protocols and will be able to analyze data to predict bugs, configure themselves and adapt to changes. Developing technology enables data collection and analysis between machines, enabling faster, more flexible and more efficient processes to produce higher quality goods at lower costs. This is expected to support production efficiency, shift economy, help in industry growth and change the profile of the workforce and ultimately change the competitiveness of companies and regions (Rüßmann et al., 2015). The term Industry 4.0, which emerged with the expectation of this future, refers to the name given to the Fourth Industrial Revolution (Lasi et al., 2014).

4 Industrial Transformation and Talent Management

We need a new generation of learning individually, so that we can keep up with the digital age, acquire the skills required by this age and use the world resources more effectively. On the other hand, due to the increasing competition, rapid change, digital transformation and productivity pressure, it is essential to redesign and improve education in business life and more accurately. While all this happens, it is not enough that education, development and learning remain the same or continue to change at the same rate. In this respect, the new generation of learning seems to be a strategy that must be put in first place in terms of the ability crisis. It is important to accelerate work to reduce the talent gap by developing new processes, technologies, tools and content in the areas of learning, knowledge generation and sharing to capture this opportunity and to make a strategic contribution to your organization.

The elements of the new generation of learning are briefly as follows (Blade, 2017):

- It is fully and fully compliant with performance targets and business strategies. From the needs analysis to the design and presentation of the learning program, to the subsequent follow-up, it must be fully in line with the company's business results.

- It is an individualized learning.
- It is an enriched learning.
- It is a technology-supported learning system.
- It is a social, sharing and participatory learning.

From the point of view of the companies, the most important point for technological developments and innovations that come to mind in terms of digital transformation should be perceived as the management of human resources, which is one of the most important sources for companies. In terms of strategic human resources along with digital transformation, valueing the personal transformations of people in the context of existing employees and/or potential employees will not only increase the competitiveness of companies, but also positively affect employer brand perception in the eyes of both employees and potential employees. As for the digitization in institutions, the first issue to be focused on is the development of strategies and practices that will dissolve the differences between the working generations. In the near future, companies should give more support to the personal transformation processes of their employees, especially their managers. Especially while the four generations working together today (X, Y, Z, Baby Boomers), each generation has a different business ethics, preference and mastery and culture.

In this respect, the strategic importance of human resources existing in companies and the traditional processes such as recruitment, placement, assignment, promotion, performance evaluation as well as the ability management and training development of strategic human resources to combine different generations in a single pot is the most important personal transformation process expected from companies. As the name implies, talent management aims to manage the power, ability and competence of employees within a company. According to Collings (2009), the systematic determination of key positions that make a significant contribution to the sustainable competitive advantage of the organization, the creation of a pool of talent with high potential and high performance employees to fill these positions and the ability of these positions to be filled with competent employees and to ensure their commitment to business is the total of activities and processes involving the development of human resource architecture. In other words, it ensures that institutions have enough people to meet their current and future business needs.

The harmony between talent management and business strategies creates a way for people to reach their potential and provide an overview of future possibilities within the organization. To do this, you need to identify and distinguish business strategies and objectives, priorities, challenges and gaps. This is the only way to recruit motivated people who will develop the knowledge and skills needed to put the organization's strategy into action. Future business plans clearly show all the gaps in the skills required and hence the ability to develop skills. This strategy provides an opportunity for all employees to develop their potential. Throughout the recruitment process, companies will recruit the most appropriate person to the position. However, it is always possible to achieve better results by improving staff skills. Measuring the performance of employees is very important to recognize the real potential of employees because they will demonstrate whether they can undertake new responsibilities. This is also an important opportunity to focus on goals and business activities, identify and correct problems and encourage performance improvement, thus improving the overall performance of the organization.

In a study conducted by Mc Kinsey in 2016, 45 % of the work that people do in return for today has been found to be done automatically by computer-aided machines with the development of technology. These results suggest that it will increase unemployment in the future, but this is not the case. Because, in the labor market, such conditions have been observed before. For example, typists have been replaced by word processing programs and cashiers have been replaced by client representatives. The only difference in the changing, transforming, disrupting or reshaping of job opportunities is that the rate of change of the required job skills is at the highest level and that this change takes place at a dizzying pace. In the age of digitalization, it will be necessary to quickly acquire new skills and use these skills more frequently to be permanent in jobs that have not yet been known (Taş et al., 2017).

Sixty-five per cent of the possible jobs of the Z generation is seen as non-existent work in the world. Educational planning cannot be carried out on a job that does not exist in the world, but training can be planned to improve the learning skills of people. Skills Revolution survey conducted by ManpowerGroup with 18,000 employers from 43 countries show a bright future in terms of employment for the young generation. According to the survey, one out of five employers (19 %) says that if the future can be adapted to the business world, technological developments will increase job opportunities. Six out of every 10 employers (64 %) stated that if the candidates have the desired skills and are ready for learning, implementation and adaptation, they will increase the number of employees and at least keep the same. More than 90 % of employers think they will be affected by trends in the digitalization of business within the next two years (Marketing Turkey, 2017).

Providing the balance between the experienced generation in the enterprise and the new generation and arranging the working conditions according to the situation of the individuals will make a difference. In this context, as business processes will be supported by technology and designed away from bureaucracy, flexible systems will be defined and environments will be created to meet the individualized demands of the employees who are raising the focus of "self". Human resources departments, which will have to abandon the standard policies, will need new policies to ensure they are fast and flexible.

While the world is experiencing a great digital transformation, the low supply of talent and the high demand for the right talents are influencing all countries and sectors around the world. As a matter of fact, since the emergence of the business world, the "talent wars" which are given to recruit and keep the right people are getting hotter. Only 40 percent of the companies surveyed said they were ready to face these challenges. This rate is 35 percent lower than last year. Therefore, in order to attract new talents, it is necessary to transform the human resources strategies of the institutions and to be much more innovative than ever and to get rid of old assumptions and outdated applications as soon as possible. It is emphasized that this is the only way to make more intelligent use of technology, create a healthier corporate culture and create a more durable workforce by successfully running the talent war (Dünya Newspaper, 2017).

5 Conclusion

In a knowledge-intensive organization, intelligence and intellectual labour replaces physical labour as the fundamental source of value and profit.

An interesting point to note is that technology has rapidly digitized some of the professions. Thirty percent of the 13 million new jobs since 2010 have required a high level of digital skill and the Millennials, defined as the Z generation, fill these digital roles much more easily. Managers who do not know how to operate the digital world in the next 5–10 years will not be able to become CEOs. But these profiles also need to be very close to business processes. We need to look at how we should improve the processes and the practices of people in the process of digitization. Employees also need to look at this vision and make themselves compatible with this system (Liu, 2017).

In all these digital transformation and personal transformation concepts, companies that are important in the generation conflicts are required to improve their communication and technology skills and to develop themselves in order to find a middle way and deal with the new generation. Accordingly, employees in this category need motivation to develop themselves. Significantly, rewarding should be one of the company's key tasks. The most important competence of strategic human resources is to motivate these employees correctly, to discover new talents, to direct them and to establish a talent management system which intersects the talents of the employees. Here, the support of senior management to ensure that talent management practices support organizational strategies, to adapt all components to support optimal performance, to manage the ability to respond to the change with a long-term perspective, to create a talent-centered corporate culture, to use talent management criteria and to effectively manage talents can be counted as the necessary skill to be ranked as.

Leaders with digital vision are in key positions because it is necessary to place an institution culture that will involve the entire institution in the process of digital change. Executives with a holistic approach play a critical role in all processes of digital transformation. We can say that the ability of corporate executives to manage change and change their companies faster than the speed at which their customers change is now more important than ever.

The most important problem of today's companies is to become the attraction "Center for High Skilled Young Workers". This can only be achieved by adopting and implementing the new conditions of the digital age.

They also want to work with people who think the same way. Companies should ensure that their culture meets these expectations. A company can exhibit a strong stance in the issues affecting its employees and demonstrate its difference not only on paper but also on culture, with leadership principles reflected on employees every day.

As a result, only carefully planned and executed strategies allow a company to realize its digital transformation and develop its own long-term goals.

Obviously, it would not be possible to make external/final customers happy without motivating employees who are regarded as internal customers.

References

Aktaş, Ş. Akıllı Üretim: Endüstri 4,0'a Hazır Mıyız?. Aktaş News-Dijital Dönüşüm. January-February-March Number 8. http://aktasholding.com/images/dergi/14/dergi.pdf, Access date: 16.10.2018.

Bulut, E., & Akçacı, T. (2017). Endüstri 4.0 ve İnovasyon Göstergeleri Kapsamında Türkiye Analizi. *Assam Uluslararası Hakemli Dergi*, 4(7), 55–77.

David G. C., & Kamel Mellahi, K. (2009).Strategic Talent Management: A review and research agenda. *Human Resource Management Review*, 19(4), 304–313, 304.

Don Tapscott Grown Up Digital (2008). How the Net Generation is Changing Your World, McGraw-Hill, New York.

Drath, R., & Horch, A. (2014). Industrie 4.0: Hit or hype? [industry forum]. *IEEE industrial electronics magazine*, 8(2), 56–58.

Drucker, P. (1993). Postcapitalist Society, Harper Business, New York; and Nonaka, l. (1991) The knowledge creating company. *Harvard Business Review*, November-December, July–August 2007 Issue, 69–104.

Dünya G. (2017) https://www.dunya.com/sektorler/teknoloji/dijitallesme-caginda-yetenek-savaslari-kizisiyor-haberi-372644, Accessed on 16.10.2018.

Eraydın, A. (1992). Post-fordizm ve değişen mekânsal öncelikler, Orta Doğu Teknik Üniversitesi, Mimarlık Fakültesi.

Ersoy, A. R. (2017). Endüstri 4.0 Sürecinde Neredeyiz. *Retrieved August*, *28*, 2017.

Florida, R. (1995). Toward The Learnıng Region. *Futures*, 27(5), pp. 527–536. Elseviet Science Ltd, Great Britain.

Görçün, Ö. F. (2017). Dördüncü Endüstri Devrimi-Endüstri 4.0, İstanbul: Beta Yayınları.

Hançer, A. (2017) Yeni İş Hayatında Yeni Nesil Öğrenme, https://www.enocta.com/blog/yeni-is-hayatinda-yeni-nesil-ogrenme/, Accessed on 17.10.2018.

Jensen, M. C. (1993). The modern industrial revolution, exit, and the failure of internal control systems. *The Journal of Finance*, 48(3), 831–880.

Lasi, H., Fettke, P., Kemper, H. G., Feld, T., & Hoffmann, M. (2014). Industrie 4.0. *Wirtschaftsinformatik*, *56*(4), 261–264.

Lazonick, W. (1990). Competitive Advantage on the Shopfloor, Harvard University Press, Cambridge, MA.

Marketing Türkiye (2017). Z kuşağı gelecekte şu anda dünyada var olmayan işlerde çalışacak,

https://www.marketingturkiye.com.tr/haberler/z-kusagi-gelecekte-su-anda-dunyada-var-olmayan-islerde-calisacak/, Accessed on 16.10.2018.

Muro, M., & Liu, S. (2017) Five takeaways on how technology has changed the American workforce, https://www.brookings.edu/blog/the-avenue/2017/11/17/five-takeaways-on-how-technology-has-changed-the-american-workforce/, Accessed on 17.10.2018.

Rüßmann, M., Lorenz, M., Gerbert, P., Waldner, M., Justus, J., Engel, P., & Harnisch, M. (2015). Industry 4.0: The future of productivity and growth in manufacturing industries. *Boston Consulting Group*, 9, https://www.bcg.com/publications/2015/engineered_products_project_business_industry_4_future_productivity_growth_manufacturing_industries.aspx . Access date:16.10.2018.

Schuh, G., Potente, T., Wesch-Potente, C., Weber, A. R., & Prote, J. P. (2014). Collaboration Mechanisms to increase Productivity in the Context of Industrie 4.0. *Procedia CIRP*, *19*, 51–56.

Schwab, K. (2016). Industry 4.0. https://www.theguardian.com/business/economics-blog/2016/jan/24/4th-industrial-revolution-brings-promise-and-peril-for-humanity-technology-davos. Access date: 20.10.2018

Sener, S., & Elevli, B. (2017). Endüstri 4.0'da Yeni İş Kolları ve Yüksek Öğrenim, Journal Of Engineer Brains. 2017.No.2, Vol.1.

Sobel, I. (1978). The human capital revolution in economic development: Its current history and status. *Comparative Education Review*, 22(2), 278–308.

Taş H. Y., Demirdöğmez M., & Küçükoğlu M. (2017) Geleceğimiz Olan Z Kuşağının Çalışma Hayatına Muhtemel Etkileri. *International Journal of Society Researches,* ISSN:2528–9527 E-ISSN: 2528–9535

Taylor, R. (1911). *The Political Prophecy in England* (No. 37). Columbia University Press, https://archive.org/stream/politicalprophec00tayluoft/politicalprophec00tayluoft_djvu.txt. Access date: 20.10.2018.

Turkoglu, E. (2018). Firmalarin Endüstri 4.0'a Hazirlik Çalişmalarinin Değerlendirilmesi: Bursa İlindeki Uygulamasi, Bahçeşehir Üniversitesi, Sosyal Bilimler Enstitüsü.

Williamson, D. (2011). Talent management in the new business world: How organizations can create the future and not be consumed by it. *Human Resource Management International Digest*, 19(6), pp. 33–36, https://doi.org/10.1108/09670731111163518. Accessed on 20.10.2018.

Yüksekbilgili, Z. (2013). Türk tipi y kuşağı. *Elektronik Sosyal Bilimler Dergisi*, 12(45), 342–353.

Hasan Huseyin Uzunbacak

The Moderating Role of Coworker Support in the Interaction Between Workplace Happiness and Innovative Work Behavior

1 Introduction

Recent organizational behavior studies focus on the effects of many variables related to the field of positive psychology on working-occupational-professional life. The question of how happiness, which is one of these concepts but is considered different from job satisfaction (Wright and Doherty, 1998: 481), or in other words, well-being affects behaviors and attitudes in business life mentally and emotionally also draws pretty much attention (Alparslan, 2016: 203). This study aims to reveal the relationship between workplace happiness, innovative work behavior and coworker support.

Workplace happiness is affected by employees' off-the-job feelings and thoughts, as well as their satisfaction with the workplace/work and experiences of positive work-related emotions more frequently than negative ones (Bakker and Oerlemans, 2011: 180). Workplace happiness, which is also described as job-related affective well-being, is defined as doing the work willingly, eagerly and energetically. Studies point out many factors such as provision of work-life balance, lack of role conflict, opportunity to participate in decision-making process, job satisfaction, feedback, team work, sense of usefulness, human-oriented organization culture, person-organization harmony and business reputation, which all together ensure employees to be happy at the workplace (Hatipoglu and Akduman, 2018: 156).

Innovative work behavior is defined as an employee's behavior which aims to achieve the initiation, intentional introduction and conduct of new and useful ideas, processes, products or procedures (De Jong, 2006: 19). According to another definition, innovative work behavior is considered as an employee's willingness to suggest new ideas for being useful to his/her organization, and to adopt and implement these ideas according to his/her role in the organization (Ceylan, 2013: 45). Studies determined that innovative work behavior has a positive relationship with many concepts such as organizational climate, leadership, empowerment and communication (Yidong and Xinxin, 2013: 444).

Coworker support is defined as, when needed, provision of an employee with information and expertise by his/her colleagues, so that the employee can gain necessary knowledge and expertise, which make for him/her easier to deal with work-related problems (Jong, 2007: 618). Coworker support, which includes interaction of an employee with other employees and his/her support behavior and intention in the workplace (Kale, 2015: 105), is also expressed as an employee' assistance to colleagues in doing their daily work and support them socially, by exhibiting attitudes and behaviors such as being friendly and warm, acting empathetically, being open to cooperation, avoiding conflict, not having gossip, not behaving arrogantly, and acting respectfully (Akgündüz and Eryılmaz, 2018: 42). Studies report that coworker support has a significant relation with the variables of intention to leave the job, job satisfaction, organizational commitment and organizational support (Ng and Sorensen, 2008: 243).

The Job Demands-Resources model suggests that a supportive working environment and positive perceptions of the work affect employees' creativity and innovation (Huhtala and Parsefall, 2007: 303). If employees have high perceptions of job resources and positive opinions about the job, then their participation in work-related activities and performance levels increase. However, employees who encounter obstacles at the workplace can experience positive emotions if they are successful in bypassing these challenges. As a result of this, they exhibit more effort to realize organizational goals and display innovative work behaviors, presenting creative ideas and suggestions (George and Brief, 1992; Eisenberger et al., 2005).

The Social Exchange Approach suggests that if employees have high perception of coworker and organizational support, they will have a high tendency to engage in work, to strive for realization of organizational goals and to exhibit behaviors that will produce beneficial and positive results (Giray, 2013: 68).

When employees encounter positive emotions, attitudes and behaviors such as happiness at the workplace, they exhibit positive behaviors such as job satisfaction and commitment. As employees are happy at the workplace, they frequently interact with colleagues, easily have physical and mental adaptation to the workplace and work, and become eager to learn new knowledge. As a result, they provide the organization with additional benefits such as increase in performance and productivity and creation of new ideas (Etikariena, 2017: 366).

In the light of the above explanations, coworker support, as an element of social support, affects happiness in the workplace, and the employee who is happy in the workplace becomes more innovative and creative. From this point of view, coworker support can play a mediatory role in the relationship between

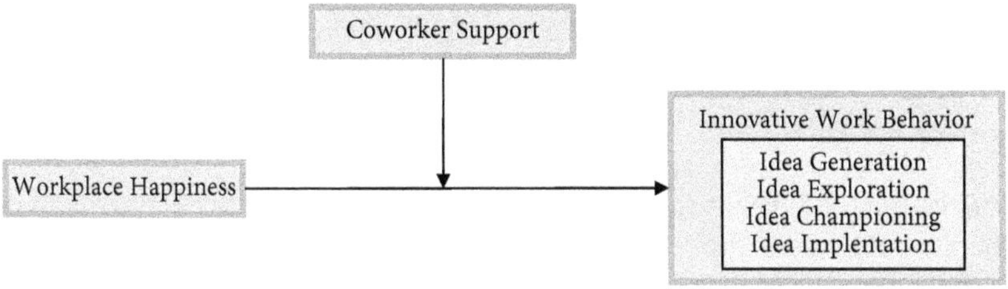

Fig. 1: Research Model

workplace happiness and innovative work behavior. In the light of this information, the research hypothesis was formed as follows:

> *Hypothesis 1: Coworker support have a mediatory role in the relationship between workplace happiness and innovative work behavior. That is to say, employees exhibit more innovative work behavior in case that they have high perception of coworker support, making them happy in the workplace, than in case that they have low perception of coworker support.*

2 Research Method

This section gives information about the research model, sample and measurement tools.

2.1 Research Model

This study aims to determine the role of coworker support in the relationship between workplace happiness and innovative work behavior. For this purpose, the research model is formed as follows.

2.2 Research Universe and Sample

The research universe consisted of white-collar employees. The sample consisted of 364 white-collar employees working in various sectors in Konya, Turkey. This study used convenience sampling method. In this context, an electronically regulated questionnaire was sent via e-mail to the employees of the enterprises that agreed to participate in the study. The questionnaire was filled by 392 employees, but 28 of them were excluded from the analysis. As a result, the analysis was performed using 364 valid questionnaire forms.

Of the participants, 49.5 % were female, 50.5 % were male, 77.5 % were married, and 22.5 % were single. In addition, 84.6 % had bachelor's degree, and

15.4 % had master's degree. The mean age and professional experience of the participants was 38.48 ± 8.55 and 14.57 ± 9.02 years, respectively.

2.3 Measures

In this study, 3 different scales were used to collect data. The scales were used in the previous studies and proven to be valid and reliable. Information on these scales is given in detail below.

Workplace Happiness: The WHO-Five Well-being Index (WHO-5) (1998 version) was developed by the Frederiksborg General Hospital Psychiatric Research Unit at the WHO Collaborating Center for Mental Health, and adapted to the Turkish by Eser (1999). The scale used in this study was a version of this scale adjusted by Alparslan (2016) based on its adaptation to the workplace. This is a six-point Likert type scale (1=Never, 6=Always), consisting of one dimension and 5 items, one of which is scored reverse. As a result of the confirmatory factor analysis (CFA) applied to the scale, it was decided to exclude the item with reverse score due to its factor load below 0.32. The goodness of fit values obtained as a result of the CFA performed over 4 items confirmed the one-dimensional structure ($\chi2$/sd= 2.48; GFI= .99; AGFI= .94; NFI= .99; NNFI= .98; CFI= .99; RMSEA= .055). The internal consistency coefficient of the scale was calculated as 0.92.

Innovative Work Behavior: The original scale developed by De Jong and den Hartog (2010) consists of four factors (generation, exploration, championing, and implementation of ideas) and 10 items. This is a 5-point Likert type scale (1=None, 5=Always) with no reverse scored item. The scale was adapted to the Turkish by Çimen and Yücel (2017). The first-order CFA results confirmed the 4-dimensional structure, and the goodness of fit values obtained were within excellent compliance limits ($\chi2$/sd= 1.48; GFI= .98; AGFI= .96; NFI= .99; NNFI= 1.00; CFI= 1.00; RMSEA= .037). The internal consistency coefficients of the scale on the basis of dimensions were 0.78; 0.90; 0.92 and 0.92.

Coworker Support: This 9-item scale with one dimension developed by Giray and Şahin (2012) is 5-point Likert type scale (1= I definitely disagree, 5= I definitely agree) in which one item is reverse scored. As a result of the CFA applied to the scale, it was decided to exclude the item with reverse score due to its factor load below 0.32. The goodness of fit values obtained as a result of the CFA performed over 8 items confirms the one-dimensional structure ($\chi2$/sd= 2.19; GFI= .98; AGFI= .95; NFI= .99; NNFI= .99; CFI= 1.00; RMSEA= .057). The internal consistency coefficient of the scale was calculated as 0.93.

The goodness of fit values and internal consistency coefficients of the 3 scales described above suggest that all scales are structurally valid and reliable.

Tab. 1: Descriptive Statistics and Relationships between Variables

Variables (N= 364)	Mean	SD	Skewness	Kurtosis	1	2	3	4	5	6
1. Workplace Happiness	4.68	.97	-.444	-.592	(.92)					
2. Idea Generation	3.53	.96	-.347	-.343	.41**	(.78)				
3. Idea Exploration	3.50	1.00	-.497	-.275	.47**	.78**	(.90)			
4. Idea Championing	3.50	1.11	-.520	-.502	.42**	.67**	.81**	(.92)		
5. Idea Implementation	3.53	1.01	-.488	-.384	.49**	.73**	.84**	.84**	(.92)	
6. Coworker Support	4.02	.75	-.568	-.352	.48**	.45**	.44**	.44**	.44**	(.93)

*p<.01 **. Values in parentheses show the reliability coefficients of the dimensions.*

3 Results

The arithmetic mean and skewness/kurtosis values of the variables discussed in the study are given in Tab. 1, which also shows the results of Pearson correlation analysis to reveal the relationships between variables. As can be seen from Tab. 1, the research data shows normal distribution. Morgan et al. (2004: 49) suggest that the skewness and kurtosis coefficients within the interval of ± 1 indicate normal distribution of the data. In this study, the skewness and kurtosis coefficients were found to be in this range.

Tab. 1 also includes arithmetic mean values of the variables. Accordingly, the participants had high levels of perceived workplace happiness (4.68 ± 0.97) and coworker support (4.02 ± 0.75). However, their innovative work behavior levels were very close to each other with respect to the scale dimensions. In general, employees had a level of innovative work behavior above the average. There are positive and moderately significant relationships between all variables ($p < 0.01$).

The hierarchical regression analysis was performed to determine the role of coworker support in the relationship between workplace happiness and innovative work behavior. Before the analysis, it was firstly investigated whether the assumptions needed to perform regression analysis were met. The Durbin-Watson coefficients between 1.5 and 2.5 and the Variance Inflation Factor (VIF) coefficients less than 10 indicate that there is no autocorrelation and multicollinearity problems (Büyüköztürk 2013). In this study, the

Tab. 2: Hierarchical Regression Analysis Results Regarding the Dimension of Idea Generation

N=364	**Idea Generation**					
Variables	**Model-1**			**Model-2**		
	B	**SE**	**β**	**B**	**SE**	**β**
Workplace Happiness	.250***	.050	.261***	.263***	.050	.274***
Coworker Support	.314***	.050	.327***	.319***	.050	.332***
Workplace Happiness*Coworker Support				.089*	.040	.101*
R	.507			.517		
R^2	.257			.267		
Adj..R^2	.253			.261		
ΔR^2	.257			.010		
F	62.507***			43.748***		

**p< .05; ***p< .001.*

Durbin-Watson coefficients ranged between 1.941 and 2.129, and the VIF values ranged between 1.028 and 1.324. Accordingly there were no autocorrelation and multicollinearity problems in the research data.

Secondly, the demographic variables were controlled, but they did not predict any of the sub-dimensions of innovative work behavior. Then the first model was formed, standardized and regressed, after assigning workplace happiness as independent variable and coworker support as moderator (moderating variable). In the second model, in addition to these variables, the interactive term was included in the regression. In the light of this information, the results of the analysis including the 4 sub-dimensions of innovative work behavior are shown in Tab. 2, Tab. 3, Tab. 4 and Tab. 5.

After the incorporation of the interactive term into the second model, the analysis revealed an increase of R^2 by .010, which was statistically significant ($p < .05$). The increase in F value was also significant [$F_{(1,360)} = 4.886$; $p<.05$]. The statistically significant result of the multiplicative outcome of the workplace happiness and coworker support indicates a mediatory effect of coworker support in the relationship between workplace happiness and the dimension of idea generation in the innovative work behavior scale ($B = 0.089$; $p < .05$).

After the incorporation of the interactive term into the second model, the analysis revealed an increase of R^2 by .012, which was statistically significant ($p < .05$). The increase in F value was also significant [$F_{(1,360)} = 6.163$; $p<.05$]. The

Tab. 3: Hierarchical Regression Analysis Results Regarding the Dimension of Idea Exploration

N=364	**Idea Exploration**					
Variables	**Model-1**			**Model-2**		
	B	**SE**	**β**	**B**	**SE**	**β**
Workplace Happiness	.338***	.051	.338***	.353***	.051	.353***
Coworker Support	.282***	.051	.281***	.287***	.051	.287***
Workplace Happiness*Coworker Support				.101*	.041	.111*
R	.534			.546		
R^2	.266			.298		
Adj.R^2	.282			.292		
ΔR^2	.286			.012		
F	72.169***			50.855***		

**p< .05; ***p< .001.*

Tab. 4: Hierarchical Regression Analysis Results Regarding the Dimension of Idea Championing

N=364	**Idea Championing**					
Variables	**Model-1**			**Model-2**		
	B	**SE**	**β**	**B**	**SE**	**β**
Workplace Happiness	.302***	.058	.271***	.320***	.058	.288***
Coworker Support	.353***	.058	.318***	.360***	.057	.324***
Workplace Happiness*Coworker Support				.126**	.046	.124**
R	.508			.522		
R^2	.258			.273		
Adj.R^2	.254			.267		
ΔR^2	.258			.015		
F	62.654***			44.979***		

**p< .01; ***p< .001.*

statistically significant result of the multiplicative outcome of the workplace happiness and coworker support indicates a mediatory effect of coworker support in the relationship between workplace happiness and the dimension of idea exploration in the innovative work behavior scale (B= 0.101; p<.05).

Tab. 5: Hierarchical Regression Analysis Results Regarding the Dimension of Idea Implementation

N=364	**Idea Implementation**					
Variables	**Model-1**			**Model-2**		
	B	**SE**	**β**	**B**	**SE**	**β**
Workplace Happiness	.365***	.051	.360***	.380***	.051	.374***
Coworker Support	.278***	.051	.274***	.284***	.051	.280***
Workplace Happiness*Coworker Support				.099*	.041	.107*
R	.548			.558		
Adj.R^2	.296			.305		
ΔR^2	.300			.011		
F	77.384***			54.224***		

**p< .05; ***p< .001.*

After the incorporation of the interactive term into the second model, the analysis revealed an increase of R^2 by .015, which was statistically significant ($p < .05$). The increase in F value was also significant [$F_{(1,360)} = 7.406$; $p < .01$]. The statistically significant result of the multiplicative outcome of the workplace happiness and coworker support indicates a mediatory effect of coworker support in the relationship between workplace happiness and the dimension of idea championing in the innovative work behavior scale ($B = 0.126$; $p < .01$).

After the incorporation of the interactive term into the second model, the analysis revealed an increase of R^2 by .011, which was statistically significant ($p < .05$). The increase in F value was also significant [$F_{(1,360)} = 5.832$; $p < .05$]. The statistically significant result of the multiplicative outcome of the workplace happiness and coworker support indicates a mediatory effect of coworker support in the relationship between workplace happiness and the dimension of idea implementation in the innovative work behavior scale ($B = 0.099$; $p < .05$).

Even though the mediatory effect of coworker support was demonstrated by regression coefficients, it was necessary to perform a simple slope test proposed by Aiken and West (1991) in order to make the role of mediator variable more visible. In the simple slope test, it should be examined whether the effect of workplace happiness on innovative work behaviors is significantly different from zero for the values with a standard deviation below and above the mean of mediator variable coworker support (Aiken and West, 1991). In this context, the slope test figures containing 4 dimensions of innovative work behavior are shown below.

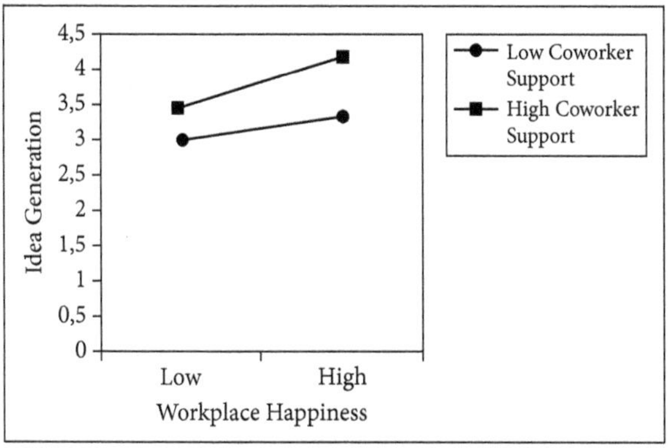

Fig. 2: Moderating Effect of Coworker support on Idea Generation

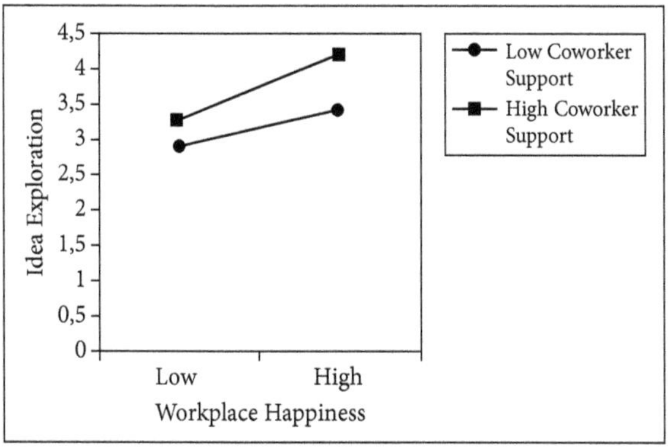

Fig. 3: Moderating Effect of Coworker Support on Idea Exploration

There are similar results in Fig. 2, Fig. 3, Fig. 4 and Fig. 5. Accordingly, regardless of cases in which employees have high or low level of coworker support, workplace happiness was found to predict positively and significantly the dimensions of innovative work behavior as follows; idea generation (B= .179, $p<.01$; B= .360, $p<.001$); exploration (B= .257, $p<.001$; B= .465, $p<.001$); championing (B= .198, $p<.01$; B= .456, $p<.001$) and implementation (B= .287, $p<.001$; B= .490, $p<.001$). As a result, when employees with high coworker support are happy in the workplace, they have more intention of producing innovative ideas, making innovative research, supporting innovative initiatives and applying innovative ideas, than those with low coworker support. Both the results of the hierarchical

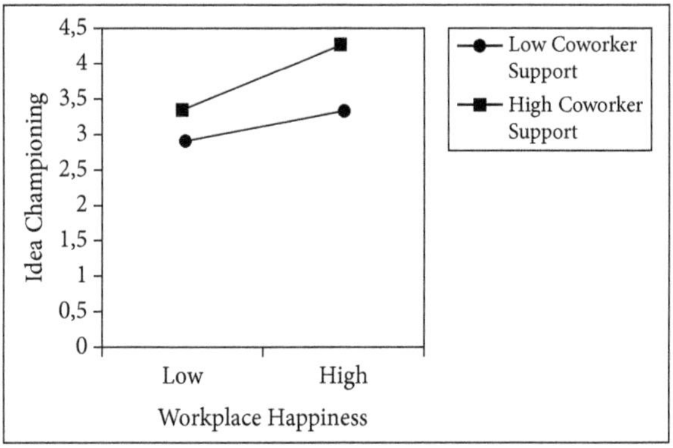

Fig. 4: Moderating Effect of Coworker Support on Idea Championing

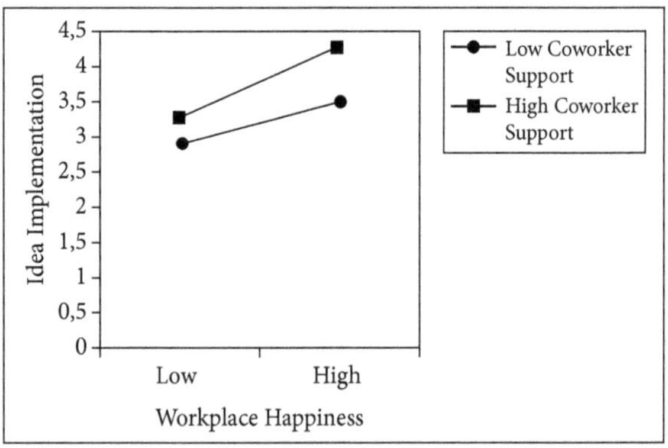

Fig. 5: Morderating Effect of Coworker Support on Idea Implementation

regression analysis with mediator variable and the findings obtained in line with the interaction figure suggest that the relationship between workplace happiness and innovative work behavior is shaped by coworker support. In this case, the hypothesis tested in the study (H_1) was accepted.

4 Discussion and Conclusion

The present study results indicate that employees who are happy at the workplace will exhibit more innovative work behavior. Indeed, these results are consistent with the other study results suggesting that happiness will increase employee performance (Wright et al., 2007: 98), and that employees with high performance will exhibit more creative and innovative work behavior (Yuan & Woodman, 2010; Akkoç et al., 2011; Oswald et al., 2015).

In addition, the present study result indicating a relationship between workplace happiness and coworker is in parallel with the results of other studies. Yalçın (2015) conducted a meta-analytic study in Turkey, and determined coworker support as one of the important variables affecting happiness of employees. Bani-Melhem et al. (2018) report that there is a positive relationship between workplace happiness and coworker support.

The hypothesis test results suggest that coworker support has a mediatory role in the relationship between workplace happiness and innovative work behavior. This finding is not observed in previous studies. However, Bani-Melhem et al. (2018) determined that coworker support mediated the relationship between workplace happiness and innovative work behavior. The mediatory effect of coworker support on the relationship between these two variables emphasizes the importance coworker support in the context of social support.

This study results show that workplace happiness and coworker support are essential components of innovative work behavior. Therefore, it is necessary for managers to perform activities and conduct studies for developing employees' perceptions of coworker support, improving teamwork culture, facilitating information share and learning, ensuring socialization and increasing perception of organizational and social support that will eliminate communication problems.

This study has important results in terms of providing infrastructure for future studies. It is recommended that researchers should evaluate this study variables together with other variables such as perceived organizational support, job satisfaction, intention to leave the job, emotional commitment, organizational culture and organizational climate.

References

Aiken, L. S., & West, S. G. (1991). *Multiple Regression: Testing andInterpreting Interactions*. SAGE: Newbury Park CA.

Akduman, G., & Hatipoğlu, Z. (2018). Mutluluk ve işe ilişkin duyuşsal iyilik algısına yönelik ülkeler bazında karşılaştırmalı bir araştırma. *Sosyal Bilimler Araştırma Dergisi*, *7*(3), 154–172.

Akgündüz, Y., & Eryılmaz, G. (2018). Does turnover intention mediate the effects of job insecurity and co-worker support on social loafing?. *International Journal of Hospitality Management*, *68*, 41–49.

Akkoç, İ., Turunç, Ö., & Çalışkan, A. (2011). Gelişim kültürü ve lider desteğinin yenilikçi davranış ve iş performansına etkisi: İş-aile çatışmasının aracılık rolü. *ISGUC the Journal of Industrial Relations and Human Resources, 13*(4), 83–114.

Alparslan, A. M. (2016). Emek işçilerinde fazladan rol davranışının öncülü: iş tatmini mi, işyerinde mutluluk mu?. *Atatürk Üniversitesi İktisadi ve İdari Bilimler Dergisi, 30*(1), 203–215.

Bakker, A. B., & Oerlemans, W. (2011). Subjective well-being in organizations. *The Oxford Handbook of Positive Organizational Scholarship*, 178–189.

Bani-Melhem, S., Zeffane, R., & Albaity, M. (2018). Determinants of employees' innovative behavior. *International Journal of Contemporary Hospitality Management, 30*(3), 1601–1620.

Büyüköztürk, Ş. (2013). *Sosyal bilimler için veri analizi el kitabı: İstatistik, araştırma deseni, SPSS uygulamaları ve yorum*. 18. Baskı. Ankara: Pegem Akademi Yayıncılık.

Ceylan, C. (2013). Algılanan Bağlılık Tabanlı İnsan Kaynakları Sisteminin Algılanan Gelişim Kültürü ve Yenilikçi İş Davranışına Etkisi. *ISGUC the Journal of Industrial Relations and Human Resources, 15*(1), 40–58.

Çimen, İ., & Yücel, C. (2017). Yenilikçi davranış ölçeği (YDÖ): Türk kültürüne uyarlama çalışması. *Cumhuriyet Uluslararası Eğitim Dergisi, 6*(3), 365–381.

de Jong, J., & den Hartog, D. N. (2010). Measuring innovative work behaviour. *Creativity and Innovation Management, 19*(1), 23–35.

Eisenberger, R., Jones, J.R., Stinglhamber, F., Shanock, L., & Randall, A.T. (2005) Flow Experiences at Work: For High Need Achievers Alone?. *Journal of Organizational Behavior, 26*, 755–75.

Etikariena, A. (2017). The effect of psychological capital as a mediator variable on the relationship between work happiness and innovative work behavior. Ariyanto, A.A., Muluk, H., Newcombe, P., Piercy, F.P., Poerwandari, E.K., & Suradijono, S.H.R. In *Diversity in Unity: Perspectives from Psychology and Behavioral Sciences, (*365–371*)*. London: Taylor & Francis Group.

George, J. M., & Brief, A. P. (1992). Feeling good – doing good: A conceptual analysis of the mood at work – Organizational spontaneity relationship. *Psychological Bulletin, 112*(2), 301–29.

Giray, D. M. (2013). İş yeri desteği: Örgüt, yönetici ve çalışma arkadaşları desteğine genel bir bakış. *ISGUC the Journal of Industrial Relations and Human Resources, 15*(3), 65–81.

Giray, M. D., & Şahin, D. N. (2012). Algılanan örgütsel, yönetici ve çalışma arkadaşları desteği ölçekleri: Geçerlik ve güvenirlik çalışması. *Türk Psikoloji Yazıları, 15*(30), 1–9.

Huhtala, H., & Parzefall, M. R. (2007). A review of employee well-being and innovativeness: An opportunity for a mutual benefit. *Creativity and Innovation Management, 16*(3), 299–306.

Joiner, T. A. (2007). Total quality management and performance: The role of organization support and co-worker support. *International Journal of Quality & Reliability Management, 24*(6), 617–627.

Jong, J. P. J. (2006). *Meer open innovatie: praktijk, ontwikkeling, motieven en knelpunten in het MKB.* Nederlands: EIM, Onderzoek voor Bedrijf & Beleid.

Kale, E. (2015). Lider desteği ve iş arkadaşları desteğinin iş performansı üzerine etkileri: iş tatmini ve yaşam tatmininin aracı rolü. *International Journal of Economic & Administrative Studies, 7*(14), 103–120.

Morgan, G. A., Leech, N. L., Gloeckner, G. W., & Barret, K. C. (2004). *SPSS for Introductory Statistics: Use and Interpretation*, Second Edition, Lawrance Erlbaum Associates: London.

Ng, T. W., & Sorensen, K. L. (2008). Toward a further understanding of the relationships between perceptions of support and work attitudes: A meta-analysis. *Group & Organization Management, 33*(3), 243–268.

Oswald, A. J., Proto, E., & Sgroi, D. (2015). Happiness and productivity. *Journal of Labor Economics, 33*(4), 789–822.

WHO (Five) Well-Being Index (1998). Psychiatric Research Unit, WHO Collaborating Center for Mental Health, Frederiksborg General Hospital, DK-3400 Hillerød.

Wright, T. A., Cropanzano, R., & Bonett, D. G. (2007). The moderating role of employee positive well being on the relation between job satisfaction and job performance. *Journal of occupational health psychology, 12*(2), 93–104.

Wright, T. A., & Doherty, E. M. (1998). Organizational behavior 'rediscovers' the role of emotional well-being. *Journal of Organizational Behavior, 19*(5), 481–485.

Yalçın, İ. (2015). İyi oluş ve sosyal destek arasındaki ilişkiler: Türkiye'de yapılmış çalışmaların meta analizi. *Türk Psikiyatri Dergisi, 26*(1), 21–32.

Yidong, T., & Xinxin, L. (2013). How ethical leadership influence employees' innovative work behavior: A perspective of intrinsic motivation. *Journal of Business Ethics, 116*(2), 441–455.

Yuan, F., & Woodman, R. W. (2010). Innovative behavior in the workplace: The role of performance and image outcome expectations. *Academy of Management Journal, 53*(2), 323–342.

Mehmet Dinc and Tahsin Akcakanat

Moderating Role of Cultural Intelligence in Interaction Between Will to Accept a Foreign Job, and an Openness to Experience Personality and Multicultural Behavior

1 Introduction

The increase in the business activities of enterprises on a global scale brings about an increase in the significance of the international mobility of highly qualified individuals and takes careers of individuals to the international arena to make them boundaryless (Carr et al., 2005). With reference to these developments and current experience, the business world increasingly needs employees who are capable of cooperating in different cultural environments and managing the specific functioning of such environments. From this standpoint, recruitment of assigned expatriates reflects a common feature of international labour mobility, and the international working efficiency of such employees constitutes an important source of competitive advantage for many enterprises. Overseas assignment is also important for many employees or executives of multinational corporations in terms of their career development (Takeuchi et al., 2005). This is because assignment in different cultural environments makes positive contribution to the business-related competencies and personal development.

This study aims at setting the framework of the process of will to accept a foreign job depending on the Evolutionary Personality Psychology Theory of Buss (1991) and the Socio-Analytic Theory of Hogan et al. (1998). Based on this purpose, the study suggests that an openness to experience personality and multicultural behaviour will affect the will to accept a foreign job offered, and this effect can be shaped by the sub-dimensions of cultural intelligence (CQ).

2 Conceptual Framework and Hypothesis Development

2.1 Openness to Experience, Multicultural Behaviour and Accepting a Foreign Job

Openness to Experience (OtE), which is one of the Big Five Personality Models, refers to a trait that separates the creative and imaginative persons from the persons who have a superficial and stereotyped perspective. It defines unique characteristics and will to change and diversity (Costa and McCrae, 1992: 653–655). While the individuals who score a high mark from the trait of Openness to Experience have a wide intellectual curiosity characterized by an individualist way of thinking free from adaptation, the individuals who score a low mark from the same trait prefer familiarity and narrow intellectual focusing (Migliore, 2011: 40).

Among the Big Five personality factors, OtE is the most relevant one to the will to take an assignment in different cultural environments and to the performance issues regarding such assignments. The evolutionary personality psychology theory forms a basis for the claims in this direction. According to the aforementioned theory, first, the Big Five personality traits including the OtE represent the universal adapting mechanisms for adapting to physical, social and especially cultural environments and meeting the requirements of such environments (Buss, 1991: 459–492). Second, individuals have the necessary personality traits to varying degrees to succeed in their objectives. Thus, individuals who have key personality traits such as OtE, which are suitable for the role ascribed in a given cultural environment are more willing to assume or take an overseas job compared to their peers who do not have this trait (Kumar et al., 2008: 323).

Multicultural Behaviour (MCB) refers to an aspect of work life that provides special benefit to the employees and executives all over the world. It focuses on a cultural skill that has become necessary for overcoming problems in the global business environment with cultural diversity. MCB means dealing with composition of a multinational workforce in the competitive free market economy, which rises new challenges for employees and executives (Parhizgar, 2002: xviii). According to Robert and Nikolay (2011: 24), MCB is defined as "the person's degree of ability to form social interaction with the individuals from different cultures."

MCB accounts for exposure of individuals to intensive interaction through formation of interaction in a different culture. With this behaviour, the individual carries on cognitive and – particularly – behavioural adaptation with respect to the different culture (Klafehn et al., 2008: 321–323). Individuals who have MCB adopted through interactions with persons from different cultures will be more prone to overseas jobs/assignments. The relation between these two variables will be regulated by the attitudinal, behavioural and cognitive aspects of CQ. Following hypotheses may be suggested given the aforementioned opinions and theories regarding the openness to experience, multicultural behaviour and will to accept a foreign job:

Hypothesis 1: Openness to experience personality trait of business administration students positively and significantly affects their will to accept a foreign job.
Hypothesis 2: Multicultural behaviour of business administration students positively and significantly affects their will to accept a foreign job.

2.2 Cultural Intelligence as a Moderator

The concept of cultural intelligence is based on the "theory of multiple intelligences" proposed by Gardner (1993). The lack of intercultural look in the Gardner's theory of multiple intelligences (1993) led Earley and Ang (2003) to develop the CQ concept (Earley and Ang, 2003: 4). They proposed the CQ approach in order to get the ability to adjust to different cultures and this concept reflected an individual's competence in collecting, interpreting different symbols and acting according to those symbols so as to function effectively in different cultural settings or in a multicultural situation (Earley and Ang, 2003: 9). Many researchers theorize CQ as a multidimensional concept, namely: Metacognitive (cognitive strategies to develop and acquire solution strategies), cognitive (information obtained on different cultures), motivational (will and self-efficacy) and behavioural (repertoire of most culturally appropriate behaviours) (Ang et al., 2007: 337; Earley and Ang, 2003: 9–11).

As an intercultural competence, CQ has been used in many studies as a moderator of different relationships. In such studies, CQ has produced results as a moderator of the relations between the variables of international assignment experience and experiential learning process (Ng et al., 2009: 517), authentic leadership and ethically grounded cultural adaptation (Vogelgesang et al., 2009: 104–105), language proficiency and task performance (Presbitero, 2016a: 1557–1558) and cultural shock and reverse cultural shock and psychological and social adaptation among international students (Presbitero, 2016b: 28).

Tendency of an individual to take an overseas job/assignment involves cognitive operations regarding a complex body of decision making and behaviours. CQ is conceptualized as a social skill showing the ability to interact in different cultural environments. According to the socio-analytic theory, social skills find meaning as getting along with others and turning the identities to actions to make achievement of goals easier (Hogan and Shelton, 1998: 135). Although this theory rather focuses on the individual forms of identity such as personality, it has included other identity sources (interactions with others, ambient context, etc.) in its scope in time. Therefore, as suggested by Shaffer and Miller (2008: 115–116), this study anticipates that the CQ, as a social skill, will regulate the relation between the individual, business and cultural factors and

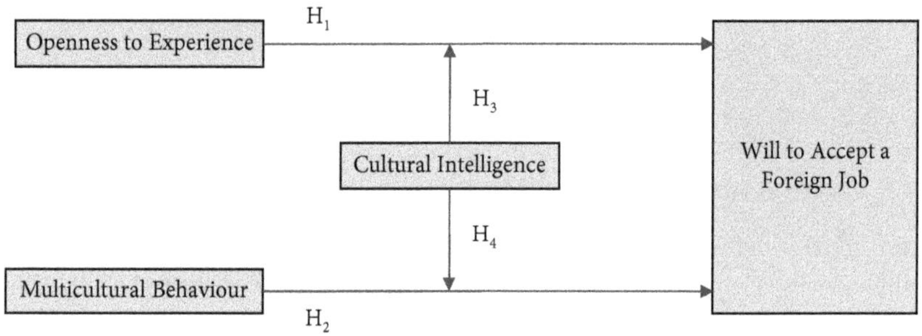

Fig. 1: Study Model

the tendency of assigned expatriates to take assignments in different cultural environments and even, the accomplishment of assignment.

Again, according to the socio-analytic theory, an individual must have certain skills to express a personality trait of him/her. For example, an individual who has the OtE trait will be less affected by intercultural uncertainty, and can flexibly use his/her cultural knowledge, motivation and behaviour according to the context in the cultural environments, which are not known to the individual (Klafehn et al., 2008: 319–320). Based on the effects of the socio-analytic theory and findings of the empirical studies summarized above, the following hypotheses can be developed on the moderator role of CQ:

Hypothesis 3: Cultural Intelligence has a moderator role on the interaction between the openness to experience personality trait of business administration students and their will to accept a foreign job.

Hypothesis 4: Cultural Intelligence has a moderator role on the interaction between the multicultural behaviour of business administration students and their will to accept a foreign job.

3 Methodology

This section provides information about the purpose of the study, sample group covered by the study, and the scales used in the study.

3.1 Purpose and Model of the Study

The main purpose of this study is to determine the effect of OtE and MCB on the students' will to accept a foreign job as well as the role of CQ on this effect. In line with this purpose, the study model has been designed as follows.

3.2 Population and Sample of the Study

Sample of the study consists of undergraduate university students. In this context, senior students of the business administration departments of Ege and Süleyman Demirel Universities represent the population of the study. Total sum of students who receive education in these departments for the spring term of the school year 2016–2017 is 416. The sampling method used in this study is the purposive sampling technique. The questionnaire was filled out by 284 students, but 43 questionnaire forms were excluded from analysis since they were not filled out completely or filled out negligently. So, the study has been conducted with 241 questionnaire forms found suitable for use.

59.6 % of the participants are female and 40.4 % are male. 42.3 % of the participants are students in Ege University, and 57.7 % are students in Süleyman Demirel University. The average age of the participants is 23.5±1.08. Age distribution of the students involved in the study was in the range of 21 to 28.

3.3 Measurement Tools

Cultural Intelligence Scale (CQS) used as a moderator in the study has been developed by Ang et al. (2007) and adapted to Turkish by İlhan and Çetin (2014). CQS is a tool to measure cultural intelligence of individuals in different cultural environments based on the self-declarations of individuals. The scale, consisting of twenty items, is a 7-point Likert-type scale (1= Strongly Disagree, 7= Strongly Agree). The scale contains no reverse scored item. Original form of the scale consists of the following four dimensions: Metacognition, cognition, motivation and behaviour. In their adaptation study, İlhan and Çetin (2014: 108) calculated the coefficient of internal consistency as .85 for the whole scale. The authors report that the coefficients of internal consistency for subscales vary between .71 and .79.

OtE, which is one of the moderators used in the study, has been measured using the 10-item questionnaire of Five-Factor Personality Scale developed by Gosling et al. (2003). This 10-item questionnaire developed by Gosling et al. (2003) has been adapted to the Turkish culture by Atak (2013). In line with the purpose of this study, only two items of the scale, which measure the OtE trait, have been used in this study. These two items included in the scale with 7-point Likert scoring (1= Strongly Disagree, 7= Strongly Agree) are *"I am open to new, complex experience"* and *"I am traditional and non-creative"* – reverse scored.

With two other questions of the scale, the individual's will to accept a foreign job and MCB have been measured. The question preferred for the will to accept a foreign job offer in a different culture was as follows: *"I would like to take a job that requires me to work in a different culture in a foreign country."* The question

Tab. 1: Goodness of Fit Values of CQS

Model	χ^2/df	CFI	NFI	NNFI	GFI	AGFI	SRMR	RMSEA
Cultural Intelligence	1.69	.98	.95	.97	.90	.87	.057	.054
Acceptable Fit*	≤5	>0.90	>0.90	>0.90	>0.85	>0.80	<0.08	<0.08
Good Fit*	≤3	>0.97	>0.95	>0.97	>0.90	>0.85	<0.05	<0.05

*Joreskog and Sorbom, (1993); Kline, (1998); Anderson and Gerbing, (1984).

used for MCB was *"I would like to socially interact with persons from different countries and different cultures."* Both questions have been derived from the study of Robert and Nikolay (2011: 27).

Among the measuring tools, only the validity of CQS has been tested by means of confirmatory factor analysis (CFA). CFA analysis could not be performed for the other scales in the questionnaire since each involves only 1 item or 2 items. The Tab. 1 below shows the analysis results of CQS.

As it can be seen in the Tab. 1, the goodness of fit values of CQS are acceptable or good. The scale works with four dimensions as in its original form. In this context, it has been concluded that CQS is a structurally valid scale.

4 Results

Results from the analysis of the collected data are presented in the headings below.

4.1 Descriptive Statistics and Relations between Variables

Arithmetic mean, standard deviation and skewness/kurtosis values of the variables used in the study have been calculated. The Tab. 2 below shows the results obtained within this scope.

When Tab. 2 has been examined, it has been concluded that the students can easily communicate in multicultural environments and they are highly prone to take an overseas job offer if they have the OtE trait. Average score of the students from the sub-dimensions of CQS, except for the sub-dimension cognition, was above 5. Accordingly, it can be said that the CQ levels of the students are quite high too.

Tab. 2 also shows the skewness and kurtosis values of the data. As it can be understood from the Table, the values are in the range of ±1. Morgan et al. (2004: 49) states that the coefficients of skewness/kurtosis in the range of ±1 are enough for normal distribution of the data. On the basis of this conclusion, parametric analysis techniques have been used in the study. Tab. 3 below shows the results of Pearson's correlation analysis performed to present the relations between the variables.

Tab. 2: Descriptive Statistics Regarding the Variables

Variables (n=241)	Mean	SD	Skewness	Kurtosis
1. Openness to Experience	5.27	1.242	-,269	-,831
2. Multicultural Behaviour	5.70	1.209	-1,007	,735
3. Metacognition	5.76	.808	-,659	,148
4. Cognition	4.31	1.015	-,320	-,049
5. Motivation	5.50	1.007	-,510	-,274
6. Behaviour	5.08	1.040	-,349	-,446
7. Will to Accept a Foreign Job	5.15	1.654	-,848	-,029

Tab. 3: Results of Pearson's Correlation Analysis

Variables (n=241)	1	2	3	4	5	6	7
1. Openness to Experience	(.72)						
2. Multicultural Behaviour	.321**	(---)					
3. Metacognition	.304**	.380**	(.82)				
4. Cognition	.188**	.368**	.330**	(.82)			
5. Motivation	.383**	.635**	.456**	.481**	(.84)		
6. Behaviour	.226**	.517**	.420**	.409**	.573**	(.87)	
7. Will to Accept a Foreign Job	.256**	.538**	.306**	.298**	.555**	.445**	(---)

**p<.01; values in parentheses show the reliability coefficients of the dimensions.

According to the results of correlation analysis given in the Tab. 3, there are positive relations among all variables at a level of p<.01 from low to medium degree. Again, when results of the reliability analysis of the scales are examined in the Tab. 3, it is seen that the coefficients of internal consistency are higher than .70 as generally accepted in the literature. According to this, it can be said that the measuring tools are highly reliable (Nunnally, 1978). The coefficient of internal consistency of the scales MCB and the will to accept a foreign job could not be found since either scale involves 1 item only.

4.2 Results of Hypothesis Testing

Simple linear regression analysis has been performed to test the hypotheses H_1 and H_2 of the study. By the end of the analysis, it has been concluded that OtE has a significant effect on the will to accept a foreign job (B= 0.341; t= 4.095;

$p<.001$; $R^2=0.066$), and H_1 has been accepted. Again, it has been determined that the MCB has a significant effect on the will to accept a foreign job (B= 0.737; t= 9.879; $p<.001$; $R^2=0.29$), the hypothesis H_2 has also been accepted.

In order to test the hypotheses no 3 and 4 of the study, the PROCESS macro for SPSS has been used. In the macro, the Model 1 has been selected to find out the Moderation effect, and the analyses have been performed with 5.000 bootstrap samples. In this context, firstly the role of CQ dimensions in the interaction between OtE and the will to accept a foreign job was tried to be determined. As a result of the analysis, it has been found that only the metacognition dimension has no moderation effect, but the other 3 dimensions of CQ have moderation effects. In respect of the interaction between MCB and the will to accept a foreign job, only the metacognition dimension has a moderation effect, while no moderation effect has been observed in the other 3 dimensions of CQ. Tab. 4 below shows the results obtained within this scope.

All of the interaction terms given in Tab. 4 have given significant results. The fact that an interaction variable gives a significant result shows that the CQ dimensions have a moderation role. In order to see this role more properly, the simple slope test proposed by Aiken and West (1991) should be carried out. Simple slope test should check whether or not the effects of OtE and MCB on the will to accept a foreign job have significantly differed from zero for the values lower or higher than the average value of cultural intelligence dimensions, which are moderator, by one standard deviation (Aiken and West, 1991). Slope test figures prepared within this scope are shown Fig. 2–5.

According to Fig. 2, the relation between OtE and the will to accept a foreign job is weaker for the students with a higher cognition level (b= 0.07, $p>.05$) compared to the students with a lower cognition level (b= 0.43, $p<.01$). In this case, it can be said that the effect of OtE on the will to accept a foreign job is shaped by the cognition dimension of CQ. So, when the students with a lower cognition level show a high OtE trait, their will to accept a foreign job shows a higher increase compared to the students with a higher cognition level. As it can be seen in Fig. 3, the relation between OtE and the will to accept a foreign job is weaker for the students with a higher motivation level (b= -0.09, $p>.05$) compared to the students with a lower motivation level (b= 0.22, $p<.05$). In this case, it can be said that the effect of OtE on the will to accept a foreign job is shaped by the motivation dimension of CQ. So, when the students with a lower motivation level show a high OtE trait, their will to accept a foreign job shows a higher increase compared to the students with a higher motivation level. According to Fig. 4, the relation between OtE and the will to accept a foreign job is weaker for the students with a higher behaviour level (b= 0.05, $p>.05$) compared to the

Tab. 4: Results of Analysis for Moderation Effect of Cultural Intelligence Dimensions

	B	SE	%95 CI	
			LLCI	ULCI
Constant	-1.91	1.72	-5,320	1,488
Openness to Experience	1.00**	0.32	0,364	1,644
Cognition	1.33**	0.40	0,534	2,137
Openness to Experience * Cognition	-0.17*	0.07	-0,321	-0,025
Constant	-4.51	1.99	-8,444	-0,594
Openness to Experience	0.95*	0.38	0,190	1,715
Motivation	1.71***	0.36	0,983	2,436
Openness to Experience * Motivation	-0.16*	0.06	-0,297	-0,025
Constant	-3.28	1.85	-6,939	0,365
Openness to Experience	0.98**	0.34	0,298	1,672
Behaviour	1.44***	0.36	0,726	2,164
Openness to Experience * Behaviour	-0.15*	0.06	-0,283	-0,019
Constant	5.95	2.81	0,414	11,498
Multicultural Behaviour	-0.42	0.50	-1,419	0,566
Metacognition	-0.84	0.50	-1,834	0,150
Multicultural Behaviour * Metacognition	0.19*	0.08	0,021	0,368

*Dependent variable: Will to Accept a Foreign Job, b = Standardized regression coefficient, SE= Standard Error, %95 CI= %95Confidence Interval, n=241 (5.000 Bootstrap Sample), *p<.05, **p<.01, *** p<.001.*

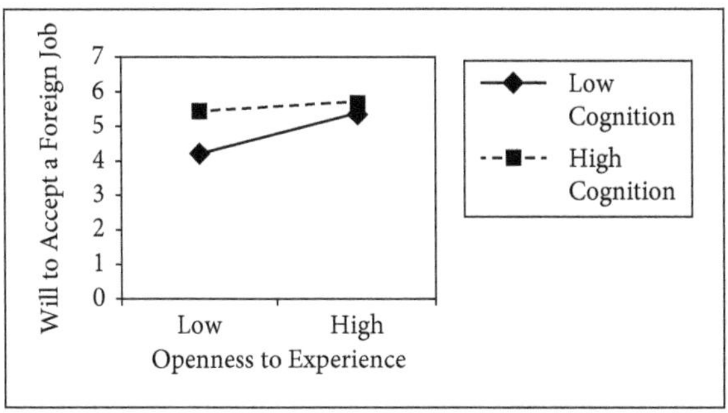

Fig. 2: Moderating Effect of Cognition Dimension

students with a lower behaviour level (b= 0.37, p<.01). In this case, it can be said that the effect of OtE on the will to accept a foreign job is shaped by the behaviour dimension of CQ. So, when the students with a lower behaviour level show a high OtE trait, their will to accept a foreign job shows a higher increase

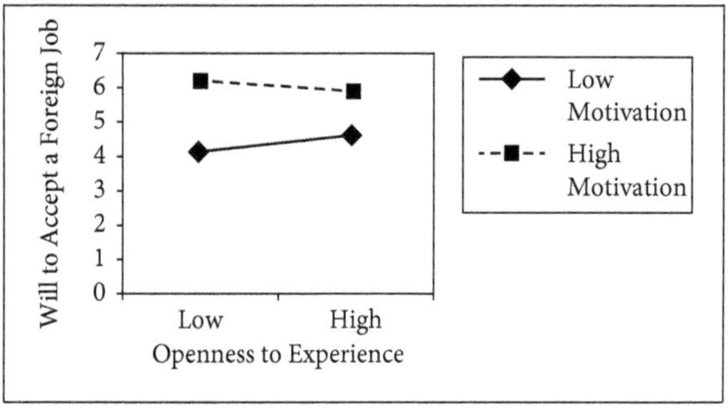

Fig. 3: Moderating Effect of Motivation Dimension

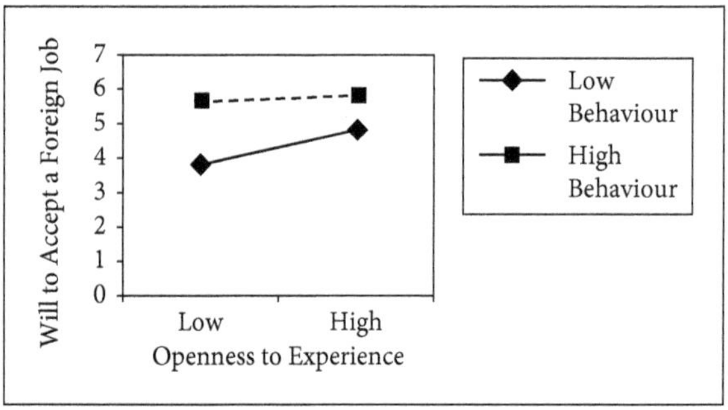

Fig. 4: Moderating Effect of Behaviour Dimension

compared to the students with a higher behaviour level. In the light of information obtained from the first 3 figures, it has been determined that the hypothesis no 3 of the study has been accepted in terms of the cognition, motivation and behaviour dimensions of CQ.

According to Fig. 5, the relation between MCB and the will to accept a foreign job is weaker for the students with a higher metacognition level ($b= 0.85$, $p<.001$) compared to the students with a lower metacognition level ($b= 0.53$, $p<.001$). In this case, it can be said that the effect of MCB on the will to accept a foreign job is shaped by the metacognition dimension of CQ. So, when the students with a higher metacognition level show a high MCB trait, their will to accept a foreign job shows a higher increase compared to the students with a lower metacognition level. This result implies that the fourth hypothesis of the study is supported only in terms of the metacognition dimension of CQ.

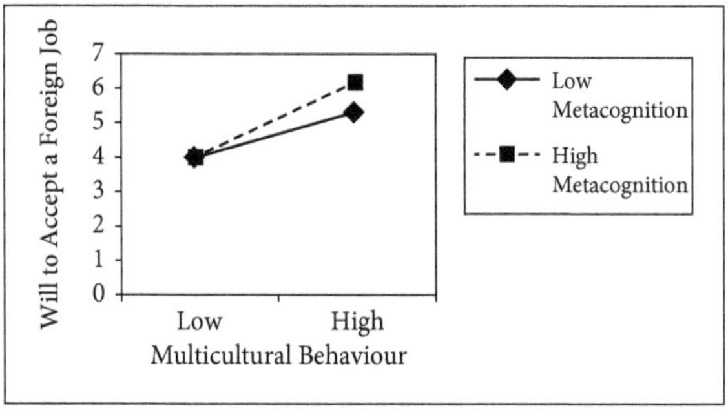

Fig. 5: Moderating Effect of Metacognition Dimension

5 Conclusion and Discussion

The primary purpose of the study is to analyse the effects of OtE and MCB on the will to accept a foreign job. Results of the model created in the study show that the OtE trait of business administration students significantly and positively affect their will to accept a foreign job. This result is consistent with the Evolutionary Personality Psychology Theory proposed by Buss (1991) suggesting that the OtE trait represents universal adapting mechanisms for adapting to physical, social and especially cultural environments and meeting the requirements of such environments in the literature. Again, this result obtained from the study supports results of many studies conducted in the literature (Kumar et al., 2008: 323; Barrick and Mount, 1991: 17–18; Shaffer et al., 2006: 116–117).

According to another result generated by the model in line with the primary purpose of the study, the MCB trait of business administration students significantly and positively affects their will to accept a foreign job. This result of the study is consistent with the Social Cognitive Theory (Bandura, 2002) proposed in the literature. This theory suggests that the MCB trait of individuals have effects on their attitudes toward their peers in different cultures and their behaviours in their own circle, and the individuals form their cognitive opinions for their current and future competencies and interests by observing the social and professional behaviours of the persons who are important for them, and in this way, they accumulate their result expectations in the observed career field (Remhof et al., 2013: 231–232).

Results of the analyses testing the hypotheses proposed for the second purpose of the study meet the expectations to a certain degree; and both the results of the multiple regression analysis with moderator, and the results obtained from single slope test and interaction charts show that three of the CQ dimensions (cognition, motivation, and behaviour) have moderation effects on the interaction between the OtE trait of business administration students and their will to accept a foreign job. In conclusion, when business administration students who have low cognitive, low motivational and low behavioural CQ levels show a high OtE trait, their will to accept a foreign job shows a higher increase compared to the students whose cognitive, motivational and behavioural CQ levels are high. These results of the study, which are contrary to expectations, may have been affected by many external factors including the fact that the business administration students are about to begin to work, they are worrying about finding a job, they are under the influence of socio-economic factors or they think that overseas employment creates attraction after all.

Only the metacognition dimension of the CQ dimensions has an effect on the interaction between the MCB trait of business administration students and their will to accept a foreign job. Therefore, it is an important result that the effect of MCB on the will to accept a foreign job is shaped by the metacognitive dimension of CQ. In fact, when the business administration students who have a high metacognitive CQ level show a high MCB trait, their will to accept a foreign job shows a higher increase compared to the business administration students whose metacognitive CQ levels are low. This result of the study is supported by the Socio-Analytic Theory (Hogan and Shelton, 1998). Furthermore, as a reflection of this theory, it meets the expectation of Shaffer and Miller (2008: 115–116) that CQ that is considered as a social skill will regulate the relation between the individual, business and cultural factors and the tendency of assigned expatriates to take assignments in different cultural environments and even, the accomplishment of assignment.

Results of the study need to be evaluated based on many constraints. First, this study has analysed only the OtE trait as a stable personality trait within the scope of Five-Factor Personality Model. Second, the study has analysed only the MCB as a variable/dynamic personality trait in the literature. It has not analysed the other variables (international experience, language proficiency, relationship networks, etc.) which are included in this group that may have an impact on the result variable. Third, the sample of the study is represented only by the business administration graduate students who are in the last stage of their education from only two state universities in only one cultural context. Fourth, since the data of the study is based on self-reports, this has created sensitivity to common variance error and social desirability bias.

References

Aiken, L. S., & West, S. G. (1991). *Multiple regression: Testing and interpreting interactions*. SAGE: Newbury Park CA.

Anderson, J. C. & Gerbing, D. W. (1984). The effect of sampling error on convergence, improper solutions, and goodness-of-fit indices for maximum likelihood confirmatory factor analysis. *Psychometrika*, *49*(2), 155–173.

Ang, S., Van Dyne, L., Koh, C., Ng, K.Y., Templer, K.J., Tay, C. et al. (2007). Cultural intelligence: Its measurement and effects on cultural judgement and decision making, cultural adaptation and task performance. *Management and Organization Review*, 3(3), 335–371.

Atak, H. (2013). On - maddeli kişilik ölçeğinin Türk kültürüne uyarlanması. *Nöropsikiyatri Arşivi*, 50, 312–319.

Bandura, A. (2002). Social cognitive theory in cultural context. *Applied Psychology: An International Review*, 51(2), 269–290.

Barrick, M. R., & Mount, M. K. (1991). The big five personality dimensions and job performance: a meta-analysis. *Personnel psychology*, *44*(1), 1–26.

Buss, D.M. (1991). "Evolutionary personality psychology". in M.R Rosenzweig & L.W. Porter (Eds.), *Annual Review of Psychology*, 42, 459–492. Palo Alto, CA: Annual Reviews Inc.

Carr, S.C., Inkson, K. & Thorn, K. (2005). From global careers to talent flow: Reinterpreting brain drain. *Journal of World Business*, 40(4), 386–398.

Costa, P.T. Jr. & McCrae, R.R. (1992). Normal personality assessment in clinical practice: The NEO personality inventory. *Psychological Assessment*, 4, 5–13.

Earley, P.C & Ang, S. (2003). *Cultural intelligence: Individual interactions across cultures*. Stanford, CA: Stanford University Press.

Gardner, H. (1993). *Multiple intelligence: The theory in practice*. New York: Basic Books.

Gosling, S., Rentfrow, P. & Swann, W. (2003). A very brief measure of the big five personality domains. *Journal of Research in Personality*, 37, 504–528.

Hogan, R. & Shelton, D. (1998). A socioanalytic perspective on job performance. *Human Performance*, 11, 129–144.

İlhan, M. & Çetin, B. (2014). Kültürel zekâ ölçeğinin Türkçe formunun geçerlik ve güvenirlik çalışması. *Hacettepe Üniversitesi Eğitim Fakültesi Dergisi*, 29(2), 94–114.

Jöreskog, K. & Sörbom, D. (1993). *LISREL 8: Structural equation modeling with the simplis command language*. Chicago, IL: Scientific Software International Inc.

Klafehn, J., Banerjee, P.M. & Chiu, C.Y. (2008). Navigating cultures: The role of metacognitive cultural intelligence. in S. Ang & L. Van Dyne (Eds.), *Handbook of Cultural Intelligence Theory, Measurement and Applications* (pp. 318–331). NY/USA: M.E. Sharpe Armonk.

Kline, R. B. (1998). *Principles and practice of structural equation modeling*. New York: Guilford Press.

Kumar, N., Rose, R.C. & Subramaniam (2008). The effects of personality and cultural intelligence on international assignment effectiveness: A review. *Journal of Social Sciences*, 4(4), 320–328.

Migliore, A.L. (2011). Relationship between big five personality traits and Hofstede's cultural dimensions a sample from India and USA. Cross-Cultural Management. An International Journal, 18(1), 38–54.

Morgan, G. A., Leech, N. L., Gloeckner, G. W. & Barret, K. C. 2004. *SPSS for introductory statistics: Use and interpretation*. Second Edition. London: Lawrance Erlbaum Associates.

Ng, K.Y., Van Dyne, L. & Ang, S. (2009). From experience to experiental learning: Cultural intelligence as a learning capability for global leader development. *Academy of Management Learning & Education*, 8(4), 511–526.

Nunnally, J. C. (1978). *Psychometrictheory*. Second edition. New York: McGraw-Hill.

Parhizgar, K.D. (2002). *Multicultural behavior and global business environments*. International Business Press, New York.

Presbitero, A.(2016a). It's not all about language ability: Motivational cultural intelligence matters in call center performance. *International Journal of Human Resource Management*, 28(11), 1–16.

Presbitero, A. (2016b). Culture shock and reverse culture shock: The moderating role of cultural intelligence in international students' adaptation. *International Journal of Intercultural Relations*, 53, 28–38.

Remhof, S., Gunkel, M. & Schlagel, C. (2013). Working in the global village: The influence of cultural intelligence on the intention to work abroad. *German Journal of Research in Human Resource Management*, 27(3), 224–250.

Robert, E. & Nikolay, D. (2011). Culture intelligence: Antecedents and propensity to accept a foreign job. *7th International Conference of ASECU Recent Economics Crisis and Future Development Tendencies*, October 6–8, 2011, 21–34.

Schaffer, M. & Miller, G. (2008). Cultural intelligence: A key success factor for expatriates. in S. Ang & L. Van Dyne (Eds.), *Handbook of Cultural Intelligence Theory, Measurement and Applications* (pp. 107–125). M.E. Sharpe Armonk, NY/USA.

Takeuchi, R., Tesluk, P., Yun, S. & Lepak, D. (2005). An integrative view of international experience. *Academy of Management Journal*, 48, 85–100.

Shaffer, M. A., Harrison, D. A., Gregersen, H., Black, J. S., & Ferzandi, L. A. (2006). You can take it with you: Individual differences and expatriate effectiveness. *Journal of Applied psychology*, *91*(1), 109–125.

Meryem Aybas

Decent Work: As a Strategy of HR Sustainability

1 Introduction

The United Nations has stated that sustainable development can become a reality only if it becomes a fundamental concern for individual companies and the business community as a whole in the sense of corporate responsibility. Because traditional financial accounting and reporting frameworks do not fully account for an institution's social and environmental activities, the sustainability needs to be broadened (Guthrie & Farneti, 2008: 362).

Today, sustainability is a new developing concept that is being discussed in many areas. It include values, governance, transparency and ethics as well as diversity, social responsibility, supporting human and employee rights, protecting the environment and contributing to society (Boudreou & Ramstad, 2005:130). In today's competitive environment, HR are consumed and exploited rather than developed and reproduced (Ehnert, 2006: 2).

In the HR literature, sustainability is seen mostly in the context of competitive advantage. However, there are some responsibilities related to HRM. In this context, the following questions may be asked in micro and macro dimensions: What can be done for sustainability on the basis of strategic HRM? Where does this concept fit into sustainable competitive advantage? How can HR strategies contribute to society in the context of decent work?

In this study, it is aimed to discuss the concept of decent work, which is important for the sustainability of human labour, how to align HRM strategies, possible compromise and conflict points. It is aimed to contribute to the literature as a theoretical review. As a result of this study, recommendations were developed for HRM managers and policy makers.

2 HR Sustainability

A sustainable organisation operates for the integration of business interests and the interests of the environment and society. It provides profit to its shareholders while protecting the environment and improving the lives of the people it interacts with (Mishra, Sarkar & Singh, 2013: 84).

The literature on sustainable HRM has evolved over the last decade and represents the initiative to review HRM practices and outcomes that are predominantly beyond financial outcomes (Kramar, 2014: 1070). Sustainable HRM is defined by Thom & Zaugg (2004: 217) as *"those long-term oriented conceptual approaches and activities aimed at a socially responsible and economically appropriate recruitment and selection, development, deployment, and downsizing of employees"*. According to Ehnert (2009: 74), sustainable HRM is the pattern of planned or emerging human resource strategies and practices intended to enable an organizational goal achievement while simultaneously reproducing the HR base over a long-lasting calendar time and controlling for self induced side and feedback effects on the HR systems and thus on the company itself. The aim of this understanding of sustainable HRM is value creation and sustainable competitive advantage, in other words long-term corporate success. However, goal orientation involves more than financial performance by including the objectives of employees and society (Ehnert, 2009: 73).

There are several approaches that explain the relationships between HR and sustainability. Sustainable work system, sustainable HRM, sustainable resource management and strategic HRM are some of these approaches (Ehnert, 2006; Ehnert, 2009). The main purpose of sustainable work systems is to understand the mechanisms and processes leading to the exploitation or development of HR, raising awareness on the negative side effects of human exploitation and work-related health problems (Ehnert, 2009: 49). In addition, the main contributions of this approach to sustainability are as follows (Ehnert, 2009: 59): control for side effects of work intensity and avoid intensive work systems, rethink temporal perspective of management, foster participation, support employees coping with ambiguities and work intensity by fostering the corresponding skills and by offering 'experiences', foster employee health, regeneration, well-being, and development.

Sustainable work system approach accepts the detrimental effects of HR developments, such as temporary employment, short term orientation, extreme performance standards, work intensification, and ambiguous job roles on individual well-being, organizational culture, family and community health and satisfaction. A central concern of this approach is the development of HRM practices leading to positive human/social consequences such as work-life balance, organizational economic outcomes and sustainable change processes (Docherty, Kira & Shani, 2009: 4; Kramar, 2014: 1077; Zink, 2014: 128).

Sustainable HRM, which is another approach that examines the relationship between sustainability and HR, looks at sustainability with a win-win logic for organizations and employees. The main contributions of this approach to HR sustainability are as follows: strengthen employee's self-responsibility and participation in decision-making, support employees' employability, use HR development, reward system, HR recruitment and HR marketing to make HRM more sustainable, work–life balance, flexible working time, sabbaticals, HR care, trust-sensitive leadership, participation of employees in decision-making processes (Ehnert, 2009: 59).

According to Ehnert (2009), the objectives of the sustainable resource management approach are based on a causal explanation for the exchange relations between organisations and their environment and develop a general theoretical approach to dealing with scarce resources. The main contributions of this approach to HR sustainability are as follows: rethink role of HRM and notion of strategic success, balance duality of efficiency and sustainability, rethink understanding of HR base and invest in it, investment in employability of HR and in 'sources of resources' (families, schools, labourmarkets), respect 'specific conditions of development, reproduction and regeneration' of the 'sources of HR', reduce feedback effects on sources of resources (Ehnert, 2009: 59).

Finally, among the research questions of strategic HRM, which is another approach related to sustainability, talent shortage externalities of HR deployment and retrenchment, downsizing enhancing social legitimacy, ethics, assumption that HR practices need to be more 'sustainable' issues are included (Ehnert, 2009: 49). The main contribution of strategic HRM is sustainability as a 'decision contributions paradigm' for strategic HRM. (Ehnert, 2009: 59).

HR has an important role to play in creating a sustainable competitive advantage. HR and business leaders define organizational effectiveness as beyond the traditional financial outcomes, the needs of the future, and the need for sustainability, including today (Boudreou & Ramstad, 2005:130). Ehnert (2009: 62–67) provides three approaches to understanding the relationship between sustainability and HRM. These are responsibility-oriented, an efficiency- and innovation-oriented, and a substance-oriented approaches. According to responsibility-oriented approach, the performance of the organization is measured in terms of various metrics such as employee well-being, community welfare and quality of life. The efficiency- and innovation-oriented approach is based on efficiency and the objective of this approach is to reduce consumption (and costs) or to increase the efficiency of resource exploitation (and value creation) via innovation. And the approach to the substance-oriented aims to protect the organization and, in particular, the HR of an organization, so that the consumption and reproduction of resources ensures the future survival of the institution.

According to Ehnert (2006: 14) the main objectives of Sustainable HRM are to balance the ambiguities and the duality of efficiency and sustainability over a long-lasting calendar time, to sustain, develop, and reproduce an organization's human and social resource base e.g. with the help of mutual exchange relationships, to evaluate and assess negative effects of HR activities on the HR base and on the sources for HR.

Sustainability is important in terms of long-term good economics as well as representing moral behaviour in organizations. Sustainability is rarely seen in strategic HR plans, and its impact on strategic HRM has received little attention. However, while organizations are increasingly adopting sustainability, HR is needed (Boudreou & Ramstad, 2005:134). HR managers are responsible for both contributing to the financial results of the organization and creating value. For this they need to reduce labour costs at the same time and increase the well-being of employees through work-life balance programs. This situation may cause them to be distressed from time to time (Kramar, 2014: 1074). According to Ehnert (2009), an important task on a macro level for sustainable HRM is to find a new balance between consumption or exploitation and the reproduction or development of future HR. On the other hand, on micro level sustainability research shows that it is necessary to maintain people's abilities, willingness to perform, self-regulation skills, and health over time (Ehnert, 2009: 75).

HR function affects employees' attrition behaviour, job satisfaction level, organizational commitment and performance. All of these factors lead to sustainability of the organizations in the long term (Mishra, Sarkar & Singh, 2013: 87).

Sustainability focuses on achieving business goals by meeting the expectations of both employees and society. HR managers may find it difficult to promote sustainable development within their organization. Applicable and concrete sustainability includes the top management commitment and institutionalization by employees (Mishra, Sarkar & Singh, 2013: 87).

3 HR Sustainability and Decent Work

Working conditions are becoming increasingly boring, dangerous or degrading worldwide. Decent work defining a work that respects the human rights of the worker is a necessary component of a strategy to eliminate multidimensional poverty and is also an important aspect of human dignity. Full employment and decent work objectives for all are central to both the United Nations and the ILO. In addition, both organizations have developed a detailed standard for full employment and decent work, and they are very compatible. Moreover, both organizations have established numerous mechanisms for technical assistance, monitoring and accountability for decent work (Frey & MacNaughton, 2016: 1–2).

The theme of work has never been central to the debate on sustainability, except in a few references to working conditions and decent work. Since 1972, the United Nations documents that underpin the actions of companies in the area of sustainability, have addressed issues on the theme of work (e.g., job security and stability, aspects of work health and safety, and contents of the Universal Declaration of Human Rights and of the Declaration on Fundamental Principles and Rights at Work) (Bolis, Brunoro & Sznelwar, 2006: 1226).

The latest documents mention the concept of decent work, as such the creation of employment for men and women, the extension of social protection, the promotion of social dialogue and the Fundamental Principles and Rights at Work; and decent work covers four strategic pillars (Ghai, 2003): *full and productive employment, rights at work, social protection and the promotion of social dialogue.*

Sustainability policies cannot ignore social aspects. The existence of negative social impacts (in terms of poor working conditions and employment relations) can also cause local people to feel helpless against environmental issues and therefore to oppose sustainability policies. There is a reciprocal relationship between work and sustainable development (Bolis et al. 2014: 1227).

Sustainable work is a vital factor in the transition towards global sustainability. The term itself, as well as its relations to work content, working conditions, and quality of life, is somewhat vague. Research in strategic HRM should also focus on making a better contribution to societal debates about the opportunities and problems of employment relations (Boxall, 2018: 25).

In the area of HRM, some researchers argue that the well-being and positive employment relationship in the academic HRM should turn into a central priority. Contemporary HR practices have unintended consequences. However, concerns about the ethical implications of the HR practices encouraging their performance while ignoring their responsibilities to their employees have been insufficient (Guest, 2017: 24). According to observations, there is a significant threat to the well-being of employees in contemporary employment relations such as job intensification, increasing technological control, increasing income inequality and increasing precarious employment (Burchell, Sehnbruch, Piasna, Agloni, 2013: 459; Boxall, 2018: 25–26).

In today's business environment, flexible employment has led to the introduction of contingency models that encourage temporary workers to focus on zero-hour contracts and talents while neglecting other employees. On the other hand, talent management provides a rationale for increased inequality reflected in the huge salaries of senior executives, while there are reimbursement increases for the rest of the labour force (Guest, 2017: 23–24).

According to Boudreou and Ramstad (2005), the service-oriented HR paradigm is combined with the traditional financial definition of organizational success. Compliance with regulations, efficiency, effectiveness, customer satisfaction are among the general objectives. However, the traditional HR service delivery paradigm is also typically about how HR is linked to sustainability (Boudreou & Ramstad, 2005:131). Decent work and sustainable oriented HR strategies are closely related. For example, the ILO Declaration recommends the elimination of child labour, forced or compulsory labour and employment discrimination, and the promotion of free association and collective bargaining. In addition to, according to the UN Global Compact, companies should protect internationally declared human rights and ensure they are not complicit in human rights abuses. Decent work can be supported through HR programs such as performance management, selection and training in organizations. For example, these programs reflect fair behaviour, respect for the rights of collective associations and work-family balance, and reward not only economic performance but also community participation or reduction of environmental emissions.

The decent work indicators on HR sustainability are as follows (Guthrie & Farneti, 2008: 361): employment, labour/management relations, occupational health and safety, training and education, diversity and equal opportunity.

Organizations create a just, equitable and healthy workforce and contribute to the welfare of the external community. Thus, it provides human sustainability (Mishra, Sarkar & Singh, 2013: 86). Decent work can be provided through HR function. HR practices with a sustainable approach include employee well-being, health and safety, work-life balance, diversity management, gender equality, talent management, fair rewards, employee development, positive internal communication, open dialogue and employee participation in society (Mishra, Sarkar & Singh, 2013: 91).

According to Kramar (2014), some proposed measures to assess sustainable HRM practices are already used in organizations. These measures include climate, well-being and work-life balance surveys, forecasting future demand, and providing capabilities through workforce planning. However, the full implementation of a sustainable HRM approach requires that these measures be systematically adopted and form part of a broad HRM strategy.

The ILO Framework Work Indicators covers ten substantive elements related to HRM policies corresponding to the four strategic pillars of the decent work agenda as following: employment opportunities, adequate earnings and productive work, decent working time, combining work, family and personal life, work that should be abolished, stability and security of work, equal opportunity and treatment in employment, safe work environment, social security, social dialogue, employers' and workers' representation (ILO, 2018).

The Global Reporting Initiative (GRI) has set several standards for sustainability. Two of these six categories are related to sustainable HRM. These are labour practices and decent work and Human Rights. Labour practices and decent work include nine performance indicators that reflect quality of work life and working environment. These indicators are mainly based on the above-mentioned Decent Work agenda (Ehnert et al., 2016: 91). The indicators included in GRI regarding sustainable HRM-Labour Practices and Decent Work are as follows (Indicators Protocol Set Labour Practices & Decent Work, 2018):

Employment
LA1 Total workforce by employment type, employment contract, and region
LA 2 Total number and rate of employee turnover by age group, gender, and region.
LA 3 Benefits provided to full-time employees that are not provided to temporary or part-time employees, by major operations.
Labour/Management Relations
LA4 Percentage of employees covered by collective bargaining agreements
LA5 Minimum notice period(s) regarding significant operational changes, including whether it is specified in collective agreements.
FP3 Percentage of working time lost due to industrial disputes, strikes and/or lock-outs, by country.
Occupational Health and Safety
LA6 Percentage of total workforce represented in formal joint management-worker health and safety committees that help monitor and advise on occupational health and safety programs
LA7 Rates of injury, occupational diseases, lost days, and absenteeism, and total number of work-related fatalities by region.
LA8 Education, training, counselling, prevention, and risk-control programs in place to assist workforce members, their families, or community members regarding serious diseases.
LA9 Health and safety topics covered in formal agreements with trade unions.
Health and safety topics covered in formal agreements with trade unions.
Training and Education
LA10 Average hours of training per year per employee by employee category.

LA11 Programs for skills management and lifelong learning that support the continued employability of employees and assist them in managing career endings.
LA12 Percentage of employees receiving regular performance and career development reviews.
Diversity and Equal Opportunity
LA13 Composition of governance bodies and breakdown of employees per category according to gender, age group, minority group membership, and other indicators of diversity.
LA14 Ratio of basic salary of men to women by employee category.

Another category of GRI related to sustainability is human rights. The social performance indicators related to this are as follows (Ehnert et al., 2016: 97):

Investment and procurement practices
HR1 Percentage and total number of significant investment agreements that include human rights clauses or that have undergone human rights screening
HR2 Percentage of significant suppliers and contractors that have undergone screening on human rights and actions taken.
Non-discrimination
HR4 Total number of incidents of discrimination and actions taken
Freedom of association and collective bargaining
HR5 Operations identified in which the right to exercise freedom of association and collective bargaining may be at significant risk, and actions taken to support these rights.
Child labour
HR6 Operations identified as having significant risk for incidents of child labour, and measures taken to contribute to the elimination of child labour
Forced and compulsory labour
HR7 Operations identified as having significant risk for incidents of forced or compulsory labour, and measures to contribute to the elimination of forced or compulsory labour

4 Conclusion

Today HR sustainability has received little interest in the organization. However, with Industry 4.0, highly-qualified labour is becoming increasingly important and unskilled labour lose their importance. In this case, sustainability will increase not only in business organizations, but also in society as a whole.

Although there is a growing attention to global codes of labour practices in improving working conditions in global production, how and why it has been systematically analysed so far has been limited (Barrientos & Smith, 2007: 716). The use of GRI standards may be useful for organizations to measure and report sustainable HRM practices.

Decent work can be supported through HR functions and practices such as performance management, selection and training in organizations. These include employee well-being, health and safety, work-life balance, diversity management, gender equality, talent management, fair rewards, employee development, positive internal communication, open dialogue and employee participation in society. All these practices and approaches are consistent with the principles of the concept of decent work. Sustainable HRM can then be used to achieve decent work.

References

Barrientos, S., & Smith, S. (2007). Do workers benefit from ethical trade? Assessing codes of labour practice in global production systems. *Third World Quarterly*, *28*(4), 713–729.

Bolis, I., Brunoro, C. M., & Sznelwar, L. I. (2014). Mapping the relationships between work and sustainability and the opportunities for ergonomic action. *Applied Ergonomics*, *45*(4), 1225–1239.

Boudreau, J. W., & Ramstad, P. M. (2005). Talentship, talent segmentation, and sustainability: A new HR decision science paradigm for a new strategy definition. *Human Resource Management: Published in Cooperation with the School of Business Administration, The University of Michigan and in alliance with the Society of Human Resources Management*, *44*(2), 129–136.

Boxall, P. (2018). The development of strategic HRM: reflections on a 30-year journey. *Labour & Industry: A Journal of the Social and Economic Relations of Work*, *28*(1), 21–30.

Burchell, B., Sehnbruch, K., Piasna, A., & Agloni, N. (2013). The quality of employment and decent work: definitions, methodologies, and ongoing debates. *Cambridge Journal of Economics*, *38*(2), 459–477.

Docherty, P., Kira, M., and Shani, A.B. (2009). 'What the World Needs Now is Sustainable Work Systems,' in Creating Sustainable Work Systems. Developing Social Sustainability (2nd ed.), eds. P. Docherty, M. Kira, and A.B. Shani, London: Routledge, pp. 1–21.

Ehnert, I. (2006). Sustainability Issues in Human Resource Management: Linkages, theoretical approaches, and outlines for an emerging field. In *21st EIASM Workshop on SHRM*.

Ehnert, I. (2009). Sustainable Human Resource Management: A Conceptual and Exploratory Analysis From a Paradox Perspective, Berlin: Physica-Verlag.

Ehnert, I., Parsa, S., Roper, I., Wagner, M., Muller-Camen, M. (2016). Reporting on sustainability and HRM: A comparative study of sustainability reporting practices by the world's largest companies. *The International Journal of Human Resource Management*, *27*(1), 88–108.

Frey, D. F., & MacNaughton, G. (2016). A human rights lens on full employment and decent work in the 2030 sustainable development agenda. *SAGE Open*, *6*(2), 2158244016649580.

Ghai, D. (2003). Decent work: Concept and indicators. *International Labour Review*, *142*(2), 113–145.

Guest, D. E. (2017). Human resource management and employee well-being: Towards a new analytic framework. *Human Resource Management Journal*, *27*(1), 22–38.

Guthrie, J., & Farneti, F. (2008). GRI sustainability reporting by Australian public sector organizations. *Public Money and management*, *28*(6), 361–366.

ILO Retrieved from, http://www.ilo.org/integration/themes/mdw/WCMS_189392/lang--en/index.htm. November15, 2018

Indicator Protocols Set Labor Practices and Decent Work (LA), Retrieved from http://www.saiplatform.org/uploads/Modules/Library/FPSS%20Labor%20Indicator%20Protocols.pdf. November 15, 2018

Kramar, R. (2014). Beyond strategic human resource management: is sustainable human resource management the next approach? *The International Journal of Human Resource Management*, *25*(8), 1069–1089.

Mishra, R. K., Sarkar, S., & Singh, P. (2013). Integrating HR functions for sustainability. Drishtikon: *A Management Journal*, *4*(2), 85–99.

Zink, K. J. (2014). Designing sustainable work systems: The need for a systems approach. *Applied Ergonomics*, *45*(1), 126–132.

Murat Yorulmaz

The Effect of the Perceived Leadership Behaviors of Ship Managers on the Contextual Performance of Seafarers

1 Introduction

Changes brought by the intense competition today affect the structures, activities and management of organizations directly. The effects of leader behaviors on management activities have attracted the interest of researchers and organizations to the concept of leadership. *Leadership* is defined as the process of mobilizing, directing and affecting employees for the purpose of reaching objectives (Hellriegel & Slocum, 1992). Leadership is the skill of directing the behaviors of group members (Fiedler, 1967), having creative morale strength, being able to persuade others to perform a certain task, providing inspiration (Casimir, 2001) and creating an environment for all these to happen. Leadership is researched regarding several of its aspects as it is an important concept related to organizational activities (Bass,1990). Especially in the literature, it is seen that several studies have been conducted to investigate the relationships between leadership behaviors and employee performance in different sectors (Judge, Piccolo & Ilies 2004; Vigoda-Gadot 2007; Veliu, Manxhari, Demiri & Jahaj, 2017). In the maritime sector, among the studies on leadership, Theotokas, Lagoudis and Kotsiopoulos (2014) applied a questionnaire on 45 ship masters from different nationalities to determine the leadership profiles of ship masters and reported that democratic and participatory leadership would be a more suitable leadership approach in ships. Olaniyan and Hystad (2016) investigated the relationship of authentic leadership with the job satisfaction, safety perception and psychological capital of seafarers. Lu, Hsu and Lee (2016) revealed the significant effect of the national culture and leadership perceptions of seafarers on their safety attitudes and behaviors. Sandhaland, Oltedal, Hystad and Eid (2017) used a sample consisting of 281 seafarers to investigate the effects of active and passive leadership behaviors on psychological job demands, situational awareness and willingness in risk-taking. Xhelilaj and Sakaj (2018) emphasized that young and inexperienced maritime officers have adopted an autocratic leadership style that is ineffective and inefficient. In the national literature Topaloğlu (2005), used a sample of 305 blue-collar shipyard employees and determined that transformative leadership affected organizational citizenship perceptions positively. Atik (2014) investigated the leadership characteristics of ship masters within the context of professional culture and based on the points of view of 269 ship masters and chief officers, masters carried the person-based, charismatic, team-based, autocratic and friendly leadership characteristics. Öter and Ayhan (2016) investigated the international literature on transformative leadership and organizational behavior in maritime establishments and emphasized that the number of studies that especially discuss the human factor and management in maritime establishments was low. It is a significant gap that studies on leadership are limited in maritime transportation, which is an indispensable part of international trade. In this context, this study was conducted to investigate the effects of task- and relationship-oriented leadership behaviors shown by ship managers among their leadership behaviors on the contextual performance of seafarers. The study also investigated whether or not there were significant differences in the contextual performance levels of seafarers in their perception of leadership behaviors and based on the sections they worked in. In the study, the leadership behaviors of ship masters, chief officers, chief engineers and second engineers who were discussed as ship managers, stationed in container ships that voyage internationally who had oceangoing capacities were investigated in the context of the points of view of the other seafarers on the ship. The significance of this study comes from that the studies on leadership in the maritime sector are limited in numbers, and there is no study which especially investigated the relationship between leadership behaviors and the contextual performance of seafarers.

2 Literature Review and Hypotheses Development

2.1 Leadership Behaviors

The first studies on leadership aimed to determine the characteristics of an effective leader by focusing on characteristics like intellect, personality and physical appearance. In this theory, which is known as the *traits approach*, it is emphasized that some people emerge as leaders with the help of the traits they have since birth. However, as the traits approach fell short in explaining an effective leader, in 1950s, researchers focused on the *behavioral leadership approach* which is based on the behaviors shown by managers in their management-related activities and revealed how the behaviors of leaders differed as effective leaders by scientific methods (Yukl, 2002). In the *situational approach* theory that proposes that effective leadership is not only shaped based on behaviors, but it also is dependent on the environment where leadership takes place, conditions and the structure of followers (Fiedler, 1967). There is not one fixed leadership behavior that is applicable for managers in every situation and will take them to success. This is because environmental factors, conditions, employees and the structure of the organization and the workplace environment determine the leadership behavior of the manager. Considering the studies in the field on leadership, it is seen that they mostly focused on the differences between task- and relationship-oriented leadership behaviors and the effects of these on organizational factors (Robbins, Judge & Breward 2003; Madlock 2008; Wagner & Hollenbeck 2015; Yücel & Akgül 2016). This study, where leadership is discussed as a form of behavior, investigated the task- and relationship-oriented leadership behaviors by considering the form of management in merchant ships which have a high level of formalization and centrality and a hierarchical organization structure.

Task-oriented leadership behavior refers to behaviors towards completing a job successfully, carrying out organizational activities and using organizational resources effectively. In task-oriented leadership behaviors, it is aimed to establish an organizational model that mobilizes the structure between the leader and their employees where information transfer channels and methods of work are well-defined (Bloisi, Cook & Hunsaker, 2003) and manage this model. The priority of the task-oriented leader is completing the defined tasks successfully. *Relationship-oriented leadership behavior* aims to satisfy the social and emotional needs of employees. For this, the leader tries to establish good relationships with their employees and meet their expectations. Relationship-oriented leaders are eager to have and maintain positive relationships with their employees (Jones & George, 2007). Task-oriented leadership behavior is based on behaviors such as planning, explanation and monitoring, while relationship-oriented leadership behavior is based on behaviors such as supporting, improvement and appreciation. Accordingly, a leader who wants to be effective and successful decides upon which among leadership behaviors is the right behavior based on the environment and conditions they are in and implements it (Yukl, 2002). Within this context, in order to determine which leadership behaviors are shown more by ship managers, the hypothesis
Hypotesis 1: There are significant differences in seafarers' perceptions on leadership behaviors was developed.

2.2. Contextual Performance

Employee performance is the degree that is obtained as a result of the assessment of a person employed to perform some tasks in an organization based on how well they perform their job (Sonnentag & Frese, 2002). In the literature,

employee performance which is effective in reaching organizational goals was usually investigated in terms of its contextual and task performance dimensions (Jawahar & Carr, 2007). *Contextual performance* refers to the employee's display of high effort in performing the task in their job description, their volunteerism and willingness in performing the task that are not in their job description, their voluntary help for and collaboration with their colleagues and their compliance with the rules determined by the organization even if these rules inconvenience them. In addition to adopting, supporting, and if needed, defending the objectives determined by the organization, it also covers commitment to the organization, representation of the organization, maintaining good relationships and being determined to reach the goals that are set (Borman & Motowidlo, 1993). *Task performance* refers to the activities and behaviors carried out by the employee as a requirement of the job they are responsible for. When employees used the professional knowledge and skills that have for facilitating or supporting the objectives of the organization, they have met their task performance requirement (Scotter, 2000). While the behaviors of the employee are in their role definition in task performance, in contextual performance, these are behaviors that provide benefits to the organization which are outside their role definition (Werner, 2000). The reason for focusing particularly on contextual performance in this study was that the level of contextual performance is an important indicator of the commitment of an employee to their organization, and it is the most prioritized parameter while organization managers are measuring total performance. Accordingly, in order to measure the differences in contextual performance levels, the hypotheses,
Hypotesis 2: There are significant differences in the contextual performance levels of seafarers based on the sections they work in was developed.

2.3. Relationship between Leadership Behavior and Contextual Performance

In several studies where the relationship between leadership and employee performance was investigated, the level of effect differed based on sectors, while in a general sense, leadership behaviors were found to have a significant effect on employee performance (Judge, Piccolo, & Ilies 2004; Vigoda-Gadot 2007; Iqbal, Anwar, & Haider, 2015). Some studies that investigated the relationships between leadership behaviors and employee performance are outlined below.

Huey and Ahmad (2009) investigated the relationships between leadership behaviors and employee performance by analyzing the data they obtained from 238 MBA students and the researchers' friends and reported that leadership behavior had a significant effect on employee performance. Yılmaz and Karahan (2010) determined that managers who displayed leadership behaviors that supported and motivated their employees and were related to their improvement increased the performance of employees. In a study that was conducted with 110 employees in the textile sector, it was reported that especially leadership behaviors that focus on vision affected employee performance to a significant extent. Yeh and Hong (2012) investigated the relationships among leadership behaviors, organizational commitment and employee performance in 420 employees of a Taiwanese shoe manufacturing firm in China. They found that leadership behaviors affected employee performance positively. Kayral (2015) conducted a study with 335 employees of a private hospital and determined that leadership skills provided an increase in the performances of employees. Çetin, Giderler and Güler (2017) found that the transformative leadership perceived by employees had a positive effect on their performances, while interactive leadership which is task-oriented did not have a significant effect on employee performance. Pradhan, Jena and Bhattacharyya (2018) carried out a study with 480 people who worked in the IT sector in India and revealed that transformative leadership affected contextual performance positively. In the light of this information in the literature, the hypotheses

Hypotesis 3: Task-oriented leadership behavior affects the contextual performance of seafarers positively and

Hypotesis 4: Relationship-oriented leadership behavior affects the contextual performance of seafarers positively were developed.

3 Method

The data that were obtained by the method of questionnaire were subjected to exploratory and confirmatory factor analyses for determining construct validity and reliability analysis for determining reliability. Using the SPSS and AMOS 22 package software, t-tests were carried out to test whether or not there were significant differences in the contextual performance levels of seafarers based on their perception of leadership behaviors and the sections they worked in, while path analyses were conducted to reveal whether or not task- and relationship-oriented leadership behaviors had a significant effect on the contextual performance levels of seafarers.

3.1 Sample and Data Collection

The study was conducted between July and October 2018 with seafarers employed by a maritime establishment which had 1170 seafarers employed, conducted container transportation and was centered in Istanbul, Turkey. The questionnaire forms were sent to ships with the help of the department of human resources and applied with seafarers who were not ship masters, chief officers, chief engineers or second engineers, who are assumed to be managers. The data that were obtained from the forms completed 240 seafarers and sent back from the ships were used in the analyses.

3.2 Measures

The first part of the questionnaire that was used in the study contained questions on the age, sex, educational status and section of employment regarding the participants, while the second part included contextual performance scales towards measurement of leadership behaviors and the contextual performance levels of the participants. As a scale of leadership behavior, the 20-item and 2-dimension scale developed by Northouse (2004) and adopted into Turkish by Giray and Güngör (2015) was preferred. In the Leadership Behavior Questionnaire, there are 10 task-oriented statements such as "my manager determines the performance criteria (standards) for their employees" or "my manager provides recommendations for employees regarding how problems will be solved" and 10 relationship-oriented statements such as "my manager communicates with their employees in person" or "my manager helps employees work together in harmony." The 8-item, single-dimension Contextual Performance Scale, which contains statements such as "I show extra care while performing my duties" or "I defend my company when others outside my company criticize it," was taken from the study by Jawahar and Carr (2007). The scales were organized based on a 5-point Likert-type scoring (1 = Absolutely Disagree, 5 = Absolutely Agree).

4 Analysis and Results

4.1 Characteristics of Respondents

93.3 % (224) of the participants were male, 6.7 % (16) were female. 38.3 % (92) of the participants were in the age range of 25–34, while 1.7 % (4) were 55 or older. 42.5 % (102) were high school graduates and 23.3 % (56) were primary school graduates. 56.7 % (136) participants were deck officers, 43.3 % (104) were machine officers, 65.8 % (158) were crew class and 34.2 % (82) were officer class. 70.8 % (170) were married, while 29.2 % (70) were single. Their duration of employment at the establishment was 8–11 years for 45.4 % (109), while 6.7 % (16) worked there for 1 year or a shorter time.

Tab. 1: Results of EFA

Dimensions	Item	Varyans (%)	KMO	Bartlett Test
TOL	10	38.463	0.931	3233.986; (p<0.01)
ROL	8	30.254		
Total	18	68.717		
CP	8	40.586	0.845	414.992; (p<0.01)

Tab. 2: CFA Fit Indices

Dimensions	χ2/sd	GFI	CFI	RMSEA
TOL & ROL	3.790	0.911	0.943	0.073
CP	1.865	0.952	0.966	0.048

4.2 Factor Analysis and Reliability

Tab. 1 shows the results of the exploratory factor analysis (EFA) that was conducted to determine the construct validity of the measurement instruments. As seen in Tab. 1, the KMO and Bartlett test values were adequate for EFA. In the EFA, where principal components analysis and Varimax rotation methods were used, the variables were analyzed to reach eigenvalues of higher than 1 and factor loads of higher than 0.50, and leadership behaviors were gathered under two dimensions, whereas contextual performance was gathered under one dimension. Two statements in the dimension of relationship-oriented leadership (ROL) were removed in order as they were overlapped in both dimensions, task-oriented leadership (TOL) explained 38.46 % and ROL explained 30.25 % of the total variance, while contextual performance (CP) explained 40.58 % of the total variance.

The fit values obtained in the confirmatory factor analysis (CFA) that was conducted to confirm the factorial structure obtained as a result of EFA are given in Tab. 2.

After it was understood that the variables in the study had sufficient values of fit, Cronbach's Alpha (CA) coefficients were examined to determine the reliability of the variables in question.

As seen in Tab. 3, the CA coefficients of the variables were higher than 0.70, which is a critical value for reliability. Tab. 3 shows the mean value, Pearson correlation, skewness and kurtosis coefficients of the variables that were determined

Tab. 3: Mean, Correlation, Skewness-Kurtosis and Reliability Coefficients of Variables

Dimensions	M	SD	CA	SKW	KUR	1	2	3
1. TOL	4.18	0.65	0.924	-.741	.264	-		
2. ROL	3.86	0.68	0.906	-.882	.311	0.689**	-	
3. CP	4.02	0.54	0.787	-.093	.231	0.447**	0.541**	-

* $p<0,05$; **$p<0.01$

Tab. 4: Paired-Samples t-Test for Leadership Behaviors

Dimensions	M	N	M. Df.	M.SD	t	df	p
TOL	4.18	240	0.32	0.38	3.522	239	0.02*
ROL	3.86						

to be valid and reliably. Based on Tab. 3, the placement of the kurtosis (KUR) and skewness (SKW) coefficients in the range of -1 to +1 shows that the data were normally distributed, while the correlation coefficients showed that there were medium-level, positive and significant relationships among the variables (Hair, Anderson, Tatham & Black, 2010).

4.3. Hypothesis Testing

The results of the paired-samples t-test that was conducted to determine the differences between the mean values of TOL and ROL perceived by the seafarers are given in Tab. 4. As seen in Tab. 4, the mean value for TOL was significantly higher than that of ROL.

According to these findings, *H1* was confirmed. The results of the independent-samples t-test that was conducted to determine the differences among the seafarers' CP levels based on the sections they worked at are given in Tab. 5. As seen in Tab. 5, deck staff had higher CP levels than machine personnel. Accordingly, *H2* was confirmed.

Structural equation modelling path analyses were carried out to test the causal relationships among the variables, and the fit values of the study model are shown in Fig. 1, while the estimate values are shown in Tab. 6.

Fig. 1 shows that the fit values of the structural equation model of the study were acceptable (Anderson & Gerbing, 1998). Tab. 6 shows that TOL did not have a significant effect on CP, while ROL had a significant effect. It was also found that ROL explained 38.2 % of the variance in CP. Accordingly, *H3* was rejected, and *H4* was confirmed.

Tab. 5: Independent-Samples t-Test for Contextual Performance Levels

Dimensions	M	N	S. D.	t	df	p
Deck Staff	4.16	136	.548	3.046	222.214	0.03*
Engine Staff	3.94	104	.546			

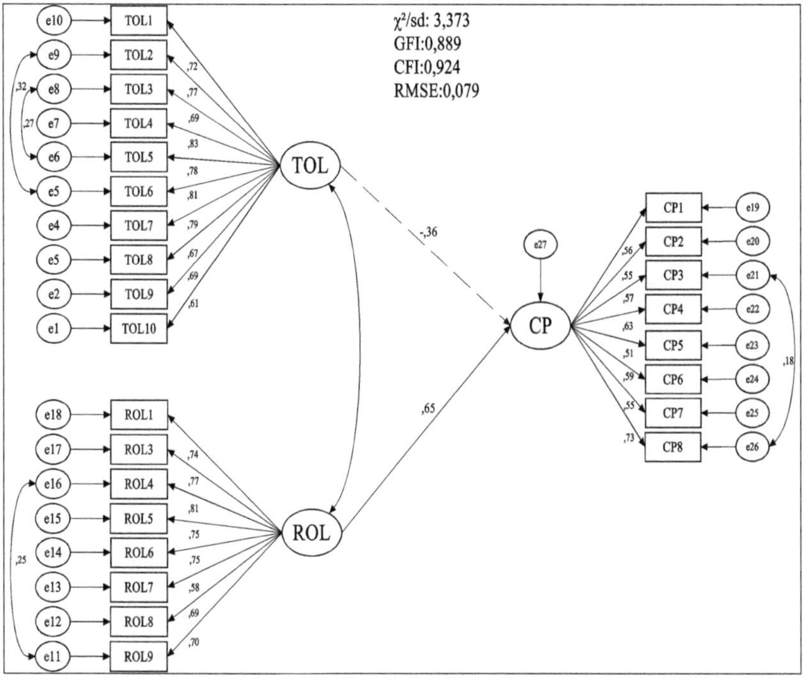

Fig. 1: Structural Equation Model of the Study

5 Conclusions and Recommendations

In this study, which was conducted to determine the effects of perceived leadership behaviors on the contextual performance of seafarers, which leadership behaviors are displayed more by ship managers and the differences in the contextual performance levels of seafarers based on the section they worked in, three (*H1, H2, H4*) of the four proposed hypotheses were confirmed, while one (*H3*) was rejected. According to the findings of the study, it was seen that ship managers displayed task-oriented leadership behaviors more. This finding

Tab. 6: Estimate Values of the Structural Equation Model of the Study

Dimensions Paths			Standardized Regression Coefficients (β)	S. E	C. R	R^2	p
CP	<---	TOL	-0.367	0.61	-1.591	-	.112
	<---	ROL	0.654	0.65	6.260	0.382	.000**

may be explained by the fact that tasks and ways of working in ships are clear, explicit and distinct. Therefore, ship managers show especially task-oriented leadership behaviors for seafarers to perform the tasks that are expected of them. Additionally, it was observed that the seafarers working on the deck had higher contextual performance levels than those of the participants who worked in the engine room. This may be explained by that contextual performance covers voluntary help towards colleagues and showing extra effort for healthy operation of all the activities of the organization in addition to main duties, and that it changes based on the physical conditions in the workplace. While engine personnel are responsible for the main and supportive machines in the engine rooms of ships, deck personnel are responsible for the entirety of the ship, its safety, navigation and management. Thus, the contextual performance levels of the deck personnel were found to be higher than those of the engine personnel. Additionally, it was found that the task-oriented leadership behaviors of ship managers did not have a significant effect on the contextual performance levels of the seafarers, while relationship-based leadership behaviors had a significant effect on contextual performance, and these explained 38.2 % of the total variance in contextual performance. This outcome suggested that a ship manager who displays an approach that values the employee will provide an increase in employee contextual performance, which is effective in reaching organizational goals. These findings were similar to those obtained in studies conducted for different sectors (Huey & Ahmad, 2009; Yeh & Hong, 2012; Çetin, Giderler & Güler, 2017; Veliu *et al.*, 2017; Pradhan, Jena & Bhattacharyya, 2018).

The results of this study are important in terms of maritime business and ship management. This is because, in order to be able to create an efficient working environment in the ships they lead, ship managers should determine what behaviors will positively or negatively affect the job performance of seafarers. That is, seafarers who work at open see ships are confined to working in a closed workplace far from their families and social life where opportunities of socializing are highly limited and there are difficult working conditions. In other words, seafarers work on ships where all life and work activities take place in the same environment. It is important to determine the factors that affect the performance levels of seafarers who work in such difficult conditions. The limitation of this study was that it was conducted with the seafarers who worked at the container ships of a maritime establishment that is operated in Turkey and seen as a corporate firm. It may be recommended for further studies that the variables in this study are investigated with seafarers from different nationalities or those who work at different types of ships and the model of this study is improved.

References

Anderson, J., & Gerbing, D. (1998). Structural equation modeling in practice: A review and recommended two-step approach. *Psychological Bulletin*, 103(3).411–423.

Atik, O. (2014). *Takım liderliğinin mesleki kültür yönünden incelenmesi: Gemi kaptanları üzerine bir araştırma*. İzmir: Dokuz Eylül Üniversitesi Yayınları.

Bass, B. (1990). From transactional to transformational leadership: Learning to share the vision. *Organizational Dynamics*, 18(3), 19–31.

Bloisi, W., Cook, C. W., & Hunsaker, P. L. (2003). *Management and organizational behaviour, European edition*. New York: The McGraw-Hill Companies.

Borman, W., & Motowidlo, S. (1993). Expanding the criterion domain to include elements of contextual performance. *Personnel Selection in Organizations*. San Francisco: Jossey-Bass, 71–98.

Casimir, G. (2001). Combinative aspects of leadership style: The ordering and temporal spacing of leadership behaviors. *The Leadership Quarterly*, *12*(3), 245–278.

Çetin, S., Giderler, C., & Güler, M. (2017). Lider yöneticilerin çalışanların motivasyonuna ve performansına etkisi: kamu kuruluşunda bir çalışma. *Kastamonu Üniversitesi İktisadi ve İdari Bilimler Fakültesi Dergisi*, 19(4), 36–49.

Fiedler, F. E. (1967). *A Theory of leadership of effectiveness*. New York: McGraw.

Giray, M. D., & Güngör, D. (2015). Görev yönelimli ve ilişki yönelimli liderlik ölçeği: geçerlik ve güvenirlik çalismasi. *Turk Psikoloji Yazıları*, 18(35), 13.

Hair, J. F., Anderson, R. E., Tatham, R. L., & Black W. C. (2010). *Multivariate data analysis* (7th. ed.). New Jersey: Prentice Hall.

Hellrıegel, D., & Slocum, J. W. (1992). *Management*. New York: Addison Wesley Publishing Company.

Huey, Y. L., & Ahmad, Z. K. (2009). The moderating effects of organizational culture on the relationships between leadership behaviour and organizational commitment and between organizational commitment and job satisfaction and performance. *Leadership & Organization Development Journal*, 30(1), 53–86.

Iqbal, N., Anwar, S., & Haider, N. (2015). Effect of leadership style on employee performance. *Arabian Journal of Business and Management Review*, 5(5) 1–6.

Jawahar, I., & Carr, D. (2007). Conscientiousness and contextual performance: The compensatory effects of perceived organizational support and leader-member exchange. *Journal of Managerial Psychology*, 22(4), 330–349.

Jones, G. R., & George, J. M. (2007). *Essentials of contemporary management* (2nd. ed.). New York: McGraw-Hill Irwin.

Judge, T. A., Piccolo, R. F., & Ilies, R. (2004). The forgotten ones? The validity of consideration and initiating structure in leadership research. *Journal of Applied Psychology*, 89(1), 36.

Kayral, İ. (2015). Öz liderlik becerilerinin, sağlık çalışanlarının iş tatminleri ve iş performanslarına etkisi. *Hacettepe Sağlık İdaresi Dergisi*, *18*(2).143–159.

Lu, C., Hsu, C., & Lee, C. (2016). The impact of seafarers' perceptions of national culture and leadership on safety attitude and safety behavior in dry bulk shipping. *International Journal of e-Navigation and Maritime Economy*, 4, 75–87.

Madlock, P. (2008). The link between leadership style, communicator competence, and employee satisfaction. *The Journal of Business Communication*, 45(1), 61–78.

Northouse, P. G. (2004). *Leadership: Theory and practice* (3rd. ed.). California: Sage Publications.

Olaniyan, O., & Hystad, S. (2016). Employees' psychological capital, job satisfaction, insecurity, and intentions to quit: The direct and indirect effects of authentic leadership. *Journal of Work and Organizational Psychology*, 32(3), 163–171.

Öter, S., & Ayan, M. (2016). Denizcilik işletmelerinde dönüşümcü liderlik ve örgütsel vatandaşlık davranışı arasındaki ilişkiler üzerine bir literatür. *Dokuz Eylül Üniversitesi Denizcilik Fakültesi Dergisi*, 8(1).129–157.

Pradhan, S., Jena, L. K., & Bhattacharyya, P. (2018). Transformational leadership and contextual performance: Role of integrity among Indian IT professionals. *International Journal of Productivity and Performance Management*, 67(2), 445–462.

Robbins, S., Judge, T., & Breward, K. (2003). *Essentials of organizational behavior*, 7. Upper Saddle River: Prentice Hall.

Sandhaland, H., Oltedal, H. A., Hystad, S. W., & Eid, J. (2017). Effects of leadership style and psychological job demands on situation awareness and the willingness to take a risk: A survey of selected offshore vessels. *Safety Science*, (93), 178–186.

Scotter, V. J. R. (2000). Relationships of task performance and contextual performance with turnover, job satisf., and affective commitment. *Human Resource Management Review*, 10(1), 79–95.

Sonnentag, S., & Frese, M. (2002). Performance concepts and performance theory. *Psychological Management of İndividual Performance*, 23(1), 3–25.

Theotokas, I., Lagoudis, I. N., & Kotsiopoulos, N. (2014). Leadership profiling of oceangoing ship masters. *The Asian Journal of Shipping and Logistics*, 30(3), 321–343.

Topaloğlu, G. (2005). *Dönüştürücü liderlik ve örgütsel vatandaşlık davranışı arasındaki ilişki*. (Unpublished Master's). Gebze Yüksek Teknoloj Enstitüsü: Gebze.

Veliu, L., Manxhari, M., Demiri, V., & Jahaj, L. (2017). The influence of leadershıp styles on employee's performance. *Journal of Management*, 31(2).59–69.

Vigoda-Gadot, E. (2007). Leadership style, organizational politics, and employees' performance: An empirical examination of two competing models. *Personnel Review*, 36(5), 661–683.

Wagner, J. A., & Hollenbeck, J. R. (2015). *Organizational behavior: Securing competitive advantage* (2nd. ed.). New York: Routledge.

Werner, J. (2000). Implications of OCB and contextual performance for human resource management. *Human Resource Management Review*, 10(1), 3–24.

Xhelilaj, E., & Sakaj, B. (2018). A Review of Leadership Behaviour of Maritime Officers in International Shipping. *Pomorstvo*, *32*(1), 76–79.

Yeh, H., & Hong, D. (2012). The mediating effect of organizational commitment on leadership type and job performance. *The Journal of Human Resource and Adult Learning*, 8(2), 50–59.

Yılmaz, H., & Karahan, A. (2010). Liderlik davranışı, örgütsel yaratıcılık ve işgören performansı arasındaki ilişkilerin incelenmesi: Uşak'ta bir araştırma. *Yönetim ve Ekonımi Dergisi*, 17(2), 145–158.

Yukl, G. (2002). *Leadership in organization* (5th. ed.). New Jersey: Prentice Hall.

Yücel, İ., & Akgül, İ. (2016). Liderlik stilleri ile örgütsel bağlılık arasındaki ilişkide iş tatmininin aracılık etkisi: Akademisyenler üzerine bir çalışma, *C.Ü. İktisadi ve İdari Bilimler Dergisi*, 17(1) 209–226.

Özge Can

Alternative Work Arrangements in Organizations: Key Dimensions and Future Directions

1 Introduction

Today, the nature of work and how the work is organized are often defined by a high degree of temporality, fragmentation, informality and contingency, generally described as alternative or non-standard work arrangements. We have been witnessing changing premises of employee involvement in organizations underlying recent employment and organizational transformations. Work becomes intermediated through diverse types of agencies including platforms, temporary work agencies, labor subcontractors, multi-employer sites, giving rise to new forms and practices for organizing across shifting and fuzzy boundaries. Within this process, regular, permanent, standard jobs are replaced by more precarious, irregular, casual and insecure forms of employment. Such emerging trends of employment pave the way to extensive occupational, organizational and social outcomes.

As opposed to these current developments, standard work arrangements have been usually identified in terms of long durations and specific locations where work is performed (Kallinikos, 2003; Felfe, Schmook, Schyns and Six, 2008). Such traditional employment relationships are described through the codes of standardized working time and continuous employment and constitute the model upon which labor contracts, laws and policies have been made (Arnold and Bongiovi, 2013). Standardized employment contract offers relatively high degrees of consistency, security, and dependability for employees and organizations (Felfe et al. 2018). In recent years, this standard work arrangement has been challenged and replaced by temporary, flexible and precarious employment forms as increasing number of employees hold jobs that differ from the standard, long-term work contracts. In the formation of non-traditional work model through years, first flexibility (the ability to make easy changes on wage levels, mobility, the use of skills and etc.) became a widespread phenomenon in the 1980s and 1990s followed by different manifestations of new and alternative arrangements including increasing informalization (unregulated labor markets), casualization (short-term employment), contractualization (outsourced work), and lately, transformed into the so-called "precarious work" which signifies a new phase in work relationships (Kalleberg, 2009; Arnold and Bongiovi, 2013).

It should be clear that all the aforementioned changes have been embedded in a historical context of newly evolving organizational forms. Alternative work arrangements have been closely associated with the emergence of "post-bureaucratic" organizational forms characterized by a concentration of core activities and outsourcing others, reduced hierarchy, diffuse control regimes, and enhanced fragmentation, complexity and instability (Farrell and Morris, 2017). Intensified competition and far-reaching technological development have facilitated the rise of these post-bureaucratic forms which differ extensively from the classic "bureaucratic forms" regarding their structure, processes and coordinating mechanisms (Morris, Farrell and Reed, 2016). Combining these characteristics in its very essence, temporary organizational forms (project-based organizations) have become an enduring part of the reality of today's business, implying that the change in the organization of work is closely intertwined with our understanding of occupations, workplaces, organizations and industries. Such a unified perspective has also been increasingly appreciated by researches from diverse fields.

Related to these developments, recently organization studies have a renewed interest on work and jobs to account for the fact that central organizational activity is undertaken by people that depend on their labor power for survival. This reengagement entails the consideration of possible conflicts, altered relationships, threatened identities and various positive and negative outcomes at work regarding how employees both individually and collectively think and behave at the workplace and beyond. It requires closer attention to fundamental changes in employment relations and the form of organizing. Perhaps more than anything, temporary, fragmented and contingent work raises vital questions about the sustainability of work and organizations. With non-standard forms of employment and work arrangements, division of labor is redefined and tensions and contradictions are more likely to arise regarding the issues including the very nature and meaning of work.

By exploring the relevant theoretical approaches, empirical findings and divergent insights, this study intends to contribute to the ongoing discussions on nonstandard work arrangements and precarious work with a specific aim of examining how their impact on the employees' attitudes and behaviors as well as organizational outcomes can be better framed and understood within the contemporary world of organizational relations. Through a systematic review of the literature and evaluation of existing findings, this chapter presents a comprehensive discussion on this essential issue and provides a number of key implications.

2 The Definition and Different Types of Nonstandard Work Arrangements

So far, many studies have highlighted the common nature and types of nonstandard work arrangements (e.g. Kalleberg, 2009; 2012; Mastracci and Thompson, 2005; Broschak and Davis-Blake, 2006; Chen and Brudney, 2009; Cappelli and Keller, 2013). According to Kalleberg et al. (2003), standard work comprises a full-time job with a fixed schedule which is controlled by the employer at a certain location. It is also expected to continue in the long-run. Even though the specifics of nonstandard work arrangements (NSWA) can vary greatly, in principle, they lack at least a number of the attributes of standard work (Broschak and Davis-Blake, 2006). Relatedly, Mastracci and Thompson (2005, p. 299) define NSWA as "those other than full-time, permanent positions and those that involve individuals whose services are acquired via a contractual arrangement with another organization".

Some other terms have also been utilized to refer the changing side of employment, all sharing the common feature of representing something in contrast to the traditional or standard work arrangement (Chen and Brudney, 2009). As an example, the new pattern of employment is commonly known under the label of "precarious work" (Kalleberg, 2009; Kalleberg and Vallas, 2017; Arnold and Bongiovi, 2013), "contingent work" (Feldman 2006; Barley and Kunda, 2006; Lemmergaard, 2011) and "temporary work" (Galais and Moser, 2009). Kalleberg describes what he means by precarious work as "employment that is uncertain, unpredictable, and risky from the point of view of the worker" (2009, p. 2). He emphasizes that even though the notion is not necessarily unique to our time, it has grown and become much more obvious in the last three decades. The term of contingent labor on the other hand describes a set of different "short-term employment settings including part-time work, temporary jobs, contracted, outsourced and home-based work" (Barley and Kunda, 2006, p. 45). It is usually limited in scope, consists of fewer working hours per week, and does not involve a lasting membership to any single organization (Feldman, 2006). The terms summarized above either refer to the different yet complementary aspects of NSWA or reveal its similar attributes under different labels.

Perhaps the best way to understand the depth and scope of NSWA is to identify its key types according to time, place, number and kind of employers. Since NSWAs can vary greatly across firms, industries and nations, researchers should be careful about the particular context such work arrangements are investigated.

One of the most widely cited source for classifying NSWA into different categories in the literature is the U.S. Bureau of Labor Statistics. According to the most updated release of the Bureau (2017), the main four types of NSWA are as follows: *Independent contractors* include all independent employees and freelancers whether self-employed or work on salary and wage. *On-call workers* are composed of workers who are called to work only when it is needed. *Temporary agency workers* are those who are paid by a professional work agency, regardless the duration of the employment. *Workers provided by contract firms* are employed by a company that provides their services to other organizations under contract. Contract firm is the lawful employer while operational management and control is left to the client organization (Cappelli and Keller, 2013).

Still, other studies offer alternative categorizations. For instance, it is suggested that NSWAs can be logically grouped into two major categories (e.g. Broschak and Davis-Blake, 2006; Broschak, Davis-Blake and Block, 2008). The first category includes independent contractors and contract workers, whether self-employed or employed by some other organization who are not legal employees of the organization for which they provide their services. The second category comprises part-time and temporary workers either being legal employees of the organization they provide services for, or those who can easily make claims for a legal status in this organization (Broschak and Davis-Blake, 2006). Another simple classification was made by Felfe and his colleagues (2008), giving references mostly to European countries rather than the U.S. The first form includes *temporary workers* having a limited-time employment with an organization, providing flexibility to both the employer and the employee. The other form consists of *freelancers* who are not a member of any company but self-employed with contracts, being employed by one or more client organizations for a specific project or assignment. Nowadays, certain occupations are dominated by freelance workers and sometimes known and trusted ex-insiders are contracted as freelancers (Farrell et al. 2017).

3 Key Factors Underlying the Use of Nonstandard Work Arrangements

There have been several attempts in the literature for identifying the key global, economic, political and social forces as the underlying factors paving the way to the current prominence of nonstandard work arrangements. The macro-level factors include neoliberalism, globalization, intensive international competition, legal and technological changes, political, institutional and economic uncertainties, growing market volatility, privatization and deregulation in markets (e.g. Kalleberg, 2009; Katz and Kruger, 2017). Besides these broad forces, the need for flexibility, level of unionization, high employment costs, potential for more efficiency gains, increased rent incentives, the motive for flattening the organization and importing relevant knowledge from outside can be listed as the specific predictors at the firm-level (e.g. Chen and Brudney, 2009; Kalleberg et al. 2003; Katz and Kruger, 2017). It can be argued that all these latter organizational-level motivations emerge from the single desire to survive in an intensively competitive environment.

Among the firm-level or demand-side factors, the effort to maximize competitive advantage and staying close to core competences through flexibility can be the most critical one (Lemmergaard, 2011). Thus, a common explanation to the increasing use NSWAs is the flexibility they provide to the organization, referring to the ability of adjusting the number of workers and the terms of their employment (Kalleberg et al. 2003). Restructuring, downsizing and outsourcing decisions are all considered as linked to this flexibility motivation as employers add more temporary workers while laying off permanent employees (Cappelli and Keller, 2013). While employers may reduce costs based on savings from salaries and wages, the most important compensation saving is regarded as the provision of employment benefits. The costs associated with hiring and laying off permanent employees may also play a role in the preference for NSWAs. Since one of the core activities of unions is protecting job security and job quality of its members, unionization is also correlated with the increased use of NSWAs. Hence, overall significant motivations to use more nonstandard workers is to provide more flexibility, to overcome possible labor shortages, to adjust to changing demand levels, to save costs on wages, training, fringe benefits and hiring and layoffs and to reduce the effect of organized labor.

Strong evidence have been presented in research regarding the pervasiveness of NSWAs across different jobs and occupations, firms, industries, and nations as a result of the predictors described above. Although nonstandard contingent work is widespread across several contexts, important differences in the content, type and extent of NSWAs have been indicated along the following factors: national context and state of labor market (e.g. Kalleberg, 2012; Kalleberg and Vallas, 2017, Keller and Seifert, 2013), specific industry (Katz and Kruger, 2017), large vs. small-size establishments, seasonal vs. non-seasonal work (Kalleberg et al. 2003), more vs. less hierarchical organizations (Pedulla, 2013), public vs. private sector (e.g. Mastracci and Thompson, 2005; Yu, 2013), service vs. manufacturing sector, online vs. offline work, and particular type of job (Kretsos and Livanos, 2016). Besides organizational and industrial setting, individual differences across workers including age, gender, family background, experience and education as well as their preference towards nonstandard work (e.g. Feldman, 2006; Katz and Kruger, 2017) create important variations in the degree of NSWAs present today.

4 How Nonstandard Work Arrangements Shape Employee Outcomes

Despite considerable research being conducted on nonstandard work arrangements investigating its individual and organizational outcomes, there has been no attempt to compare, review and evaluate the accumulated empirical findings in a systematic way. Thus, this section represents such an evaluation based on three main issues: Attitudes and behaviors of workers employed under NSWAs, dissimilar outcomes based on different types of NSWAs, and consequences of blending standard and nonstandard workers in the same organizational setting.

A significant part of the ongoing research concerning the effects of NSWAs have focused on whether and how nonstandard workers think and behave. In view of that, several positive and negative attitudes towards work have been surveyed. As one of the recent examples, Katz and Kruger (2017) investigated how satisfied various types of nonstandard workers are with their respective employment arrangement. They found that a large number of employees working under different NSWA categories prefer a permanent job with regularly scheduled hours. On the other hand, workers who become independent contractors and freelancers were found to be in favor of their current work arrangement. This contrast between the two groups might imply that while some individuals seek contingent and temporary works to gain independence and to be their own boss, the others engage in such work out of necessity and unavailability of a standard job alternative.

Job satisfaction and commitment levels of nonstandard workers have also been examined in several studies. For instance, in their study on German employees, Felfe and his colleagues (2008) found that form of employment emerges as a new focus of commitment along with the existing organizational and occupational foci. Similar to the aforementioned findings by Katz and Kruger (2019), they provided evidence that except for self-employment situations, commitment in alternative forms of employment is not as high as commitment in traditional forms, suggesting that temporary work may not be that attractive for individuals. Another study discloses that contingent employees' performance appears to be more closely related with job satisfaction than those in conventional employment relationships, and the correlation between job satisfaction and work performance is highest for typical temporary workers than freelancers (Marler et al.

2002). In another interesting study, longitudinal analysis reveals that commitment to the client organization can be damaging for temporary agency workers, providing evidence for both beneficial and negative effects of organizational commitment for them based on a shorter vs. longer time frames (Galais and Moser, 2009).

Evidence has also been provided on work outcomes other than job satisfaction and commitment. For example, in their study on UK television industry, Farrell and Morris (2017) found that almost all freelance workers in the industry declare work intensification, reduction in benefits, the feeling of job insecurity and reduced solidarity. The growth of perceived job insecurity by more precarious work has been a recurring theme in the whole literature, as it was evident in Kalleberg's pivotal study in 2009. Moreover, it is suggested that NSWAs do not only influence work attitudes and predict work-related outcomes but they also have a wide range of consequences outside the workplace including deteriorating personal and family well-being as well as community life in the form of weakened social engagements (Kalleberg, 2009).

Finally, Kalleberg and Vallas (2017) argue that individuals are likely to adopt different, fractured responses to precarious work in the form of exit, voice and loyalty instead of identical responses. They claim that while responses of exit and voice mostly relate to working-class communities and occupations, loyalty is more associated with high educated, office employees who are more likely to engage in market logic and "career management" ideology.

A second and wider set of studies aims either to compare employee outcomes based on different types of NSWA or to examine the impact of contingent and temporary workers on traditional, standard employees. As an important example for both, five employment arrangements (one standard and four alternative forms) were compared in a comprehensive study by Van Aerden and his colleagues in 2015. They found that these five work types show significant relationships with separate indicators of job satisfaction, ability to stay in employment, climate of perceived safety and work-related well-being, emphasizing the importance of the degree of intrinsic work associated with different alternative work arrangements.

Combining the two research aims, Pedulla's study (2013) reveals how three types of alternative work have different outcomes for the traditionally employed workers in the same workplace. He provides evidence that the presence of temporary workers is negatively associated with perceived job security, perceived social status, and organizational trust of standard workers. His findings also suggest that differences exist among the impact of diverse types of contingent workers. Namely, independent contractors (as opposed to temporary or on-call workers), are not evaluated as competitors or potential replacements by standard workers. Consequently, no significant relationship was found between the presence of freelancers and standard workers' outcomes.

Finally, several empirical studies suggest that the workplace balance is usually a very sensitive one and it becomes a challenge to construct fairness and harmony among the two groups. As evidence to that, higher proportions of nonstandard workers in an organization are found to be connected to unfavorable attitudes toward supervisors and coworkers, higher turnover intentions, and lower level of work-related helping behaviors for entire workforce (Broschak and Davis-Blake, 2006). Evidence also shows that a blended workforce affects manager-employee relations negatively, decrease standard employees' loyalty, and increase their intention to quit their job and participate in a trade union (Davis-Blake et al. 2003). Another piece of support on the likely negative effects of contingent workers on standard workers was presented by Banerjee and her colleagues (2012). According to this study, although contingent workers have little effect on the workload perceptions of traditional employees, their presence strongly reduces their perceived job security, job satisfaction and organizational loyalty.

5 Implications and Suggestions for the Future of Employment Relationships

It is rather surprising that despite the amount of evidence on the growth and prevalence of NSWAs around the world and their possible impact on particular employee attitudes, limited discussion has been provided on their implications on the current and future state of worker-organization relationships. How certain jobs, occupations and organizational processes are being radically transformed by these strong forces and what should be expected for the near future remains to be explored. Above anything else, increasingly precarious, temporary and contingent work arrangements across different industries and economies pose challenges for the organizations in sustaining effective and positive work relationships. The understanding of the frustrations, problems and conflicts of nonstandard workers is the essential first step to build sustainable work relationships which is critical for both the individuals and the organization itself.

Particularly, I believe that there is an urgent need for consideration of possible human resource management (HRM) strategies that can be designed and implemented to reduce the negative health-related, psychological and social impacts of being a contingent and/or temporary worker. It is important for organizations to pay attention to establishing equality and mutual trust-based relationships among all worker types, regardless of the label they are given. The review of the relevant literature suggests that usually there is a huge distance and lack of communication between standard and nonstandard workers, giving rise to tensions that can be detrimental for organizations. Gaining flexibility, cost reduction and agility might come with a huge loss of sense of belonging, engagement and motivation to work. As Mallon and Duberley claim (2000), new work forms require not just changed behavior from individuals but also from organizations. If organizations gain from the existence of nonstandard workers, they also need to provide something to contribute.

As another key discussion topic, the alternative work arrangements appear to become more complex by each passing day with respect to the emergence of different work forms making it challenging for both researchers and practitioners to sort out and predict possible consequences. There is a need for creating alternative initiatives to alleviate the tensions associated with NSWAs including establishing new values about work altogether. As the role of organizations and their HRM function in dealing with nonstandard workers remains a question mark, future research should investigate how HR practices must be designed to accommodate the needs of individuals involved in NSWA. For instance, there should be a real debate on whether the arrangements imposed by the employer are reasonable and desirable for the employees. Overall, following the rare yet rightful calls by researchers in the literature (e.g. Pfeffer, 2010), existing tensions should be redefined towards developing sustainable relationships between employees and organizations by emphasizing mutual interdependencies and collaborations.

References

Arnold, D., & Bongiovi, J. R. (2013). Precarious, Informalizing, and Flexible Work: Transforming Concepts and Understandings. *American Behavioral Scientist*, *57*(3), 289–308.

Banerjee, M., Tolbert, P. S., & DiCiccio, T. (2012). Friend or Foe? The Effects of Contingent Employees on Standard Employees' Work Attitudes. *International Journal of Human Resource Management*, *23*(11), 2180–2204.

Barley, S. R., & Kunda, G. (2006). Contracting: A New Form of Professional Practice. *Academy of Management Perspectives*, *20*(1), 45–66.

Broschak, J. P., & Davis-Blake, A. (2006). Mixing Standard Work and Nonstandard Deals: The Consequences of Heterogeneity in Employment Arrangements. *Academy of Management Journal*, *49*(2), 371.

Broschak, J. P., Davis-Blake, A., & Block, E. S. (2008). Nonstandard, Not Substandard: The Relationship among Work Arrangements, Work Attitudes and Job Performance. *Work & Occupations*, *35*(1), 3.

Bureau of Labor Statistics. (2017). *Contingent and Alternative Employment Arrangements*. Retrieved November 25, 2018, from https://www.bls.gov/news.release/pdf/conemp.pdf.

Cappelli, P., & Keller, J. R. (2013). A Study of the Extent and Potential Causes of Alternative Employment Arrangements. *ILR Review 66*(4): 874–901.

Chen, A., & Brudney, J. L. (2009). A Cross-Sector Comparison of Using Nonstandard Workers: Explaining Use and Impacts on the Employment Relationship. *Administration & Society*, *41*(3), 313–339.

Davis-Blake, A., Broschak, J. P., & George, E. (2003). Happy Together? How Using Nonstandard Workers Affects Exit, Voice, and Loyalty among Standard Employees. *Academy of Management Journal*, *46*(4), 475–485.

Farrell, C., & Morris, J. (2017). Neo-bureaucratic Organisational Forms, Technology, Control and Contingent Work: The Case of UK TV. *New Technology, Work & Employment*, *32*(2), 115–130.

Feldman, D. C. (2006). Toward a New Taxonomy for Understanding the Nature and Consequences of Contingent Employment. *Career Development International 11*(1), 28–47.

Felfe, J., Schmook, R., Schyns, B., & Six, B. (2008). Does the Form of Employment Make a Difference?—Commitment of Traditional, Temporary, and Self-employed Workers. *Journal of Vocational Behavior*, *72*, 81–94.

Galais, N., & Moser, K. (2009). Organizational Commitment and the Well-being of Temporary Agency Workers: A Longitudinal Study. *Human Relations*, *62*(4), 589–620.

Kalleberg, A. L. (2009). Precarious Work, Insecure Workers: Employment Relations in Transition. *American Sociological Review*, (1), 1–22.

Kalleberg, A. L. (2012). Job Quality and Precarious Work: Clarifications, Controversies, and Challenges. *Work and Occupations*, *39*(4), 427–448.

Kalleberg, A. L., Reynolds, J., & Marsden, P. V. (2003). Externalizing Employment: Flexible Staffing Arrangements in US Organizations. *Social Science Research 32*, 525–552.

Kalleberg, A. L., & Vallas, S. P. (2017). Probing Precarious Work: Theory, Research, and Politics. *Research in the Sociology of Work*, *31* (1).

Kallinikos, J. (2003). Work, Human Agency and Organizational Forms: An Anatomy of Fragmentation. *Organization Studies*, *24*(4), 595–618.

Katz, L. F. & Krueger, A. B. (2019). The Rise and Nature of Alternative Work Arrangements in the United States, 1995–2015, *ILR Review*, 72(2), 382–416.

Keller, B., & Seifert, H. (2013). Atypical Employment in Germany. Forms, Development, Patterns. *Transfer: European Review of Labour and Research*, *19*(4), 457.

Kretsos, L., & Livanos, I. (2016). The Extent and Determinants of Precarious Employment in Europe. *International Journal of Manpower, 37*(1), 25–43.

Lemmergaard, J. (2011). Questioning the Assumption that Contingent Work Arrangements Reshape Organizations and Relationships. *Team Performance Management: An International Journal,* (5/6), 244.

Marler, J. H., Barringer, M. W., & Milkovich, G. T. (2002). Boundaryless and Traditional Contingent Employees: Worlds Apart. *Journal of Organizational Behavior, 23*(4), 425–453.

Mastracci S.H., & Thompson, J. R. (2005). Nonstandard Work Arrangements in the Public Sector. *Review of Public Personnel Administration,* 25(4), 299–324.

Morris, J., Farrell, C., & Reed, M. (2016). The Indeterminacy of 'Temporariness': Control and Power in Neo-bureaucratic Organizations and Work in UK Television. *Human Relations, 69*(12), 2274–2297.

Pedulla, D. S. (2013). The Hidden Costs of Contingency: Employers' Use of Contingent Workers and Standard Employees' Outcomes. *Social Forces, 92*(2), 691–722.

Pfeffer, J. (2010). Building Sustainable Organizations: The Human Factor. *Academy of Management Perspectives, 24*(1), 34–45.

Van Aerden, K., Moors, G., Levecque, K., & Vanroelen, C. (2015). The Relationship between Employment Quality and Work-related Well-being in the European Labor Force. *Journal of Vocational Behavior, 86,* 66–76.

Yu, W-H (2013). It's Who You Work With: Effects of Workplace Shares of Nonstandard Employees and Women in Japan. *Social Forces, 92*(1), 25–58.

Ahmet Sait Özkul and Ömer Lütfi Antalyalı

The Moderator Role of Negative Environment Perceptions in the Effect of Achievement Motivation on Work Values in Entrepreneurship[1]

1 Introduction

Hazan and Shaver (1990), who conducted the pioneering study of the attachment theory in the field of organization, discussed the attachment system that functions in the organizational environment in terms of individual differences. With this pioneering study, a basis emerged for discussing the relationships between various dimensions of workplace performance and styles of attachment. Later, authors reached the idea that the type of emotional attachment between the leader and their followers and in group dynamics and relationships could be similar to those in their childhood, adolescence or adulthood period towards their parents, friends and romantic partners (Mikulincer and Shaver, 2016: 473). It may be argued that, for individuals who act with a motivation to succeed in entrepreneurship, the ways of perceiving the environment or workplace (setting) they are in will be reflected in their values. Nevertheless, the relationship among the adult attachment styles, work values and achievement motivations of university students receiving education on entrepreneurship was investigated, and important findings were reached. In this context, it is believed that the findings related to the relationships in question will make significant contributions to the literature on management, organization and business/business management.

2 Attachment Theory and Styles of Adult Attachment

According to the attachment theory, relationships that individuals form at early ages with their caregivers have a determining role in their feelings, thoughts and

1 The previous version of this study was the manuscript titled "*The Moderator Role of Negative Environment Perceptions in the Effect of Achievement Motivation on Work Values in Entrepreneurship*" which was presented at the 25th National Conference of Management and Organization organized by Başkent University. This manuscript was later turned into a book chapter after broadening based on criticisms and recommendations.

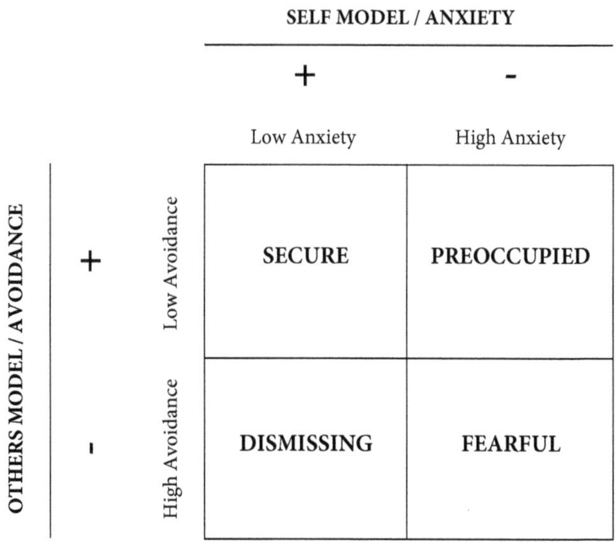

Fig. 1: Four Category Models. Source: (Sümer, 2006: 2)

behaviors at further stages of their lives (Selçuk et al., 2005: 2). Bartholomew and Horowitz (1991) and Brennan, Clark and Shaver (1998) defined four different styles of attachment based on the dimensions of anxiety and avoidance. As seen in Fig. 1, the main dimensions are formed by the relationships between the anxiety dimension and the self model and between the avoidance dimension and the others model. A secure style of attachment is defined in the avoidance (positive others model) dimension with a low level of anxiety (positive self model). A fearful style of attachment, which is the opposite of the one above, is described by high levels in both dimensions (negative self and negative others). A preoccupied style of attachment is defined as high anxiety (negative self) and low avoidance (positive others). Finally, a dismissing style of attachment is described with low anxiety (positive self) and high avoidance (negative others) (Sümer, 2006: 2).

3 The Theory of Basic Needs and Achievement Motivation

McClelland described *need for achievement* as the individual's effort to become very good based on some certain standards (McClelland, 1961). While the need for achievement includes the individual's needs to obtain an achievement with high standards, overcome difficult/complicated tasks and do what they do better than others (Daft, 2008: 529), it also involves the desire of the individual to surpass self (Heintz and Steele-Johnson, 2004). Those with a high need for achievement are individuals with stronger tendency for independence (Hofstede, 1991), distinguish themselves from their peers regarding willingness to show a higher performance and seek situations where they are responsible with the purpose of creating new/innovative solutions (McClelland, 1961, 1975, 1985). Achieved entrepreneurs usually come from among individuals who have high needs for achievement (Brant, 2005; Shane, Locke and Collins, 2012). Additionally, McClelland (1965) stated that individuals with high needs for achievement are more entrepreneurial than those with low levels of such needs.

4 Work Values

Work is significant throughout a person's life in terms of time. Individuals within this time period/process develop a set of values as in their other activities (İnançoğlu, 2002: 150). Additionally, the most effective role is taken on by spiritual-religious factors in the individuals' perception of life being stripped from a simple act and turned into a worldview and/or understanding of the world by patterns of moral expression (Ülgener, 1981: 14). Therefore, work ideology/understanding covers the attitudes, beliefs and ideas of the members of a community, and such concepts are accepted as work values. Work values not only determine the characteristics wanted and desired by a group or community but also express the approach of the individual towards work (Özkul, 1997: 15).

5 Participants

The study was carried out in the class for "entrepreneurship" which was offered as a common elective course in the spring semester of the academic year of 2016–2017 at the Faculty of Economics and Administrative Sciences at Süleyman Demirel University. Among the students, those who had the idea of "building own business" were considered to be those who "had intent for entrepreneurship", while those who did not share the idea were considered to be those who "did not have intent for entrepreneurship".

6 Data Collection Tools

All the scales used a 7-point Likert-type scoring.

Work Objectives Test: Tevrüz et al. (2010) shortened the scale (WOT – Work Objectives Test) that was developed by Tevrüz and Turgut (2004) and examined it with 3 dimensions. In the 12-item scale, 3 items measure normative, 2 items measure earthly and 6 items measure individual values. The Cronbach's alpha

coefficients that were calculated in this study for reliability were 0.65 for normative values, 0.70 for earthly values and 0.80 for individual values.
ECR-RS: ECR-RS (Experiences in Close Relationships - Revised Short Form) was developed by Fraley et al. (2006) by shortening ECR-R and adapted into Turkish by Antalyalı and Özkul (2016) (Yakın İlişkilerde Yaşantılar Envanterinin Kısa Formu). The 9-item scale has 2 dimensions, 3 items measure the anxiety dimension, while the other 6 measure the avoidance dimension. The Cronbach's alpha reliability coefficients were calculated as 0.76 for anxious attachment and 0.77 for avoidant attachment.
Achievement Motivation: The *Achievement Motivation* scale which was developed by the first author of this study and is now at the stage of publication was adapted from the scales created by Steers and Braunstein (1976) and Yamaguchi (2003). It is one-dimensional and consists of 6 items. The Cronbach's alpha coefficient that was calculated for reliability was 0.75.

7 Data Analysis

The data were analyzed using the SPSS and STATA package software. The moderating effect was analyzed using the PROCESS macro that makes calculations based on the least squares method of regression that was developed to be integrated into the SPSS and SAS programs by Andrew F. Hayes, one of the professors of the Department of Psychology at Ohio State University, and described by Hayes (2013) himself in detail.

8 Findings

The mean, standard deviation, Skewness and Kurtosis values of the measured variables, scale reliability coefficients and correlations among the variables are summarized in Tab. 1.

53.8 % of the participants were male, 46.2 % were female, and the mean age of the participants was 21.11. The values on the diagonal of Tab. 1 show the Cronbach's alpha reliability coefficients of the scales. Relatively, the scale with the lowest reliability was on normative values (0.653), while the one with the highest reliability was on individual values (0.802). The Skewness and Kurtosis values in all the variables to be used in the analyses were in the range of -1.5 to 1.5 as stated by Tabachnick and Fidell (2013) as conditions of normal distribution. So, parametric tests were used. Among the mean values calculated over 7, the highest mean values were in work values, while the lowest were in the levels of anxious and avoidant attachment levels. The correlation between age and achievement

Tab. 1: Descriptive Statistics, Reliability and Correlation Findings

Variable	Age	1	2	3	4	5	6
Achievement Motivation (1)	0.25**	**(0.754)**					
Normative Values (2)	0.15	0.11	**(0.653)**				
Earthly Values (3)	0.06	0.06	0.61**	**(0.699)**			
Individual Values (4)	0.04	0.12	0.66**	0.60**	**(0.802)**		
Anxious Attachment (5)	0.03	-0.14	-0.17	-0.28**	-0.27**	**(0.755)**	
Avoidant Attachment (6)	-0.08	-0.19*	-0.02	0.03	-0.11	0.03	**(0.770)**
Mean	21.11	5.05	5.62	5.82	5.56	3.03	3.20
SD	1.28	1.03	1.11	1.18	1.09	1.39	1.06
Skewness	1.45	0.03	-0.61	-0.62	-0.69	0.31	0.27
Kurtosis	3.21	-0.75	-0.22	-0.89	-0.20	-0.80	-0.16

The values on the diagonal line are the Cronbach's alpha reliability coefficients of the scale.
**$p<0.01$, *$p<0.05$

motivation ($r=0.25$, $p<0.01$) is not expected. Moreover, it is known that those with high achievement motivation levels are more successful entrepreneurs (McClelland, 1965; Brant, 2005; Shane, Locke and Collins, 2012). Students of older ages might have selected the entrepreneurship course with more tangible intentions as they had high levels of achievement motivation. As the coefficient is low and no measurement was made towards measuring entrepreneurship success, this finding will no longer be discussed.

The correlation among the normative, earthly and individual work values was very high ($r>0.60$, $p<0.01$). Additionally, the negative relationships between anxious attachment and earthly values ($r=-0.28$, $p<0.01$) and individual values ($r=-0.27$, $p<0.01$) were noteworthy. Moreover, within the scope of the study, whether the participants had an intent for entrepreneurship or not was measured by one question as described in the "participants" section. Independent-samples t-test was used to determine whether or not there were any differences in the findings obtained from the variables based on both gender and presence of intent for entrepreneurship, and the results are shown in Tab. 2.

The work values of the women and those who had intent were higher in comparison to the men and those who did not have intent in all 3 dimensions (normative, earthly and individual) ($p<0.05$). No significant difference was observed in the other variables ($p>0.05$). The finding that the women had higher work

Tab. 2: Difference Tests Based on Intent for Entrepreneurship and Gender

Values	**Intent for Entrepreneurship[a] A Ort (ss)**	**No Intent for Entrepreneurship[b] B Ort (ss)**	**A-B Difference (t)**	**Male[c] C Ort (ss)**	**Female[d] D Ort (ss)**	**C-D Difference (t)**
Achievement Motivation	**5.08** (1.15)	**5.00** (1.01)	0.42	**4.96** (1.10)	**5.14** (0.93)	-1.00
Normative Values	**5.89** (1.00)	**5.14** (1.14)	3.75^{**}	**5.37** (1.24)	**5.91** (0.87)	-2.69^{**}
Earthly Values	**6.07** (1.07)	**5.39** (1.23)	3.16^{**}	**5.62** (1.26)	**6.04** (1.05)	-1.96^{*}
Individual Values	**5.78** (1.05)	**5.18** (1.07)	2.97^{**}	**5.31** (1.20)	**5.85** (0.89)	-2.73^{**}
Anxious Attachment	**2.89** (1.35)	**3.27** (1.44)	-1.47	**3.07** (1.47)	**3.01** (1.29)	0.23
Avoidant Attachment	**3.30** (1.12)	**3.02** (0.94)	1.44	**3.17** (1.13)	**3.26** (0.96)	-0.48

[a] N=76, [b] N=44, [c] N=64, [d] N=55, $^{**}p<0.01$, $^{*}p<0.05$

values in comparison to the men was in agreement with the findings in previous studies (Tevrüz et al., 2010).

This study questioned the extent to which the levels of work values of an individual determine whether they have intent to become an entrepreneur or not. A logistic regression analysis was conducted by using the STATA statistical package software. A significant result was not expected as there would be a high correlation between the variables in a regression analysis that uses the normative, earthly and individual values in combination. The three-variable model was tested anyway, and it was concluded that the model was not significant ($p>0.05$).

Each work value was separately defined as the independent variable, and logistic regression analysis was carried out to determine its relationship with intent for entrepreneurship. Normative values were the best in predicting intent for entrepreneurship ($R^2=0.08$, $B=0.65$, $p<0.01$, odds ratio=1.91, $p<0.01$). Earthly values ($R^2=0.06$, $B=0.50$, $p<0.01$, odds ratio=1.65, $p<0.01$) and individual values ($R^2=0.05$, $B=0.51$, $p<0.01$, odds ratio=1.67, $p<0.01$) could predict intent for entrepreneurship alone. The model error was insignificant for all the analyses ($p>0.05$). Each of the work values could separately predict whether or not a person had an intent for entrepreneurship. Those with higher work values had higher probabilities of having intent for entrepreneurship.

As seen in Tab. 1, there was no significant relationship between achievement motivation and work values ($p>0.05$). Additionally, , in individuals with negative perception of their environment (highly avoidant attachment), attachment motivation would form more earthly values. The hypothesis "as the avoidant attachment levels of people increase, the effects of their achievement motivations on their earthly values also increase" was formed, and it was tested by using Model 1 in the SPSS PROCESS macro. As earthly values varied based on gender and intent for entrepreneurship, the analyses were controlled for these variables. The findings are shown in Tab. 3.

There was no direct effect of the avoidant attachment level of the individual on their levels of earthly values ($p>0.05$). The model where avoidant attachment is included as a moderator variable was significant ($\Delta R^2=0.05$, $F(1,113)=7.06$, $p<0.01$). The effect of the interaction between avoidant attachment and achievement motivation on the levels of earthly values was positive and significant ($\beta=0.28$, $SE=0.10$, $t=1.44$, $p<0.01$). As the avoidant attachment levels of the participants increased, the effects of their achievement motivations on their earthly values also increased. The effects of achievement motivation on earthly values on different levels of avoidant attachment are shown under Tab. 3 for three levels. While a negative effect was observed in those with low avoidant attachment levels (M-sd), this effect was not significant (effect coefficient=-0.21,

Tab. 3: The Moderator Role of Avoidant Attachment in the Effect of Achievement Motivation on Earthly Values

Independent Variable	***B***	***SE***	***t***	***p***	***LLCI***	***ULCI***
R^2=0,15, F(5,113)=4,93, p<0,01, ΔR²=0,05, F(1,113)=7,06, p<0,01						
CO: Gender	0.31	0.21	1.44	0.15	-0.11	0.73
CO: Intent for Entrepreneurship	-0.68	0.22	-3.06	< 0.01	-1.12	-0.24
Constant	6.34	0.49	12.96	< 0.01	5.37	7.31
Achievement Motivation	0.07	0.10	0.72	0.47	-0.13	0.27
Avoidant Attachment	0.00	0.10	0.00	0.99	-0.20	0.20
Ach. Mot. X Avoidant Attc.	0.28	0.10	2.66	< 0.01	0.07	0.48
	Effect	***SE***	***t***	***p***	***LLCI***	***ULCI***
The effects of achievement motivation on earthly value levels on different levels of avoidant attachment						
-1 *ss*	-0.21	0.15	-1.43	0.16	-0.52	0.08
M	0.07	0.10	0.71	0.47	-0.13	0.27
+1 *ss*	0.36	0.14	2.51	0.01	0.08	0.65

LL = lower limit; CI = 95 % confidence interval; UL = upper limit.
The gender and entrepreneurship intent variables were controlled in the analyses.
The method of 1000 samples bootstrap that was cleaned off bias error was used. Regression coefficients were not standardized. The achievement motivation and avoidant attachment variables were standardized based on the mean (mean centered) before the analysis

p>0.05). The effect coefficient was close to zero in those with moderate avoidant attachment levels (M), as well as being statistically insignificant (effect coefficient=0.07, p>0.05). In those with high levels of avoidant attachment (M+sd), there was a positive and significant effect (effect coefficient=0.36, p<0.05). The variation of the effects of achievement motivation on levels of earthly values based on avoidant attachment levels is shown in Fig. 2.

Avoidant attachment moderated the effects of attachment motivation on earthly values. In those with high levels of avoidant attachment, success motivation affected levels of earthly values positively. There was no significant effect among those who had moderate or low levels of avoidant attachment.

9 Conclusion

According to this study, where important findings were obtained regarding the effects of psychological factors in administrative and organizational field studies, women pay more importance to work values than men. In this case, it may be stated that the role of women in the struggle in life in the names of themselves,

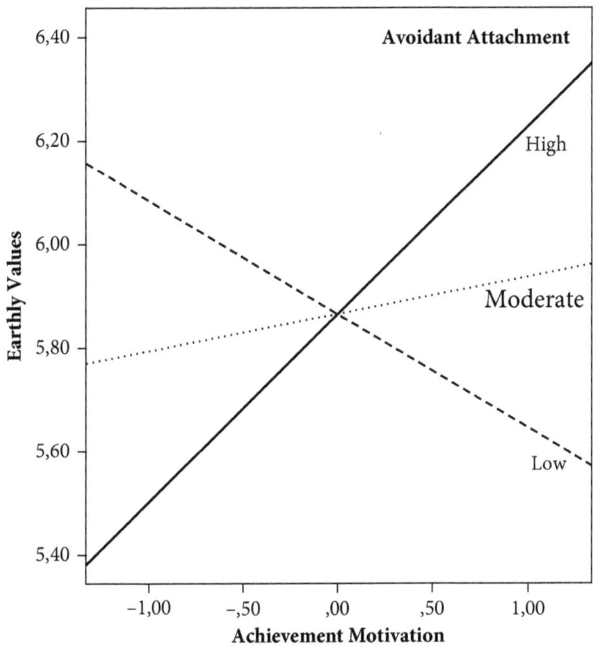

Fig. 2: The Effects of Achievement Motivation on Levels of Earthly Values Based on Avoidant Attachment Levels

their environments and their future has a tendency to increase day by day in terms of consciousness/feelings/practice.

Another important result was about the intent for entrepreneurship. Those who intend to become entrepreneurs pay more importance to work values. Such that, as stated in the findings section, even the intent of the individual towards entrepreneurship may be predicted by looking at the level of importance they pay to work values. Accordingly, the perceptions of individuals who are preparing for professional life on work values should be discussed by considering their entrepreneurship tendency/training, economic conditions, personality traits and the social environment they have grown up in.

In the relationship between adult attachment styles and work values, as the anxious attachment levels decreased, earthly and individual values increased. It may be stated that individuals with low anxiety about their self are more likely to embrace individual work values that will support their personal development, satisfy their needs/desires and make their time efficient/fun. In addition to this, it may also be stated that individuals with low anxiety levels also value earthly work values that may be summarized as earning one's living and obtaining status. In this context, it may be argued that individuals in the "positive self – positive others" model pay importance to earthly values while earning their living and statuses by trusting others and maybe for others' benefit, while individuals in the "positive self – negative others" model pay importance to individual values for protecting themselves as they do not trust others.

The most important result of the study, which is a recommendation for all organizations that are active in the business world, education and management, was that the moderator role of avoidant attachment in the effects of achievement motivation on the earthly (living and status) dimension of work values was demonstrated. In other words, in people who have negative perceptions about their environment (those who attach avoidantly), as achievement motivations increase, tendency to pay importance to earthly values such as status, prestige, money, power, safety of future and economic freedom will also increase, such people will no longer need their environment, and they will desire to build a life that is more independent and self-sustained. This way, it may be recommended for all managers, leaders and/or mentors who see their employees who provide contributions to the organization as intellectual capital to assess individuals that will take an active role in the professional world by considering psychological factors. This study, which revealed the interaction of the achievement motivations, attachment styles and work values of individuals who will join the professional world, should also be carried out with individuals who are already in the professional world. This way, in the sense of organizational psychology, individuals who are/will be active on all levels of management will be able to *analyze their followers/employees in a more qualified way.*

References

Antalyalı Ö. L., ve Özkul, A. S. 2016. Örgüt ve yönetim araştırmaları için yakın ilişkilerde yaşantılar envanterinin kısa formunun YİYE II K psikometrik açıdan değerlendirilmesi. Balkan Journal of Social Sciences, Aralık, 640–655.

Brant, J. 2005. What one man can do. Inc., Eylül, 145–153.

Daft, R. L. 2008. Management. (8.b.). Ohio: Thomson South-Western.

Fraley, R. C., Niedenthal, P. M., Marks, M. J., Brumbaugh, C. C., ve Vicary, A. 2006. Adult attachment and the perception of emotional expressions: Probing the hyperactivating strategies underlying anxious attachment. Journal of Personality, 74, 1163–1190.

Hayes, A. F. 2013. An introduction to mediation, moderation, and conditional process analysis: A regression-based approach. New York: Guilford Press.

Heintz, P. J., ve Steele-Johnson, D. 2004. Clarifying the conceptual definitions of goal orientation dimensions: Competence, control and evaluation. Organizational Analysis, 12, 5–19.

Hofstede, G. 1991. Cultures and organizations: Software of the mind. Basingstoke: McGraw-Hill.

İnançoğlu, E. 2002. Çalışma değerlerinin örgütsel değişime dirence etkisi. 10. Ulusal Yönetim Organizasyon Kongresi Bildiri Kitabı. Akdeniz Üniversitesi, Antalya, 23–25 Mayıs, 146–160.

McClelland, D. C. 1961. The achieving society. New York: Van Nostrand Reinhold.

McClelland, D. C. 1965. Achievement and entrepreneurship: A longitudinal study. Journal of Personality and Organizational Behavior, 1(4), 389–392.

Mikulincer, M., ve Shaver, P. R. 2016. Attachment in adulthood. Second Edition, New York & London: The Guildford Press.

Özkul, M. 1997. Çalışma sosyolojisi. Isparta.

Selçuk, E., Günaydın, G., Sümer, N., ve Uysal, A. 2005. Yetişkin bağlanma boyutları için yeni bir ölçüm: Yakın ilişkilerde yaşantılar envanteri-II'nin Türk örnekleminde psikometrik açıdan değerlendirilmesi, Türk Psikoloji Yazıları, 8(16), 1–11.

Shane, S., Locke, E. A., ve Collins, C. J. 2012. Entrepreneurial motivation. Human Resource Management Review, 13(2), 257–279.

Steers, R., ve Braunstein, D. 1976. A behaviorally based measure of manifest needs in work settings, Journal of Vocational Behavior, 9(2), 251–265.

Sümer, N. 2006. Ergenlikte ebeveyn tutum ve davranışlarının bağlanma kaygısındaki rolü, Hacettepe Üniversitesi, 11. Ergen Günleri Konuşma Metni.

Tabachnick, B. G., ve Fidell, L. S. 2013. Using Multivariate Statistics. Sixth Edition, Boston: Pearson.

Tevrüz, S., ve Turgut, T. 2004. Çalışma amaçlarının tesbiti ve çalışma amaçları testinin geliştirilmesi. Öneri, 6(22), Haziran, 33–44.

Tevrüz, S., Turgut, T., ve Çinko, M. 2010. Bir merakın peşinde: amaç'tan başarı'ya. 1. Baskı, İstanbul: Beta.

Ülgener, S. F. 1981. İktisadî çözülmenin ahlâk ve zihniyet dünyası, İkinci Baskı, İstanbul: Der Yayınları.

Yamaguchi, I. 2003. The relationships among individual differences, needs and equity sensitivity. Journal of Managerial Psychology, 18(4), 324–344.

Resul Baltaci and Canan Cetin and Burcak Vatansever Durmaz

Servant Leadership

1 Introduction

Servant Leadership (SL) is an oxymoronic term (Sendjaya & Sarros, 2002, p. 57) coined by Robert Greenleaf (1904–1990) in his seminar work "The Servant Leader" published in 1970 (Spears, 1996, p. 33). It is a paradox because it embodies a concept (service) contrary to image of a leader who, in fact, is expected to influence (Northouse, 2016, p. 225; Spears, 2010b, p. 26). Although the idea of a leader who serves and a servant who leads may challenge traditional perspectives to leadership, dynamic conceptual relationships between servanthood and leadership as well as complementary roles (Rachmawati & Lantu, 2014, p. 388) have attracted attention of academics and practitioners recently (Sendjaya & Sarros, 2002, p. 57; Spears, 1996, p. 34). It is also paradoxical that despite recent attraction, the idea that leaders must serve their constituents has been around much longer. To show this point, Sendjaya (2015, p. 16) cites Nair (1994) pointing to ancient monarchs who for over a thousand years had at least professed the importance of service to leadership. They acknowledge that they were in the service of their country and their people – even if their actions were not consistent with this. Modern coronation ceremonies and inaugurations of heads of state, all involve the acknowledgement of service to God, country, and the people. Politicians define their roles in terms of public service, too. In other words, leadership has long been associated with service.

Laub (1999, pp. 11–13) cites Biblical references of SL, as practiced by Jesus Christ by washing feet of his disciples. Jesus taught that a leader's greatness is measured by a total commitment to serve fellow people (Rachmawati & Lantu, 2014, p. 389; Sendjaya & Sarros, 2002, p. 58). Lynch and Friedman (2013, p. 90) reviewed the Torah, and defined Moses as servant leader, too. However, despite long lasting roots and its introduction a few decades ago, there is still no consensus about a definition and theoretical framework of SL (van Dierendonck, 2011, p. 1229).

According to Greenleaf (1977), servant leaders are ones who put other people's needs, aspirations and interests above their own. Their main motivation and deliberate choice is to serve first, contrary to lead first (Laub, 1999, p. 14; Spears, 1996, p. 33). Greenleaf (1977, p. 6) claims that "The servant-leader *is* servant first … It begins with the natural feeling that one wants to serve, to serve *first*. Then conscious choice brings one to aspire to lead. That person is sharply different from one who is *leader* first, perhaps because of the need to assuage an unusual power drive or to acquire material possessions. For such it will be a later choice to serve – after leadership is established. The leader-first and the servant-first are two extreme types. Between them there are shadings and blends that are part of the infinite variety of human nature. The difference manifests itself in the care taken by the servant-first to make sure that other people's highest priority needs are being served. The best test, and difficult to administer, is: Do those served grow as persons? Do they, *while being served*, become healthier, wiser, freer, more autonomous, more likely themselves to become servants? *And*, what is the effect on the least privileged in society; will they benefit, or, at least, not be further deprived?

Burns (1978) asserted similar ideas about leadership: "(Transforming) leadership occurs when one or more persons engage with others in such a way that leaders and followers raise one another to higher levels of motivation and morality…But transforming leadership ultimately becomes *moral* (italics in original) in that it raises the level of human conduct and ethical aspiration of both leader and led, thus it has a transforming effect on both" (cited in Rachmawati & Lantu (2014, p. 388), and Sendjaya & Sarros, 2002, p. 58)

Robert Greenleaf spent most of his career at AT&T in the fields of management, R&D, and education for 38 years. After his retirement, he started a second career that focused on role of education. He worked as a consultant for businesses, educational and professional organizations, which provided him with leadership experience, understanding of management challenges, and insight into practitioner issues. His writings reflected his involvement in movements that addressed social disparity, and spiritual association with the Quaker (Society of Friends) faith, a commitment evidenced in his numerous writings (Boyum, 2006, p. 2)

The idea of the servant as a leader came partly out of his experience in shaping his large organization. However, what actually crystallized his ideas was reading a metaphorical story, *Journey to the East*, by Hermann Hesse (Sendjaya & Sarros, 2002, p. 58; van Dierendonck & Patterson, 2010, p. 3). It tells the story of a group of pilgrims who are on a journey to discover the ultimate eastern order. The pilgrims undergo many trials and struggles but a loyal servant named Leo sustains them. Leo eventually leaves the journey, which results in the rising of various self-proclaimed leaders from among the pilgrims. Although the mission to discover the order ultimately fails, one pilgrim later reunites with the faithful servant Leo and discovers that Leo was the actual leader of the eastern order that they sought (Hesse (1956) cited in Boyum, 2006, p. 3).

2 The Philosophical Background of SL

The premises servant leading a group and leader serving a group stand opposite to each other though they imply a linear relationship between the act of service and the position of the leader. What motivates the leader in SL (to serve first) fundamentally distinguishes it from other leadership approaches. The primary reason for existence of leaders is to serve first, not to lead first. It is through that act of serving that the leaders lead other people to be what they are capable of becoming (Sendjaya & Sarros, 2002, p. 60). Thus, it functions as the antithesis of leadership approaches which prioritizes power and welfare – ones who believe in "leaders first" (Lynch & Friedman, 2013, p. 87).

Having attracted attention of academics recently, various perspectives of SL are read in the literature. Russell and Stone (2002, p. 145) argue SL takes place when leaders assume the position of servant in their relationships with fellow workers. Patterson (2003, p. 5) defines it as leaders who lead an organization by focusing on their followers, such that the followers are the primary concern and the organizational concerns are peripheral, and his/her behaviors and attitudes are congruent with this follower focus. Page and Wong (2000, p. 70) characterizes servant leader as a leader whose primary purpose for leading is to serve others by investing in their development and well-being for the benefit of accomplishing tasks and goals for the common good. Hale and Fields (2007, p. 397) discuss SL as an understanding and practice of leadership that places the good of those led over the self-interest of the leader, emphasizing leader behaviors that focus on follower development, and de-emphasizing glorification of the leader. Rude (2003), as cited in Nwogu (2004), defines SL as distancing oneself from using power, influence and position to serve self, and instead gravitating to a position where these instruments are used to empower, enable, and encourage those who are within one's circle of influence (Tonwe, n.d., p. 2). Coetzer, Bussin, and Geldenhuys (2017, p. 1) define SL as a multidimensional leadership theory that starts with a desire to serve, followed by an intent to lead and develop others to ultimately achieve a higher purpose objective to the benefit of individuals, organizations, and societies.

As it reads, the common argument of all descriptions is their emphasis on servant leader's attentiveness to concerns of their followers. Servant leaders put followers first, empower them, and help them develop their full personal capabilities (Northouse, 2016, p. 225). It is important to realize that according to Greenleaf the servant-leader is "primus inter pares" (i.e., first among equals), who does not use his or her power to get things done but who tries to persuade and convince staff (van Dierendonck, 2011, p. 1231).

Greenleaf believed that one can learn to be a servant leader. Some of the effective methods for this purpose include encouraging people in their own service impulses, doing your best to live your own life as a servant leader, accepting people for who they are, focusing on personal examples of SL within each person's life, and sharing a variety of learning tools on SL (Spears, 2010a, p. 14). It is also important to stress that SL is not a "quick fix" approach, not something that can be quickly instilled within an institution. At its core, SL is a long-term transformational approach to life and work that has the potential for creating positive change throughout the society (Spears, 2002, p. 4).

3 Characteristics of SL

The lack of an accurate definition of SL by Greenleaf has given rise to many interpretations. At present, the models developed by Spears (1995), Laub (1999), Russell and Stone (2002), and Patterson (2003) are among the most influential (von Dierendonck, 2011, p. 1231).

After carefully considering Greenleaf's writings, Spears (2010b, pp. 27–29) has identified a set of ten characteristics of the servant leader, which comprise the first conceptualization of SL (Northouse, 2016, pp. 227–229):

- *Listening:* Communication is an interactive process that includes sending and receiving messages. However, servant leaders communicate first by listening to what is said (and unsaid) to identify the will of a group. Listening also includes hearing one's own inner voice.
- *Empathy:* The servant leader strives to understand and empathize with others. People need to be accepted and recognized for their special and unique spirit.
- *Healing:* The healing of relationships is a powerful force for transformation and integration. One of the great strengths of SL is the potential for healing one's self and one's relationship to others. Greenleaf argues that in helping followers become whole, servant leaders themselves are healed.
- *Awareness:* General awareness strengthens the servant leader. It includes understanding oneself and the impact one has on others. With awareness, servant leaders are able to step aside and view themselves and their own perspectives in the greater context of the situation.
- *Persuasion:* Servant leaders rely on persuasion in making decisions. They seek to convince others, rather than coerce compliance, which makes one of the clearest distinctions with the traditional authoritarian model.
- *Conceptualization:* Servant leaders seek to nurture their abilities to dream great dreams. This ability requires one to think beyond day-to-day realities, provide a visionary concept for an institution.

- <u>*Foresight:*</u> Foresight is a characteristic that enables the servant leader to understand the lessons from the past, the realities of the present, and the likely consequence of a decision for the future. It is also deeply rooted within the intuitive mind.
- <u>*Stewardship:*</u> CEO's, staffs, and trustees all play significant roles in holding their institutions in trust for the greater good of society. SL, like stewardship, assumes first and foremost a commitment to serving the needs of others.
- <u>*Commitment to the growth of people:*</u> Servant leader is deeply committed to the personal and professional growth of each and every individual within his/her organization. In practice, this can include (but is not limited to) concrete actions such as making funds available for personal and professional development, taking a personal interest in the ideas and suggestions from everyone, encouraging worker involvement in decision-making, and actively assisting laid-off employees to find other positions.
- <u>*Building community:*</u> The servant leader senses that much has been lost as a result of the shift from local communities to large institutions as the primary shaper of human lives. Thus, he/she seeks to identify some means for building community among those who work within a given institution. He/she builds community to provide a place where people can feel safe and connected with others, but are still allowed to express their own individuality.

Following his study to collect an agreed upon list of characteristics of SL to develop an instrument for assessing the level at which leaders and workers perceive that these characteristics are displayed in their organizations, Laub (1999, pp. 49–51) concludes six clusters of SL characteristics shown in Tab. 1. Laub (2003, p. 3) defines the servant organization as an organization in which the characteristics of SL are displayed through the organizational culture and are valued and practiced by the leadership and workforce.

Tab. 2 shows one of the most comprehensive models of SL developed by Russell and Stone (2002, pp. 147–152). It has 9 functional attributes and 11 additional attributes of SL. The biggest problem with this model is the differentiation between functional attributes and accompanying attributes. It is unclear why certain attributes are allocated to a particular category (van Dierendonck, 2011, p. 1232).

As presented in in Fig. 1, Patterson (2003) discusses SL in seven constructs of virtues: agapao love, humility, altruism, vision, trust, empowerment, and service. According to her, SL is about virtues, which describe elements of someone's character that embody excellence (von Dierendonck, 2011, p. 1232). *Agapao* love means to love in a social or moral sense and includes embracing the judgment and

Tab. 1: SL and the Servant Organization (OLA) Model (Laub, 2003, p. 3)

The servant leader…	
Values people	by believing in people. by serving other's needs before his or her own. by receptive, non-judgmental listening.
Develops People	by providing opportunities for learning and growth. by modeling appropriate behavior. by building up others through encouragement and affirmation.
Develops People	by building strong personal relationships. by working collaboratively with others. by valuing the differences of others.
Displays Authenticity	by being open and accountable to others. by a willingness to learn from others. by maintaining integrity and trust.
Provides Leadership	by envisioning the future. by taking initiative. by clarifying goals.
Shares Leadership	by facilitating a shared vision. by sharing power and releasing control. by sharing status and promoting others.

Tab. 2: SL Attributes (Russel and Stone, 2002, p. 147)

Functional attributes		**Accompanying attributes**	
1. Vision	6. Modeling	1. Communication	7. Persuasion
2. Honesty	7. Pioneering	2. Credibility	8. Listening
3. Integrity	8. Appreciation of others	3. Competence	9. Encouragement
4. Trust	9. Empowerment	4. Stewardship	10. Teaching
5. Service		5. Visibility	11. Delegation
		6. Influence	

the deliberate assent of the will as a matter of principle, duty, and propriety. This love is shown by leaders who consider each of their followers as a total person – one with needs, wants, and desires. Humility requires not being self-focused, and rejects self-glorification. Altruism is concern for welfare of another. Vision refers to the idea that the leader looks forward and sees the person as a viable and worthy person, believes in the future state for each individual, and seeks to assist each one in reaching that state. Trust is essential in SL in that the values of integrity and honesty build interpersonal and organizational trust and leads to credibility. Servant

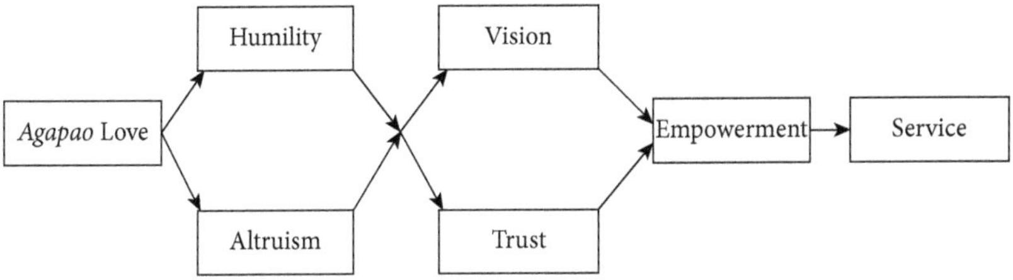

Fig. 1: Patterson's Model of SL Characteristic (2003, p. 10)

leaders lay the foundation of trust, and trust holds the servant-led organization together. They empower followers to find their own paths, and they, in turn, are inspired to help others find their best paths. The servant leader is called to serve and to see life as a mission of service, and this calling to service induces an acceptance of the responsibility for others (Patterson, 2003, pp. 11–27).

Finally, van Dierendonck (2011, p. 1232) distinguishes six characteristics of servant leader behaviors. Servant leaders empower and develop people, they show humility, are authentic, accept people for who they are, provide direction, and are stewards who work for the good of the whole.

Tab. 3 provides a summary of studies illustrating lack of agreement among researchers on what specific characteristics define SL. While there are some common characteristics, none of the studies conceptualize the SL the same. It also shows how SL is both treated as a trait phenomenon (e.g., courage, humility) and behavioral process (e.g., serving and developing others). Despite lack of agreement, these studies provide the groundwork for development of a model of SL (Northouse, 2016, p. 231)

4 Model of SL

To clarify the phenomenon of SL and provide a framework for understanding its complexities, Northouse (2016, pp. 231–238) developed a model (as illustrated in Fig. 2) based on Liden, Wayne, Zhao, and Henderson (2008) and Liden, Panaccio, Hu, and Meuser (2014) that has three main components: *antecedent conditions, servant leader behaviors,* and *leadership outcomes.*

Three existing conditions have an impact on SL:

- *Context and culture:* The nature of given organizational context and a particular culture affect the way SL is carried out.
- *Leader attributes:* Individual traits of the leader (desire to serve or motivation to lead) shape how individuals demonstrate SL.

Tab. 3: Key Characteristics of SL (van Dierendonck, 2011, p. 1241)

Van Dierendonck (2011)	Laub (1999)	Wong & Davey (2007)	Barbuto & Wheeler (2006)	Dennis & Bocarnea (2005)	Liden, Wayne, Zhao, & Henderson (2008)	Sendjaya, Sarros, & Santora (2008)	Van Dierendonck & Nuijten (2011)
-Empowering and developing people	-Develops people	-Serving and developing others -Consulting and involving others		-Empowerment -Trust	-Empowering -Helping subordinates grow and succeed	-Transforming influence	-Empowerment
-Humility	-Shares leadership	-Humility and selflessness	-Altruistic calling	-Humility	-Putting subordinates first	-Voluntary subordination	-Humility -Standing
-Authenticity	-Displays authenticity	-Modeling integrity and authenticity				-Authentic self -Transcendental spirituality	-Authenticity
-Interpersonal acceptance	-Values people		-Emotional healing	-Agapao love	-Emotional healing	-Covenantal relationship	-Forgiveness
-Providing direction	-Providing leadership	-Inspiring and influencing others	-Persuasive mapping	-Vision	-Conceptual skills	-Courage – -Accountability	
-Stewardship	-Builds community		-Organizational stewardship -Wisdom	-Creating value for the community -Behaving ethically	-Responsible morality	-Stewardship	

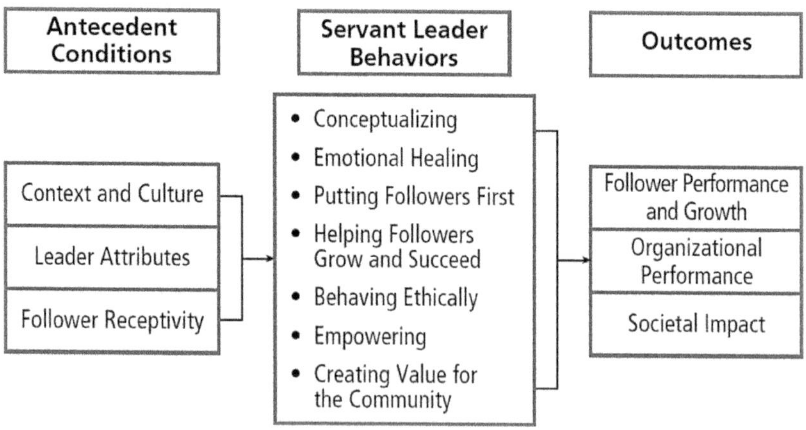

Fig. 2: Model of SL (Northouse, 2016, p. 232)

- *Follower receptivity:* The question "Do all followers show a desire for SL?" influences the impact of SL on outcomes such as personal and organizational job performance.

The middle component of the model identifies seven servant leader behaviors.

Conceptualizing refers to the servant leader's thorough understanding of the organization – its purposes, complexities, and mission – to be able to think through and solve multifaceted problems.

Putting followers first is the sine qua non of the SL. It means using actions and words that clearly demonstrate to followers that their concerns are a priority, including placing followers' interests and success ahead of those of the leader.

Emotional healing involves being sensitive to the personal concerns and well-being of others.

Helping followers grow and succeed refers to knowing followers' professional or personal goals and helping them to accomplish those aspirations by making their career development a priority.

Behaving ethically is doing the right thing in the right way. It is holding to strong ethical standards, including being open, honest, and fair with followers.

Empowering refers to allowing followers the freedom to be independent, make decisions on their own, and be self-sufficient.

Creating Value for the Community. Servant leaders create value for the community by consciously and intentionally giving back to the community. They are involved in local activities and encourage followers to also volunteer for community service.

The third component of the model refers to the potential outcomes of SL.

- *Follower Performance and Growth*. The expected outcome for followers is greater self-actualization. That is, followers will realize their full capabilities when leaders nurture them, help them with their personal goals, and give them control. Also, it is expected to have a favorable impact on follower in the way they do their work. Another expected result is that followers themselves may become servant leaders.
- *Organizational Performance.* In addition to positively affecting followers and their performance, SL has an influence on organizational performance. It also positively affects the way organizational teams function.
- *Societal Impact.* Another outcome expected of SL is that it is likely to have a positive impact on society.

5 Relationship with Other Theories

There are seven leadership theories that reveal the most overlap with SL, namely, transformational, authentic, ethical, Level 5, empowering, spiritual, and self-sacrificing leadership theories (van Dierendonck, 2011, p. 1235). Both transformational leadership and SL emphasize the importance of appreciating and valuing people, listening, mentoring or teaching, and empowering followers. Nevertheless, transformational leadership and SL do have points of variation. There is a much greater emphasis upon service to followers in the SL paradigm.

Furthermore, while both leaders are influential, servant leaders allow extraordinary freedom for followers to exercise their own abilities. They also place a much higher degree of trust in their followers than would be the case in any leadership style that required the leader to be somewhat directive (Stone, Russel & Patterson, 2004, p. 354). Transactional leadership may appear to share similar characteristics to SL, too, however a distinct feature is that the transactional leader's actions may or may not benefit the follower (Burns (1978) cited in Boyum (2006, p. 3)), and may even be associated with harmful gain, like that of Adolf Hitler, Saddam Hussein (Whetstone, 2002, p. 387).

Yukl (2013, pp. 347–348) lists transforming, servant, authentic, and spiritual leadership under the category of ethical leadership theories, which emphasize the importance of integrity and ethical behavior. He notes integrity, altruism, humility, empathy and healing, personal growth, fairness and justice, and empowerment as the values emphasized in these theories. These theories all share some features in common with theories of transformational and charismatic leadership, together with important differences (Yukl, 2013, p. 353). SL is distinguished from others by explaining why primary concern of the leaders should be to nurture, develop, and protect followers through the extra focus it has on the needs of followers and service by the leader.

6 Conclusion

Research on SL has made several contributions to the field of leadership (Northouse, 2016, p. 240). First, while there are other leadership approaches that include an ethical dimension, SL is unique in the way it makes service the central component of the leadership process. It also provides a counterintuitive and provocative approach to the use of influence, or power, in leadership. Nearly all other theories of leadership treat influence as a positive factor in the leadership process, but SL does just the opposite. It argues that leaders should not dominate, direct, or control; but rather, leaders should share control and influence. Third, rather than imply that SL is a panacea, research on SL has shown there are conditions under which SL is not a preferred kind of leadership. Findings indicate that SL may not be effective in contexts where followers are not open to being guided, supported, and empowered.

This approach has several limitations, too (Northouse, 2016, p. 241). First, the paradoxical nature of the title "SL" creates semantic noise that diminishes the potential value of the approach. Because the name appears contradictory, SL is prone to be perceived as fanciful or whimsical. In addition, being a servant leader implies following, and following is viewed as the opposite of leading.

There is also debate among SL scholars regarding the core dimensions of the process, as illustrated in Tab. 3. To date, researchers have been unable to reach consensus on a common definition or theoretical framework for SL. Third, a large segment of the writing on SL has a prescriptive overtone that implies that good leaders "put others first". While advocating an altruistic approach to leadership is commendable, it conflicts with individual autonomy and other principles of leadership such as directing, concern for production, goal setting, and creating a vision. Fourth, focusing too much on the needs of followers might cause the leaders to ignore the needs of the organization (Lynch & Friedman, 2013, p. 89). Finally, Tonwe (n.d., p. 6) cites researchers questioning the practicality and applicability of the theory to real-world situations since it ignores accountability and differing levels of competence among individuals in the work place, as well.

In conclusion, Whetstone (2002, p. 390) cites DiStefano (1995) that SL requires a paradigm shift. This may be why some object that it is unrealistic. It is dismissed as a paradigm of weakness, not fitting with our egocentric natures, our assertiveness, or our will to power. It is not only different, but also threatening to those wielding or seeking power in hierarchical structures.

References

Boyum, G. (2006) The historical and philosophical influences on Greenleaf's concept of Servant Leadership: setting the stage for scientific theory building. Regent University SL Research Roundtable Proceedings. Retrieved from https://www.regent.edu/acad/global/publications/sl_proceedings/2006/boyum.pdf on 24 February 2019.

Coetzer, M.F., Bussin, M. & Goldenhuys, M. (2017) The functions of a servant leader. *Administrative Sciences*, 7 (5), 1–32, http://dx.doi.org/10.3390/admsci7010005.

Greenleaf, R. (1977) *Servant Leadership a journey into the nature of legitimate power and greatness*. Paulist press. Retrieved from https://www.essr.net/~jafundo/mestrado_material_itgjkhnld/IV/Lideran%C3%A7as/The%20Servant%20as%20Leader.pdf.retrived 20 October 2018.

Hale, J.R. & Fields, D.L. (2007) Exploring Servant Leadership across cultures: a study of followers in Ghana and the USA. *Leadership*, 3 (4), 397–417.

Laub, J.A. (1999) Assessing the Servant Organization Development of the Servant Organizational Leadership Assessment (SOLA) Instrument. A Dissertation Submitted to the Graduate Faculty at Florida Atlantic University in Partial Fulfillment of the Requirements for the Degree doctor of education.

Retrieved from https://www.servantleaderperformance.com/wp-content/uploads/2018/04/1999-Laub-Dissertation.pdf on 23 February 2019.

Laub, J.A. (2003) From paternalism to the servant organization: expanding the organizational leadership assessment (OLA) model. Regent University Servant Leadership Research Roundtable Proceedings. Retrieved from https://www.regent.edu/acad/global/publications/sl_proceedings/2003/laub_from_paternalism.pdf on 23 February 2019.

Lynch, J.A. & Friedman, H.H. (2013) Servant leader, spiritual leader: the case for convergence. *Journal of Leadership, Accountability and Ethics*, 10 (2), 87–95.

Northouse, P.G. (2016) *Leadership theory and practice.* 7th edition. Los Angeles: Sage Publications.

Page, D. & Wong, T.P. (2000). A conceptual framework for measuring servant-leadership. In S. Adjibolosoo (Ed.), *The human factor in shaping the course of history and development* (pp. 69–110). Lanham, MD: University Press of America. Retrieved from http://www.drpaulwong.com/wp-content/uploads/2013/09/Conceptual-Framework.pdf.on 23 October 2018.

Patterson, K.A. (2003) SL: a theoretical model. Unpublished doctoral dissertation. Regent University, Virginia Beach, VA.

Rachmawati, A.W. & Lantu, D.C. (2014) Servant Leadership Theory Development and Measurement. Procedia. *Social and Behavioral Sciences*, 115, 387–393.

Russell, R.F. & Stone, A. G. (2002) A review of Servant Leadership attributes: developing a practical model, *Leadership & Organization Development Journal*, 23 (3), 145–157, https://doi.org/10.1108/01437730210424.

Sendjaya, S. & Sarros, J.C. (2002) Servant Leadership: its origin, development, and application in organizations. *Journal of Leadership and Organization Studies*, 9 (2), 57–64.

Sendjaya, S. (2015) *Personal and organizational excellence through Servant Leadership: learning to serve, serving to lead, leading to transform*. Springer International Publishing, Switzerland.

Spears, L.C. (1996) Reflections on Robert K. Greenleaf and Servant Leadership. *Leadership & Organization Development Journal*, 17 (7), 33–35.

Spears, L.C. (2002) Tracing the past, present, and future of Servant Leadership. In L.C. Spears & M. Lawrence (Eds.), *Focus on leadership: Servant-leadership for the 21st century* (pp. 1–16). New York: Wiley. Retrieved from https://civicleadership. lipscomb.edu/uploads/41763.pdf.on 21 October 2018.

Spears, L.C. (2010a) Servant Leadership and Robert K. Greenleaf's legacy. In van Dierendonck D. & Patterson K. (Eds) *Servant Leadership Developments in Theory and Research*. Palgrave Macmillan, London pp. 11–24.

Spears, L.C. (2010b) Character and Servant Leadership: Ten Characteristics of Effective, Caring Leaders. *The Journal of Virtues & Leadership*, 1 (1), 25–30.

Stone, A. G., Russell, R.F., & Patterson, K. (2004) Transformational versus Servant Leadership: a difference in leader focus, *Leadership & Organization Development Journal*, 25 (4), 349–361, https://doi.org/10.1108/01437730410538671.

Tonwe, D.A. (n.d) Revisiting the Servant Leadership phenomenon. Retrieved from http://www.unimaid.edu.ng/oer/Journals-oer/Social/General/Paper%20E%207.pdf on 23 October 2018

Whetstone, J.T. (2002) Personalism and moral leadership: the servant leader with a transforming vision. *Business Ethics:A European Vision*, 11 (4), 385–392.

van Dierendonck D. & Patterson K. (2010) Servant Leadership. In van Dierendonck D., Patterson K. (Eds.) In *Servant Leadership Developments in Theory and Research*. Palgrave Macmillan: London.

van Dierendonck, D. (2011) Servant Leadership: A Review and Synthesis. *Journal of Management*, 37 (4), 1228–1261. DOI: 10.1177/0149206310380462

Yukl, G. (2013) *Leadership in organizations*. 8th edition. Boston: Pearson Education.

Tahsin Akcakanat

The Role of Professional Vitality in the Relationship Between Organizational Trust and Career Satisfaction

1 Introduction

In recent years, the health of employees is highly emphasized, as it is considered that it will directly affect the performance of the labor force. The health of the employees affects their productive use of physical capacity and their vitality (Strijk et al., 2013: 66). In addition, health and vitality of the employees make them feel more energetic, stronger and more sufficient by revealing a reducing effect on the sense of fatigue, and an increasing effect on their psychological strength, determination towards work and their diligence. (Schaufeli W. & Bakker A. (2003)2003: 5). The first research on the vitality of employees was made in early 1960s. When we look at the researches made in this period and after that, it is seen that researches are carried out in terms of subjective vitality and these researches are concentrated on academicians. However, in the 2000s, the studies continued with vitality variable in working life (professional vitality), as well as the research on vitality from a subjective perspective (Aydınlı Kulak, 2016: 228).

Professional vitality has attracted more attention of researchers in the last few years in organizational behavior literature because of the positive results of the organizational outcomes. Professional vitality is defined as the source of energy that increases the performance and the success of the employees in organizations and the experience in which the employees feel energetic, lively, vigorous and strong (Ryan and Frederick, 1997; Hennekam, 2016: 17–18). Professional vitality is an empowerment experience in which employees try to improve, prolong and revitalize the conditions they perceive as energy-boosting and to reduce or prevent the conditions they perceive as vitality-reducing (Collins, 1993: 219). In another definition, professional vitality is expressed as the approach of employees to their works with the feelings of passion, vigor, facility and satisfaction (Harvey, 2002: 30). Professionally vital employees are considered enthusiastic, compassionate, dedicated, strong, creative, flexible, risk-taking and productive individuals (McLauglin, 1999: 390). Harvey defined professional vitality in four sub-dimensions: vigor, passion, facility and job satisfaction (2002: 32–37).

According to Harvey, passion is the controlled willingness of the employee in order to have a strong desire to achieve their purpose and to complete a job. Vigor is defined as a high level of mental, physical and emotional energy which is conceived by passion. Facility refers to the ability of an employee to use the skills and competencies the individual has when carrying out their work related activities. Job satisfaction, which is the last sub-dimension, is defined as the state of satisfaction and success of the employee through vigor and facility, as a result of the passion of the employee.

Organizational trust, which is the second variable of the research, is expressed as being sure of the decisions and practices of the organization, and supporting these situations, even in risky situations (Lewicki et al., 1998: 439). Organizational trust defines the positive justice and ethical expectations of the employees regarding the roles, relationships, behaviors, approach to incidents, experiences and their attitudes based on the sense of belonging to each other in the organization (Akdoğan and Köksal, 2014: 27). According to Nylan and Marlowe (1997), organizational trust is discussed in two dimensions as trust in supervisor and trust in organization. Trust in supervisor expresses the expectations of the employees, which are affected by individual expectations, interpersonal relations, economic changes, social situations and ethical values, approaches and contexts, from the supervisor to treat fairly and to act in accordance with ethical principles (Hosmer, 1995). Trust in organization is defined as the confidence of the employees that the organization will take actions for the benefit of the employees or at least these actions will not harm them (Mayer et al., 1995: 714). In order to constitute a sense of trust in the organization, it is necessary to fulfill the promises made by the organization according to the legal and business contract (McKnight et al., 1998: 478).

Job satisfaction, which is the third variable of the study, is defined as the individuals' perception of expectations about their career satisfaction, achievements and careers they want to achieve in the future. Job satisfaction is summarized as perceptions of individuals about their current career achievements and their expectations for future progress (Gattiker and Larwood, 1988: 573; Vianen et al., 2009: 236). Greenhaus et al. defined job satisfaction as satisfaction of the individual with the level of achieving the goals determined by themselves in their career and stated that job satisfaction is affected by professional achievements, professional goals, income-related goals, professional progress, and new experience acquisitions (act. Yüksel, 2005: 305). The relationship between trust in organization, professional vitality and career satisfaction is based on Holland's Career Choice, Herzberg's Dual Factor and Lent, Brown and Hackett's Social Cognitive Career Theories. According to Career Choice Theory, career satisfaction is based on the experience, ability, value and success of employees. However, the presence of motoric (basic ability levels), intellectual, supportive, adaptable, convincing and aesthetic environmental conditions in which employees are involved, affect the career satisfaction of employees (Holland, 1959: 35–36). The Dual Factor Theory states that the factors such as taking on authority and responsibility, being appreciated, achieving success, attractiveness of the work, providing progress and promotion opportunities increase the eagerness, desires and ambitions of the employees (Dinham and Scott, 1998: 363). Another theory on which the research is based is Social Cognitive Career Theory. According to this theory, the provision of support and resources for the employees to achieve their individual goals has an impact on their career satisfaction. The absence of these supports prevents employees from achieving their goals and reduces their satisfaction (Verbruggen and Sels, 2010: 4). Within the scope of these theories, employees' trust in their organizations improves the sense of belonging of employees and leads to positive outcomes such as passion for work (Chughtai and Buckley, 2008: 581). Furthermore, it has been shown that high levels of trust in employees can result in positive emotions and moods that can be generalized in an institution (Dasborough et al., 2009). Employees will work more willingly, eagerly and passionately. As a result, the satisfaction level for jobs and careers will increase. As a matter of fact, the researches show that as the perceptions of trust towards the supervisors and the organization of the employees increase, their professional vitality also increases. At the same time, the perception of organizational trust and professional vitality increase the levels of career satisfaction (Chu et al., 2015: 1342; Baruch, 2014: 525). In addition, the relationship between organizational trust, professional vitality and career satisfaction enables the development of the social environment of employees, which helps them to improve their careers (Burt, 1992: 125). In the light of these explanations, the following hypotheses were proposed in the study:

Hypothesis 1: There is a mediating role of dimensions such as (a) passion, (b) vigor, (c) facility, (d) job satisfaction on the effect of trust in supervisor on career satisfaction.
Hypothesis 2: There is a mediating role of dimensions such as (a) passion, (b) vigor, (c) facility, (d) job satisfaction on the effect of trust in organization on career satisfaction.

2 Methodology of the Research

In this part of the chapter, detailed information about the model, population and sample and the scales used in the study are included.

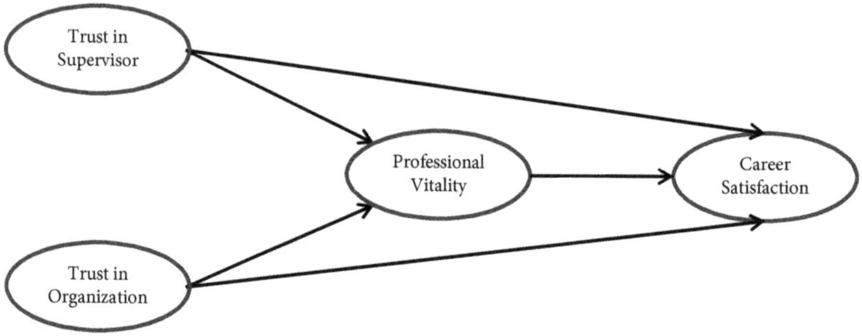

Fig. 1: Model of the Research

2.1 Model of the Research

The aim of the study is to determine the role of professional vitality in the effect of trust in supervisor and organization that constitute organizational trust on career satisfaction. The research model designed for this purpose is given below. In the model, four dimensions of professional vitality are designed as mediator variables.

2.2 The Population and Sample of the Research

The population of the research consists of white-collar employees who experience professional vitality in the forefront. The sample is composed of 485 employees working in one of the leading companies in the construction products sector of our country. Convenience sampling method, which is one of the random sampling selection methods, is used. The link of the virtual questionnaire has been delivered to the employees through the enterprise's e-mail network. Of the 1293 employees, 502 completed the questionnaire and the questionnaire's rate of return is 38%. In the examinations, it was decided that 17 questionnaire forms should be left out of the analysis due to the fact that many blank questions were left and the same answers were given. As a result, the data that was obtained from 485 employees is used in the study. The results regarding the demographic characteristics of the employees who participated in the study, are presented in Tab. 1.

As can be seen from Tab. 1, a significant portion of the body that constitutes the sample (58.4%) consists of male employees. In terms of marital status variable, married and unmarried workers show almost equal distribution. In terms of education level, the rate of bachelor's degree (54.6%) is very high as

Tab. 1: Information Regarding the Demographic Characteristics of the Participants

N= 485		N	%
Gender	Female	202	41.6
	Male	283	58.4
Marital Status	Married	248	51.1
	Single	237	48.9
Educational Qualification	High School	74	15.3
	Vocational School	68	14.0
	Bachelor Degree	265	54.6
	Postgraduate	78	16.1

expected. The average age of the employees who participated in the study was 32.3 (SD = 8.18), the average term of employment was 5.9 years (SD = 3.66), and the average of the total working time was 10.3 years (SD = 5.07).

2.3 Measures

Within the scope of the research, questionnaire technique was used to determine the relationships between variables. In this direction, three scales were used in the study. In addition, a form consisting of five questions was used to determine the demographic characteristics of the participants. Detailed information about the scales used in the research is given below.

Organizational Trust Scale: The scale developed by Nyhan and Marlowe (1997) and adapted to Turkish by Demircan (2003) consists of 2 dimensions and 12 items. Dimensions are called trust in the supervisor (first 8 items) and trust in the organization (last 4 items). 5-point likert-type grading method was used in the scale and 1 = Strongly Disagree, 5 = Strongly Agree. There are no items with a reverse score in the scale. The internal consistency coefficient of the scale was calculated by Nyhan and Marlowe (1997) as $\alpha = .96$. Examples of the items included in the scale are "I have full confidence in the accuracy of what my supervisor has said on any subject" and, "I have full confidence that this business will treat me fairly".

Professional Vitality Scale: The scale developed by Harvey (2002) and adapted to Turkish by Uzunbacak and Akçakanat (2018), consists of 17 items and 4 subdimensions. The dimensions that compose the scale are named as passion, vigor, facility and job satisfaction. There are 4 items in passion, vigor and job satisfaction dimensions and 5 items in facility dimension. Harvey (2002) calculated the internal consistency coefficient for the whole scale as .87 and between .68 and .84 for dimensions. In the adaptation study performed by Uzunbacak and

Tab. 2: Values for Goodness of Fit of the Scales

Model	#	χ^2/df	CFI	NFI	NNFI	GFI	AGFI	SRMR	RMSEA
Career Satifaction	5	2,65	.99	.99	.98	.99	.96	.023	.074
Trust	12	2,88	.97	.97	.97	.92	.88	.063	.071
Professianl Vitality	17	2,06	.95	.93	.94	.88	.83	.065	.093
Research Model	34	2,88	.97	.96	.97	.86	.84	.054	.059
Acceptable Fit*		≤5	>0.90	>0.90	>0.90	>0.85	>0.80	<0.08	<0.08
Good Fit*		≤3	>0.97	>0.95	>0.97	>0.90	>0.85	<0.05	<0.05

Akçakanat (2018), the internal consistency coefficient of the whole scale was calculated as .89, and .71 to .80 on the basis of dimensions. 5-point likert-type grading method was used in the scale and 1 = Strongly Disagree, 5 = Strongly Agree. There are no items with a reverse score in the scale. Examples of the items included in the scale are "I have an inner sense of mission for doing this job" and "I am full of energy during the working day".

Career Satisfaction Scale: The scale developed by Greenhaus et al. (1990) and adapted to Turkish by Avcı and Turunc (2012), consists of 5 items and one dimension. Avcı and Turunc (2012) calculated the internal consistency coefficient of the scale as .91. 5-point Likert-type grading method was used in the scale and 1 = Strongly Disagree, 5 = Strongly Agree. There are no items with a reverse score in the scale. Example of items included in the scale is "My achievement in my career makes me happy".

2.4 Validity and Reliability

In order to test the structural validity of the data collection tools used in the study, confirmatory factor analysis (CFA) was performed by using Lisrel 8.80 program. The CFA results can be seen in Tab. 2.

When the values for goodness of fit of the 3 scales in Tab. 2 are examined, it is concluded that they are all structurally valid scales. Internal consistency coefficients were calculated to measure the reliability levels of the scales. The results are shown in Tab. 3.

Tab. 3 shows that the internal consistency coefficients for all variables were above the acceptable limit of .70 (Nunnally, 1978). In light of all this information, all scales used in the study were found to be structurally valid and reliable scales.

3 Findings

Tab. 4 shows the arithmetic mean, skewness/kurtosis and correlation values of the variables subject to the study. As can be seen from Tab. 4, research data shows

Tab. 3: Internal Consistency Coefficients of the Scales

Variables	Number of Item	α
Career Satisfaction	5	.87
Trust in Supervisor	8	.90
Trust in Organization	4	.88
Passion	4	.71
Vigor	4	.70
Facility	5	.78
Job Satisfaction	4	.79

*Joreskog ve Sorbom, (1993); Kline, (1998); Anderson ve Gerbing, (1984).

Tab. 4: Descriptive Statistics and Relationships between Variables

Variables (N= 485)	Mean	SD	Skew.	Kurt.	1	2	3	4	5	6	7
1. Career Satisfaction	3.76	.85	-.512	-.411	(.87)						
2. Trust in Supervisor	3.91	.67	-.340	-.401	.405**	(.90)					
3. Trust in Organization	3.73	.91	-.433	-.427	.447**	.607**	(.88)				
4. Passion	3.59	.61	-.454	.356	.452**	.441**	.447**	(.71)			
5. Vigor	3.43	.62	-.307	-.286	.427**	.453**	.469**	.701**	(.70)		
6. Facility	3.95	.46	.025	-.344	.383**	.462**	.423**	.575**	.639**	(.78)	
7. Job Satisfaction	3.56	.82	-.492	-.353	.629**	.430**	.513**	.599**	.617**	.480**	(.79)

*** $p< .01$. Values in parentheses show the reliability coefficients of the dimensions.*

normal distribution. According to Morgan et al. (2004: 49), if the skewness and kurtosis coefficients are within ± 1 range, it can be said that the data shows normal distribution. In this study, skewness coefficients are also in this range. Tab. 4 shows arithmetic mean values of the variables. Accordingly, it is observed that the level of career satisfaction of the employees (3.76 ± .85) is above the medium level but not too high. According to Tab. 4, trust in the supervisor (3.91 ± .67) and trust in the organization (3.73 ± .91) were higher than the average level. The point that draws attention here is that the employees feel more trust in their supervisors than the organization. When Tab. 4 is examined in terms of the dimensions of professional vitality, it is seen that all means are above the medium level. The most remarkable average here is in the facility dimension (3.95 ± .46). When Pearson correlation analysis results are examined in Tab. 4, positively, medium strength level and $p<.01$ level significant relationships between all variables were found.

A regression analysis was performed by Bootstrap method to determine the hypothesis of the study, in other words, the role played by the professional vitality in the relationship between trust in supervisor, trust in organization and career satisfaction. In the analysis of mediation models, Baron and Kenny (1986)'s traditional approach is used very frequently in the literature. However, in recent times, the modern approach (Bootstrap) has been proposed that allows for more accurate results for the analysis of mediation models. Modern approach, unlike the Baron and Kenny's approach, does not see it as necessary to fulfill the requirements of the steps listed one after another, and foresees that the mediation effect (indirect effect) can be mentioned even if these conditions are not met. In other words, if the indirect effect is significant, it is considered sufficient to accept the mediation model. Accordingly, if the lower and upper trust interval values corresponding to the indirect effect value do not cover the value of zero, then the indirect effect is considered significant and the mediation effect is observed (Gürbüz and Bayık, 2018). This analysis was performed via SPSS PROCESS plugin. In order to reveal the mediating effect in the analysis, Model 4 was chosen. Bootstrap regression analysis results are shown in Tab. 5.

According to Tab. 5, it is seen that the indirect effect of trust in supervisor on career satisfaction through passion is significant (B = .149, 95% BCA CI [.107, .199]); the indirect effect of trust in supervisor on career satisfaction through vigor is significant (B = .138, 95% BCA CI [.095, .187]); the indirect effect of trust in supervisor on career satisfaction through facility is significant (B = .115, 95% BCA CI [.071, .167]); the indirect effect of trust in supervisor on career satisfaction through job satisfaction is significant (B = .239, 95% BCA CI [.191, .292]) and H_{1A}, H_{1B}, H_{1C} ve H_{1D} hypotheses were deemed to have accepted. Again, when Tab. 5 is examined, it is found that the indirect effect of trust in organization on career satisfaction through passion is significant (B = .140, 95% BCA CI [.097, .189]); the indirect effect of trust in organization on career satisfaction through vigor is significant (B = .130, 95% BCA CI [.087, .179]); the indirect effect of trust in organization on career satisfaction through facility is significant (B = .100, 95% BCA CI [.061, .144]); the indirect effect of trust in organization on career satisfaction through job satisfaction is significant (B = .278, 95% BCA CI [.227, .333]) and in this case, H_{2A}, H_{2B}, H_{2C} and H_{2D} hypotheses were also accepted.

Tab. 5: Results of the Bootstrap Regression Analysis

Variables	**Passion**			**Career Satisfaction**		
	B	*LLCI*	*ULCI*	*B*	*LLCI*	*ULCI*
Model 1						
Trust in Supervisor	.401***	.327	.473	.322***	.214	.431
Passion (Mediator)				.471***	.352	.591
R^2	.194			.256		
Bootstrap Indirect Effect	Trust in Supervisor →Passion→Career Satisfaction *B* = .149, 95% BCA CI [.107, .199]					
	Vigor			**Career Satisfaction**		
	B	*LLCI*	*ULCI*	*B*	*LLCI*	*ULCI*
Model 2						
Trust in Supervisor	.417***	.344	.490	.336***	.225	.446
Vigor (Mediator)				.420***	.299	.539
R^2	.205			.238		
Bootstrap Indirect Effect	Trust in Supervisor→Vigor→Career Satisfaction *B* = .138, 95% BCA CI [.095, .187]					
	Facility			**Career Satisfaction**		
	B	*LLCI*	*ULCI*	*B*	*LLCI*	*ULCI*
Model 3						
Trust in Supervisor	.317***	.263	.371	.366***	.253	.478
Facility (Mediator)				.459***	.294	.623
R^2	.213			.213		
Bootstrap Indirect Effect	Trust in Supervisor→Facility→Career Satisfaction *B* = .115, 95% BCA CI [.071, .167]					
	Job Satisfaction			**Career Satisfaction**		
	B	*LLCI*	*ULCI*	*B*	*LLCI*	*ULCI*
Model 4						
Trust in Supervisor	.522***	.424	.620	.208***	.113	.304
Job Satisfaction (Mediator)				.580***	.501	.568
R^2	.185			.418		
Bootstrap Indirect Effect	Trust in Supervisor→Job Satisfaction→Career Satisfaction *B* = .239, 95% BCA CI [.191, .292]					
	Passion			**Career Satisfaction**		
	B	*LLCI*	*ULCI*	*B*	*LLCI*	*ULCI*
Model 5						
Trust in Organization	.299***	.245	.352	.284***	.205	.363
Passion (Mediator)				.438***	.320	.556

(continued on next page)

Tab. 5: (continued)

Variables	Passion			Career Satisfaction		
	B	*LLCI*	*ULCI*	*B*	*LLCI*	*ULCI*
R^2	.199			.279		
Bootstrap Indirect Effect	Trust in Organization→Passion→Career Satisfaction *B* = .140, 95% BCA CI [.097, .189]					
	Vigor			**Career Satisfaction**		
	B	*LLCI*	*ULCI*	*B*	*LLCI*	*ULCI*
Model 6						
Trust in Organization	.317***	.264	.371	.294***	.213	.375
Vigor (Mediator)				.382***	.262	.501
R^2	.220			.260		
Bootstrap Indirect Effect	Trust in Organization→Vigor→Career Satisfaction *B* = .130, 95% BCA CI [.087, .179]					
	Facility			**Career Satisfaction**		
	B	*LLCI*	*ULCI*	*B*	*LLCI*	*ULCI*
Model 7						
Trust in Organization	.214***	.173	.255	.322***	.242	.402
Facility(Mediator)				.435***	.277	.593
R^2	.179			.246		
Bootstrap Indirect Effect	Trust in Organization→Facility→Career Satisfaction *B* = .100, 95% BCA CI [.061, .144]					
	Job Satisfaction			**Career Satisfaction**		
	B	*LLCI*	*ULCI*	*B*	*LLCI*	*ULCI*
Model 8						
Trust in Organization	.459***	.390	.527	.157***	.083	.231
Job Satisfaction (Mediator)				.563***	.481	.646
R^2	.264			.416		
Bootstrap Indirect Effect	Trust in Organization→Job Satisfaction→Career Satisfaction *B* = .278, 95% BCA CI [.227, .333]					

*** p< .001. n= 485, LLCI = Lower level confidence interval; ULCI = Upper level confidence interval. Bootstrap resampling= 5000.

4 Conclusion and Discussion

Organizational trust is as important as to ensure the continuity of organizational success (Asunakutlu, 2006: 17); in addition to being closely related to organizational outcomes such as job satisfaction and performance, it also plays an important role in the realization of the goals of employees and the organization, and in the conduct of organizational activities and processes (Shockley-Zalabak et al., 2000: 8). Therefore, the main purpose of this study is to investigate the relationship between organizational trust and professional vitality and career satisfaction.

As a result of the analyses, it was found that all sub-dimensions of professional vitality and career satisfaction levels of the employees, who have high level of trust in the supervisor and the organization, are also high. Again, the positive effect of all sub-dimensions of professional vitality on career satisfaction is determined. In addition, it is determined that the sub-dimensions, – passion, vigor, facility and job satisfaction – of professional vitality take the role of mediator between the trust in supervisor and organization and career satisfaction. All these results are consistent with the results of previous studies (Hennekam, 2016; Chu et al., 2015; Baruch et al., 2014). The findings of this study show that organizational trust and professional vitality are the precursors of career satisfaction.

Within the context of the significance of professional vitality, it is important that practitioners make the work meaningful, implement practices that increase the sense of trust and justice, and support creativity and innovation. This research has important results in terms of providing infrastructure for future studies. It should be taken into consideration that the research is a cross-sectional study and that the data is collected from only one sector. It is considered that when variables such as organizational support perception, life satisfaction, organizational citizenship behavior, workplace happiness, significance of work, organizational culture and organizational climate are taken together with the variables in the study, more generalizable results will be obtained.

References

Akdoğan, A. A., & Köksal, O. (2014). Aidiyet algısının örgütsel vatandaşlık davranışı üzerindeki etkisinde yöneticiye güvenin aracılık rolü. *Atatürk Üniversitesi Sosyal Bilimler Enstitüsü Dergisi*, *18*(1), 25–43.

Anderson, J. C., & Gerbing, D. W. (1984). The effect of sampling error on convergence, improper solutions, and goodness-of-fit indices for maximum likelihood confirmatory factor analysis. *Psychometrika*, *49*(2), 155–173.

Avcı, U., & Turunc, Ö. (2012). Dönüşümcü liderlik ve örgüte güvenin kariyer memnuniyetine etkisi: Lider-üye etkileşiminin aracılık rolü. *Alanya İşletme Fakültesi Dergisi*, *4*(2), 45–55.

Aydınlı Kulak, F. (2016). Mesleki canlılık. Ed. P. Kanten ve S. Kanten içinde *Örgütsel Davranışın Aydınlık ve Karanlık Yüzü* (227–237), Ankara: Nobel Akademik Yayıncılık.

Baron, R. M., & Kenny, D. A. (1986). The moderator–mediator variable distinction in social psychological research: Conceptual, strategic, and statistical considerations. *Journal of Personality and Social Psychology*, *51*(6), 1173–1182.

Baruch, Y., Grimland, S., & Vigoda-Gadot, E. (2014). Professional vitality and career success: Mediation, age and outcomes. *European Management Journal*, *32*(3), 518–527.

Burt, R. S. (1992). Structural holes: The social structure of competition. Cambridge, MA: Harvard University Press.

Chughtai, A. A., & Buckley, F. (2009). Linking trust in the principal to school outcomes the mediating role of organizational identification and work engagement. *International Journal of Educational Management*, *23*(7), 574–589.

Collins, R. (1993). Emotional energy as the common denominator of rational action. *Rationality and Society*, *5*(2), 203–230.

Dasborough, M. T., Ashkanasy, N. M., Tee, E. Y., & Herman, H. M. (2009). What goes around comes around: How meso-level negative emotional contagion can ultimately determine organizational attitudes toward leaders. *The Leadership Quarterly*, *20*(4), 571–585.

Demircan, N. (2003). *Örgütsel güvenin bir ara değişken olarak örgütsel bağlılık üzerindeki etkisi: Eğitim sektöründe bir uygulama*. Yayımlanmamış Doktora Tezi, Gebze Yüksek Teknoloji Enstitüsü, Sosyal Bilimler Enstitüsü, Gebze.

Dinham, S., & Scott, C. (1998). A three domain model of teacher and school executive career satisfaction. *Journal of Educational Administration*, *36*(4), 362–378.

Gattiker, U. E., & Larwood, L. (1988). Predictors for managers' career mobility, success, and satisfaction. *Human relations*, *41*(8), 569–591.

Greenhaus, J. H., Parasuraman, S., & Wormley, W. M. (1990). Effects of race on organizational experiences, job performance evaluations, and career outcomes. *Academy of Management Journal*, *33*(1), 64–86.

Gürbüz, S., & Bayık, M. E. (2018). Aracılık modellerinin analizinde modern yaklaşım: Baron ve Kenny yöntemi artık terk edilmeli mi? 6. Örgütsel Davranış Bildiriler Kitabı, Süleyman Demirel Üniversitesi: Isparta.

Harvey, T. A. (2002). *Professional vitality and the principalship: a construct validity study*. Unpublished doctoral dissertation, University of Maine.

Hennekam, S. (2016). Vitality of older workers and its relationship with performance, career satisfaction and career success. *Management & Avenir*, *83*(1), 15–32.

Holland, J. L. (1959). A theory of vocational choice. *Journal of Counseling Psychology*, *6*(1), 35–45.

Hosmer, L. T. (1995). Trust: The connecting link between organization theory and philosophical ethics. *The Academy of Management Review, 20*(2), 379–403.

Jöreskog, K., & Sörbom, D. (1993). *LISREL 8: Structural equation modeling with the simplis command language.* Chicago, IL: Scientific Software International Inc.

Kline, R. B. (1998). *Principles and practice of structural equation modeling.* New York: Guilford Press.

Lewicki, R. J., Mc Allister D. J., & Bles D. J. (1998). Trust and distrust: New relationships and realities. *The Academy of Management Rewiew, 23*(3), 438–458.

Mayer, R. C., Davis, J. H., & Schoorman, F. D. (1995). An integrative model of organizational trust. *The Academy of Management Review, 20*(3), 709–734.

McLaughlin, P. S. (1999). Vitality o f mid-career faculty: The case for public comprehensive universities. (Doctoral dissertation, Claremont, CA: Claremont Graduate University).

McKnight, D. H., Cummings, L. L., & Chervany, N. L. (1998). Initial trust formation in new organizational relationships. *The Academy of Management Review, 23*(3), 473–490.

Morgan, G. A., Leech, N. L., Gloeckner, G. W., & Barret, K. C. (2004). *SPSS for introductory statistics: Use and interpretation*, Second Edition, London: Lawrance Erlbaum Associates.

Nunnally, J. C. (1978). *Psychometric theory.* New York: McGraw-Hill.

Nyhan, R. C., & Marlowe, H. A. (1997). Development and psychometric properties of the organizational trust inventory. *Evaluation Review, 21*(5), 614–635.

Ryan R.M. and Frederick C. (1997). On energy, personality, and health : Subjective vitality as a dynamic reflection of well-being. *Journal of Personality, 65*(3), 529–566.

Schaufeli, W. B., & Bakker, A. B. (2004). Utrecht Work Engagement Scale.Utrecht, Netherlands: Occupational Health Psychology Unit Utrecht University.

Shockley-Zalabak, P., Ellis, K., & Cesaria, R. (2000). IABC Research Foundation unveils new study on trust. *Communication World, 17*(6), 7–9.

Strijk, J. E., Proper, K. I., van Mechelen, W., & van der Beek, A. J. (2013). Effectiveness of a worksite lifestyle intervention on vitality, work engagement, productivity, and sick leave: results of a randomized controlled trial. *Scandinavian Journal of Work, Environment & Health, 39*(1), 66–75.

Uzunbacak, H. H., & Akçakanat, T. (2018). Mesleki canlılık ölçeği Türkçe formunun geçerlik ve güvenirlik çalışması. *Journal of Social & Humanities Sciences Research*, *5*(28): 322–3230.

Verbruggen, M., & Sels, L. (2010). Social-cognitive factors affecting clients' career and life satisfaction after counseling. *Journal of Career Assessment*, *18*(1), 3–15.

Yüksel, İ. (2005). İş-aile çatışmasının kariyer tatmini, iş tatmini ve iş davranışları ile ilişkisi. *Atatürk Üniversitesi İktisadi ve İdari Bilimler Dergisi*, *19*(2): 301–314.

Mehmet Yorulmaz and Burhanettin Uysal

A Comparison of Public Health Insurance: The Case of Turkey and the United States of America

1 Introduction

In almost all developed countries, it is noticeable that the state has an effective role in health, and plays a leading role in the funding of health services and its regulatory and legislative role (Hayran 1998).

The method of payment has measurable effects on subjects such as the diagnosis of the disease, the form and quantity of the service, the amount and types of prescribed medications, the length of hospitalization, and the frequency of analysis requests (İstanbulluoğlu 2010).

The Health Insurance System in the US (United States) and Turkey have many aspects which segregated from each other. In our chapter, after addressing the historical development of health insurance in the US, we will review the Medicare and Medicaid, current public health insurances, and referring to the history of health insurance in Turkey after the Health Transformation Program will be mentioned to the impact of public insurance.

2 Public Health Insurance of the US

2.1 The Historical Development of Health Insurance

Practices of public health insurance in the US began in 1965. But current private health insurance practices were based in earlier years. The first private health insurance in the US was introduced in the state of Dallas, 1929, and in the following years the Blue Cross Plan, and later, it replaced the Blue Shield Plan (Oral 2003). Because of the increase in the demand after World War II, private insurances became widespread, and service areas developed. The US did not include public health insurance until the 1960s (Belek 1994). But, in 1965s the public health insurance application could start. Financing was provided as Medicare (Medical Care Insurance) and Medicaid (Medical Aid). In the 1980s, insurance coverage expanded. The DRG (Diagnosis-Related Groups), a reimbursement system for hospitals in 1983, was put into service. The child health insurance government program was developed in 1997.

In 2001, centers of Medicare and Medicaid were established, and insurance coverage extended. In 2010, the ACA (Affordable Care Act) aimed to give low-income families, expanding the insurance coverage of insurance companies and providing better service to the inhabitants. The increasing of coverage areas among insurance corporations led to progress in the competition and thus to better service (Kırılmaz et al. 2017). In 2015, the performance-based payment of physicians given to the service quality, thus avoiding useless examinations and treatment, and both patient satisfaction and financial gains ensured. In 2017, the healthcare systems, also called Obama Care, led to dissatisfied public with many people uninsured, and Donald Trump was on the agenda.

The US has a free market-type health system that is managed by liberal policies, provides private sector-based services and has a health insurance system for these purposes (Kılıç 1994). It has no equal and comprehensive health insurance for the total population. It finances public expenditure through taxes. US healthcare system – with the national health insurance model in terms of services offered to the elderly; with Beveridge model in terms of healthcare provided for veterans and kids of veterans – is like the Bismarck model in terms of health services provided to workers and 9.1% because of lack of health insurance (Daştan and Çetinkaya, 2015).

The Department of Health and Human Services in the US is a body responsible for protecting, treating and protecting the health of citizens. HHS (Health & Human Services) affiliates are Medicaid and Medicare Service Services, Centers for Disease Control and Prevention, National Health Institute, Health Resources and Services Administration, Health Service Research and Quality Board, Food and Drug Management, Medicaid and Medicare Development Center, Patient-Centered Results Research Institute (Sargutan et al. 2010).

2.2 Medicare Program

The insurance of Medicare is covered by the insured, employer and government. Insurers and employers for Medicare A earn 1.45% of the insured's earnings during their employment; self-employed employees also pay 2.9% of their earnings. The contribution of the state is seen in covering the expenses for non-insured persons. They must be registered with Medicare in order for the state to contribute to sickness insurance. In addition, their annual income should be below the national poverty line, and assets for a person, such as bank accounts, bonds, stocks, etc., should not exceed $4,000 and not more than $6,000 for a couple. These households and their cars are not included in these calculations. (Kılıç 1994)

People older than 65 years of age, those with disabilities under the age of 65, people with chronic kidney disease, patients with ALS (Amyotrophic Lateral Sclerosis) can benefit from the program. This program does not cover all medical expenditures. In Medicare system, people can purchase supplementary health packages. Private insurance companies (such as Medigap) cover costs that Medicare does not cover. The system's financing is by some payroll taxes funded by the workers and the premiums deducted from the social security checks. Medicare & Medicaid Services Centers manage the program. Medicare comprises four parts (www.medicare.gov, 20.12.2018).

2.2.1 Medicare A Program

Those who have exceeded 65 years of age will avail from providing no monetary contribution to Medicare A: (www.medicare.gov, 20.12.2018)

- Residents in the US for at least five years,
- Those who receive pension from social insurance or railways,
- Those who do not complete their primes although they have the conditions of getting monthly from social insurances or railways,
- Wives (including those who divorced) or officers who are included in the Medicare plan.

Those who have not exceeded 65 years of age and who will avail from providing no monetary contribution to Medicare A:

- Residents in the US for at least five years,
- Those who receive disabled salary for at least 24 months from social insurances or railway administration,
- Chronic kidney patients who have kidney transplantation or who are living with dialysis,
- ALS (Amyotrophic Lateral Sclerosis).

2.2.2 Medicare B Program

It is an arbitrary insurance plan for individuals to reach extra health services. Those who are eligible for Medicare A can register for Medicare B at a monthly payment. First, for Medicare A they are required to spend seven months (first registration period). If the person is under the age of 65, the first registration time starts three months in advance.

The services included in the Medicare B program: (www.medicare.gov, 20.12.2018)

- Services offered by medical doctors and other healthcare providers,
- Preventive services,
- Laboratory services,
- Health services in rural areas,
- Emergency services,
- Outpatient services,
- Home care services,
- Dialysis services,
- Radiation therapy,
- Tissue and organ transplantation,
- Prosthesis and medical equipment,
- E-health services.

For all women in the insurance plan once a year; examinations and tests for protection from uterine cancer, urology examination and investigations against prostate cancer for men over 50 years of age, influenza for all people, vaccination for preventive health services such as hepatitis, bone densitometry for women, mammography against breast cancer for women over the age of 40, examinations and treatments for diabetes patients are health services that the participant can meet by paying 20%. The Medicare B program does not provide for the payment of comprehensive health services, such as eye care and eyeglasses purchases, audio aids, outpatient treatments and prescriptions and any physical care. (www.medicare.gov, 20.12.2018)

2.2.3 Medicare C Program

The program came into force in 1998 and also called the Choice of Health Plan. Health care organizations are Medicare-approved managed care services by preferential service provider organizations and private companies. The person makes a direct (out-of-pocket) payment for the service he/she receives. It provides extra coverage for people in the program. (www.medicare.gov, 20.12.2018)

2.2.4 Medicare D Program

It implemented the Prescription Discount Card in the United States Congress in 2003 and was put into practice in 2006. Outpatient treatment reduced prescription drug costs. Seniors older than 65 years automatically joined. Participation in the Medicare prescription drug plan is optional. The participant can avail the program during the period in which he/she paid extra primes. (www.medicare.gov, 20.12.2018)

2.2.5 Health Services Outside Medicare Coverage

- Acupuncture,
- Dental treatments and prostheses,
- Plastic surgery,
- Care services (bathing, etc.),
- Health care outside the country,
- Audio prostheses,
- Orthopedic footwear,
- Outpatient prescriptions,
- Foot care,
- Some eyeglasses according to the eye examination and number,
- Physical examination,
- Some radiology shots,
- Vaccinations are not in scope.

According to 2017 data, 58 million people benefit from the Medicare program. Considering that the US population is 325.7 million (US Census Bureau 2017), Medicare approximately covers 6% of the population. Medicare serves for the program with 15000 nurses, 1.2 million physicians and other healthcare professionals in 6000 hospitals (www.cms.gov, 25.12.2018).

2.3 Medicaid Program

Medicaid is a social welfare program that supports other health programs, those who have inadequate income, and provides medical and hospital expenses for individuals who are below the poverty line defined by the states. Medicaid creates its program by financing and organizing its own health programs within the boundaries defined by each state and according to national guidelines. The program varies from state to state. Immigration status, residence status, American citizenship, budgets of individuals, and compliance with procedures established by the state are important for taking part in the program (www.medicaid.gov, 21.12.2018)

In 2015, Medicaid provided health insurance for 97 million low-income people, including 33 million children, 27 million adults, 6 million elderly and 10 million people for disabilities (according to Congressional Budget Office (CBO)). In 2017, 28 million children experienced a decline in the number of services provided by 72 million people (Centers for Medicare & Medicaid Services). In the US, 40% are still below the level of poverty who benefit from this program.

The program of Medicaid may include healthcare payments such as dental, home care, physical therapy, prosthetic devices, eyeglasses and eye care, outpatient prescriptions.

People included in the Medicaid program: (www.medicaid.gov, 21.12.2018)

- Low-income families,
- Pregnant women,
- Children and adolescents,
- Some people with disabilities,
- Parents and caretakers of young children,
- Elders,
- Low-income adults,
- 40% of those without mental health,
- 40% of all births.

Services covered by Medicaid program (www.medicaid.gov, 21.12.2018):

- Outpatient and inpatient health services,
- Health-care services in pregnant women,
- Vaccination,
- Inspection service,
- Nurse-care service,
- Private care and nursing services at home,
- Family planning,
- Outpatient polyclinics,
- Mental health services,
- Mammography,
- Colonoscopy,
- Protective services,
- Laboratory and medical imaging services,
- Diagnostic services under preventive healthcare,
- Ambulance service,
- Nurse and midwife service,
- Nurse and treatment services for children under 21,
- Children and adolescents fully receive the vision, auditory, dental, health screening, and diagnosis and treatment services.

Seeming at the expenditure and enrollment rates in the Medicaid program, children account for less than one-fifth of the expenditures, although they account for over two out of five people in Medicare. Elderly and people with disabilities account for half of the registered people for the high need for health

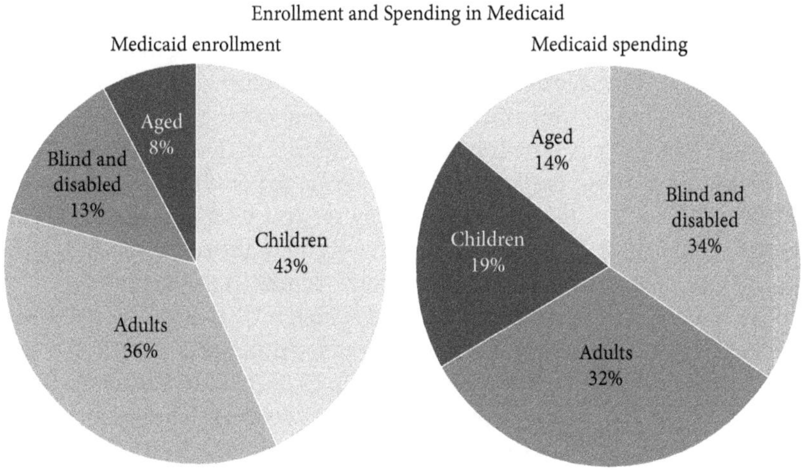

Fig. 1: Medicaid Program Enrollment and Spending Rates. Source: Spending and enrollment estimates for FY2015 from the Congressional Budget Office's March 2016 Medicaid Baseline

services, despite being a one-fifth of the registered people (www.medicaid.gov, 21.12.2018).

The groups in which states can receive financial aid are:

- Children under 18 years of age in families with a poverty line below 38% (poverty limit is $25,975 in a family of three),
- Pregnant women with a poverty line below 38%,
- Parents eligible for cash achieve prosperity life standards,
- Elderly and disabled people enrolled in the Supplemental Security Income Program,
- The contribution of the states to the federal government for the Medicaid program varies from 50% to 78% according to their wealth.

3 Turkey Public Insurance

3.1 The Historical Development of Health Insurance

It divides the development of health services in Turkey into two as before and after the Republic (Çakmak et al. 2017). In this study, after referring to the post-republic health services, the current health transformation and general health insurance will be mentioned.

With the proclamation of the Republic, Refik Saydam had been the Minister of Health. He gave importance to preventive health services; he did not see therapeutic services as a state duty and left it to local administrations. He signed laws such as Law no. 1593 'Umumi Hıfzıssıhha Kanunu' with Law no. 1219 'Tababet ve Şuabatı Sanatlarının Tarzı İcrasına Dair Kanun'. Having embraced the model of vertical integration, the Ministry of Health is responsible for the country's health policy and health services, providing services related to preventive and curative practices, and the struggle against infectious diseases as malaria, syphilis and tuberculosis as well as offering medical education (Akdur 1999).

The second Minister of Health of the Republican Era, was Behçet Uz who prepared the First Ten-Year Health Plan. He adopted all health services as a state duty. In 1961, he issued no. 224, named 'Sağlık Hizmetlerinin Sosyalleştirilmesi Kanunu' adopted and aimed to present the health services in a continuous, widespread and integrated manner. For this purpose, he opened health houses, health centers, district, and provincial hospitals, and an integrated structure was gradually being established into the presentation of health services in a province. It was decided that it would be impossible to finance all services by the state and decided to provide financing through stamps and salt (Aksakoğlu 2008).

In Turkey, 1992, by Law no. 3861 issue, Yeşil Kart application provided free health services for low-income families by the public (Akder 1999).

In 2003, the Ministry of Health went into structuring undertaking the Health Transformation Program (HTP). The Health Transformation Program provided an effective, efficient, and fair service delivery and financing. It contains the components such as providing primary care services in family, autonomous management in hospitals, giving priority to protective services, a planner and supervisory Health Ministry organization, quality accreditation, well-trained and motivated health personnel, friendly service, effective and graded referral chain, improvement of decision-support systems, and the establish of health information systems. In this context, for citizens to receive equal healthcare service, the Social Security Institution, the General Directorate of Bağ-Kur and the General Directorate of Retirement Fund merged on 20.06.2006 to provide access to health services through a single service provider. In the hospitals of the Ministry of Health, it introduced the Performance-Based Payment System. It introduced family medicine and intended every individual in the country to perform health checks depending on a physician, registered in 2017 over 95% of the population to a family physician and reached 98% of the population with General Health Insurance. The provision and prescription management system, MEDULA was put into operation and introduced health budget law to Health Application Notification (HAN) pricing (Türkiye Sağlıkta Dönüşüm Programı İlerleme Raporu 2008)

For developing and improving quality in the healthcare system of Turkey, there is a need to know of and focus on many prerequisites such as planning of quality and showing a systematic approach (Yorulmaz 2014). On the other hand, it is important to organize the number and distribution of physicians figuring the population density with polyclinic numbers of the region (Demirkıran and Şahin 2010). It can examine the actors involved in the Turkish health system under four main headings in line with their functions. These titles are in the form of policy-making, administrative decision-making actors, financing actors and service delivery actors (Tengilimoglu et al. 2017):

- Politics creation, mainly the Ministry of Health, the state planning organization, private part, and non-governmental organizations assume roles. The stage of preparation of the legal basis of the policies provided by the Grand National Assembly of Turkey and the Constitutional Court and the Council of Higher Education offers consultancy services in the stage of training and planning of health manpower.
- The Ministry of Health and provincial health directorates are the administrative decision-making actors.
- Finance actors composed of the Ministry of Finance, Social Security Institution, private insurances, and complementary health insurances and international organizations.
- Services provided by public and private hospitals.

4 Comparison of Health Systems of Turkey and the US

In our study, after testing the health system of Turkey and the US, we will hold this chapter as a benchmark indicator of the health of the two countries. It will compare the health indicators of the two countries subject to current health expenditures, population rates and health workers providing service. This comparison shows the positive or negative differences between the two countries by recognizing the shortcomings in the health system and is important to determine the examples that were applied between the two countries. It also reflects the cultural, social, economic, political and administrative differences between countries in the health system. Since the aim is to provide better quality and efficient service with the applications developed in this context, the analyses should be done well. A correct comparison leads to the betterment of policies of governments, reducing their error rate while making their strategies and programs, and making future directions.

Tab. 1: International Comparison of Current Health Expenditure in GDP (%). Source: OECD Health Data, 2017

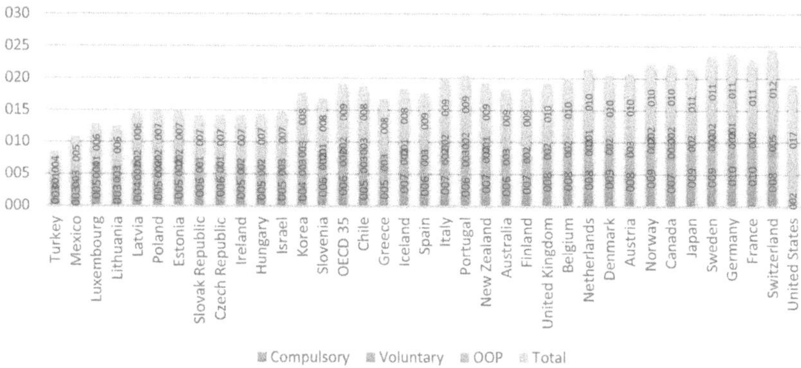

Tab. 1 shows the GDP ratio of Turkey and the US health spending. Looking at this ratio of the amount allocated to health spending from US, GDP in Turkey seems to be on too. The proportion allocated to Turkey in 2017, while only 4.23% of GDP to health spending, this rate has been 17.15% for the US. In 1999, total health spending in Turkey was 5 million, the ratio of total health expenditure to gross domestic product 4.7%. In 2016, health expenditures were 119,756 million and the rate of gross domestic product was 4.23% (https://data.oecd.org, 28.12.2018).

If we are to compare the two countries in terms of the population according to OECD data, while Turkey's population of 80.8 million people in 2017, the US has a population of 325.7 million. The US has almost four times the population of Turkey, hence at the top in terms of health spending. In 2015, while the number of elderly population in Turkey was 6 million 193 thousand, the number of elderly US population reached to 47 million 819 thousand. When we look at the OECD in 2016, 8% of the population in Turkey and 15% of the population in the US aged 65 and over. The average life expectancy is around 78 years in Turkey and although almost the same in the US, the elderly population in the US was more than Turkey. The population is aging in both countries, which means a rising in health expenditures because of the increase in the aging demand of the population for health services. When we look at the average life balance with health spending although the US spends the most on health investment in countries, has a lower life expectancy than Turkey. This figure is even lower than that of the OECD. When we look at other countries except for the US, a positive deviation is observed between health expenditures and the average life expectancy. According to the regression

Tab. 2: International Comparison of the Number of Physicians per 100.000 People, 2017. Source: OECD Health Data, 2017

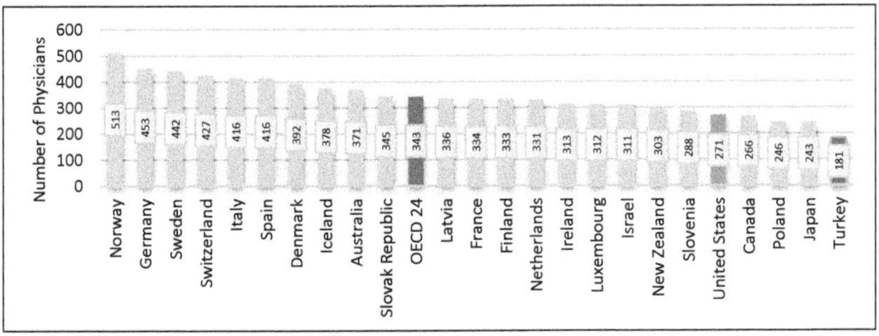

analysis performed in health expenditures, the effect of every $100 increase on the average life expectancy was 0.42 years. Therefore, it is observed that there is a positive relationship with the average life expectancy (Mathers et al. 2003).

Because of 2 nurses per thousand people in Turkey and 11.3 nurses in the US, it shows that the number of nursing staff is inadequate within the health system in Turkey. In addition, the number of trained and skilled health staff in the US is higher than in Turkey. Nurse and technicians make ultrasound shots and many interventions by practitioners, which shows us its advanced health staff. Nurses apply the treatment given by the practitioners, and in Turkey it shows the quality of education, considering they are not decision-makers.

The OECD data on the number of hospital beds in Turkey was investigated; the number fell 2.8 beds per 1000 people in 2017, this figure is 2.8 in the US, a significant difference is not seen and figures are close to each other.

If we look at the number of health occupation members per capita based on the statistics on the population of the countries, per 100,000 people in the US falling in 2017 to 271 practitioner lags that number fell to 181 in Turkey (Tab. 2).

According to the average index by OECD, the number of physicians per 100,000 people of Turkey is approximately half of the OECD24 average. However, the US data are also lower than the average of the OECD24.

Tab. 3 shows programs that public insurances include such as Medicaid, Medicare, and the Children's Health Insurance Program (CHIP).

While under protecting public insurance most of the insured population in Turkey, 2002, this ratio is 24.1% in the US. When looked at the spendings of Turkey in 2016, 78% of the public, 16% out-of-pocket payments, and private insurance and payment is 5%. According to OECD data, these rates in the US are 49% in public,

Tab. 3: International Comparison of Current Health Expenditure Distribution by Type of Financing, 2015. Source: OECD Health Data, 2017 (The data of Turkey and the US belong to 2016)

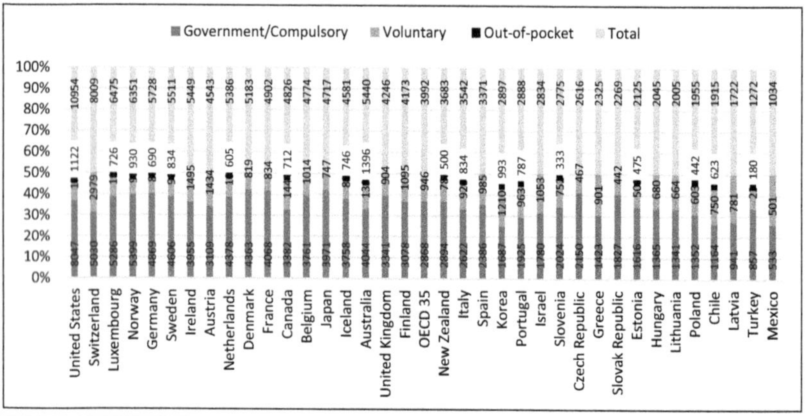

11% in out-of-pocket payments, 40% in private insurance and payments. As we can see it, in Turkey including scope the general health insurance of the individuals with the success of the health transformation program, most of the population benefit with public health services. In the US, it is almost halved by private companies. While it is 5% penetration of private health insurance in Turkey, the ratio is 63% in the US. This is because of health insurance covering the entire population of Turkey is not needing another assurance, in 2016 share of total private health expenditure was 23% in Turkey, was 52% in the US (World Health Organization 2016).

In Turkey socialization Law No. 224 and in all subsequent laws protecting the citizens health is state's responsibility, the US Constitution have not included the right to health of individuals and it did not see as a state duty. The weight of public health services in Turkey, together with the importance given to cultural patterns and Islam's tolerance and helping although it has always existed from past to present. The US has not included the public and provided health services in a profit-driven manner.

5 Conclusion

The working population in Turkey has assurance in the social and health area provided by the state through the primes paid. That there is no guarantee provided by the state in the US creates insecurity by creating an ambience of uncertainty in individuals such as social risks and retirement. In the US while it requires five years of residence and citizenship to avail health insurance, refugees in Turkey also seem to avail health services of the refugees. This also shows Turkey needs both religious obligations and the positive effects of the importance given to social cohesion and solidarity in terms of human rights.

Turkey, has the lowest proportion of health spending in the budget in the OECD countries. Besides, health service satisfaction rate is high with the impact of the spread of general health insurance. Although there is a high level of health care financing in the US healthcare service, the satisfaction rate is low for lack of comprehensive health insurance. Regarding health services, according to the OECD countries average, Turkey is low in terms of the number of hospitals and hospital beds, the number of practitioners, nurses and midwife's number. To improve their health status indicators, Turkey should allocate more proportion from budget to health and should increase the number of health professionals such as qualified practitioners, nurses and midwives, and establish a strong health system infrastructure.

If the US extends public health insurances and provides them for the benefit of more people and ignores the advantages of increasingly advanced technology and health manpower number, citizens are ensured to receive quality health care. In both countries, there is no referral system. It should bring a referral system in the US and Turkey to prevent unnecessary costs.

References

Akdur R, (1999). Türkiye'de Sağlık Hizmetleri ve Avrupa Topluluğu Ülkeleri İle Kıyaslanması. Ankara, http://www.recepakdur.com/upload/ab_turkiye_kiyaslamasi.pdf, 26.12.2018.

Aksakoğlu G, (2008). Sağlıkta Sosyalleştirmenin Öyküsü. Memleket Siyaset Yönetim Dergisi. 8, pp. 7–62.

Belek İ, (1994). İstanbul Sosyal Devletin Krizi ve Sağlığın Ekonomi Politiği, İstanbul www.cms.gov, 25.12.2018.

Çavmak Ş, Çavmak D, 2017. Türkiye'de Sağlık Hizmetlerinin Tarihsel Gelişimi ve Sağlıkta Dönüşüm Programı, Sağlık Yönetimi Dergisi, 1 (1), pp. 48–57.

Daştan İ., Çetinkaya V, (2015). OECD Ülkeleri ve Türkiye'nin Sağlık Sistemleri, Sağlık Harcamaları ve Sağlık Göstergeleri Karşılaştırması. SGD-Sosyal Güvenlik Dergisi, 5 (1), pp. 104–134. Retrieved from http://dergipark.gov.tr/sgd/issue/28889/308995, 27.12.2018.

Demirkıran M., Şahin B, (2010). Pratisyen Hekimlerin İlaç Seçimlerini Etkileyen Faktörlere İlişkin Değerlendirmeleri. Hacettepe Sağlık İdaresi Dergisi. 13 (1), pp. 1–28.

Hayran O, (1998). Sağlık Hizmetlerinin Özel ve Kamusal Yönü. Sağlık Hizmetleri El Kitabı. Nobel Tıp Kitabevleri. pp. 49–61.

İstanbulluoğlu H., Mahir, G., Recai, O, (2010). Sağlık Hizmetlerinin Finansman Yöntemleri. Dirim Tıp Gazetesi. 85 (2), pp. 86–99.

Kılıç B, (1994). Amerika Birleşik Devletleri Sağlık Sistemi. Toplum ve Hekim. 9(64–65), pp. 64–65.

Kırılmaz H., Amarat M., Ünal Ö, (2017). Türkiye ve Amerika Birleşik Devletleri Sağlık Sistemlerinin Karşılatırmalı Analizi. Strategic Public Management Journal. 3 (6), pp. 78–104.

Mathers CD., Murray CJL., Salomon JA, et al. (2003). Healthy life expectancy: comparison of OECD countries in 2001. Australia and New Zealand Journal of Public Health. 27, pp. 5–11.

Oral Aİ, (2003). ABD ve İngiltere Kamu Sağlık Sigortası Programları Üzerine Karşılaştırmalı Bir Değerlendirme. Sosyal Bilimler Dergisi.2(2): pp. 61–78.

Sağlık Bakanlığı (SB) 2008. Türkiye Sağlıkta Dönüşüm Programı İlerleme Raporu. Ağustos. Sağlık Bakanlığı Yayın No:749, Ankara

Sargutan, AE. (2010). 84 Ülke ve Türkiye'nin Karşılaştırmalı Sağlık Sistemleri–Kavram Metot ve Uygulamalar, Sağlık Sektörlerinin Genel Sistem ve Mali Yapıları, Sağlık Sistemi Tipleri ve Özellikleri, 84 Ülkenin Sağlık Sektörleri Sağlık Sistemleri ve Mali Yapıları, Türkiye Sağlık Sektörü Sağlık Sistemi ve Mali Yapıları, www.sargutan.com, 27.12.2018.

Tengilimoğlu D., Akbolat, M., Işık, O, (2017). Sağlık İşletmeleri Yönetimi. Ankara: Nobel Yayıncılık pp :147–149.

Yorulmaz M, (2014). Evaluation of the ISO 9001:2000 Quality Management System Application in the Hospital Management System. 03 June 2014, 10th International Academic Conference, Vienna.

World Health Organization (WHO), 2016

www.medicaid.gov, 21.12.2018

www.medicare.gov, 20.12.2018

www.oecd.org, 27.12.2018

www.saglik.gov.tr, 17.11.2018

List of Figures

List of Tables

ngramcontent.com/pod-product-compliance
Content Group UK Ltd.
Milton Keynes, MK11 3LW, UK
922120926
K00042BA/1122

9 783631 782828